TOP 10: THE FORTY-NINERS
A PREQUEL TO TOP 10

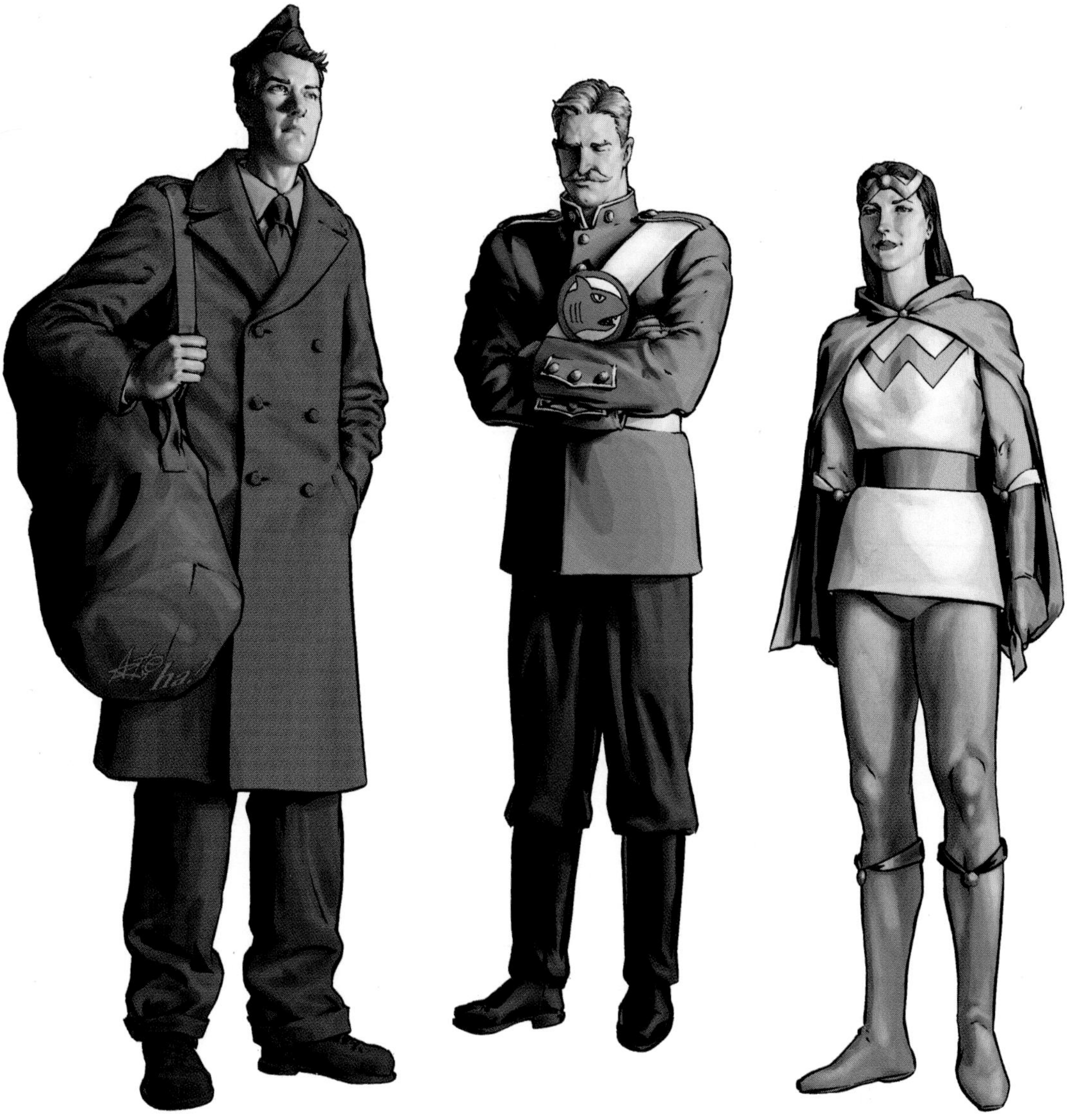

Gene Ha

JIM LEE
Editorial Director

JOHN NEE
VP – Business Development

SCOTT DUNBIER
Executive Editor

KRISTY QUINN
Assistant Editor

TOP 10:THE FORTY-NINERS Published by America's Best Comics, LLC, © 2005 America's Best Comics, LLC, 888 Prospect St., Suite 240, La Jolla, CA 92037. All rights reserved. TOP 10, all characters, the distinctive likenesses thereof and all related elements are trademarks of America's Best Comics, LLC. The stories, characters and incidents mentioned in this book are entirely fictional. Printed on recyclable paper. America's Best Comics does not read or accept unsolicited submissions of ideas, stories or artwork. Printed in Canada. FIRST PRINTING.

TOP 10 — THE FORTY-NINERS

ALAN MOORE
writer

GENE HA
artist

ART LYON
colorist

TODD KLEIN
lettering, logos
and design

created by Alan Moore and Gene Ha

AMERICA'S
BEST COMICS

NEOPOLIS POLICE DEPARTMENT

NPD

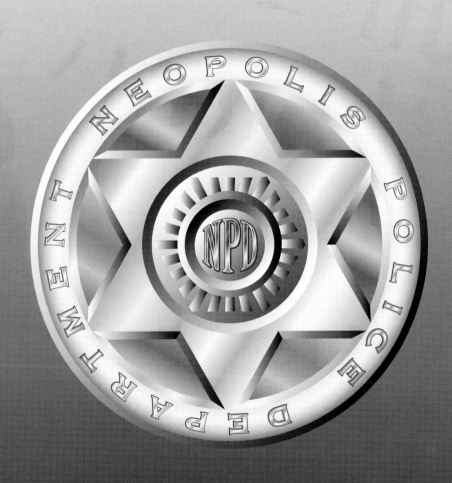

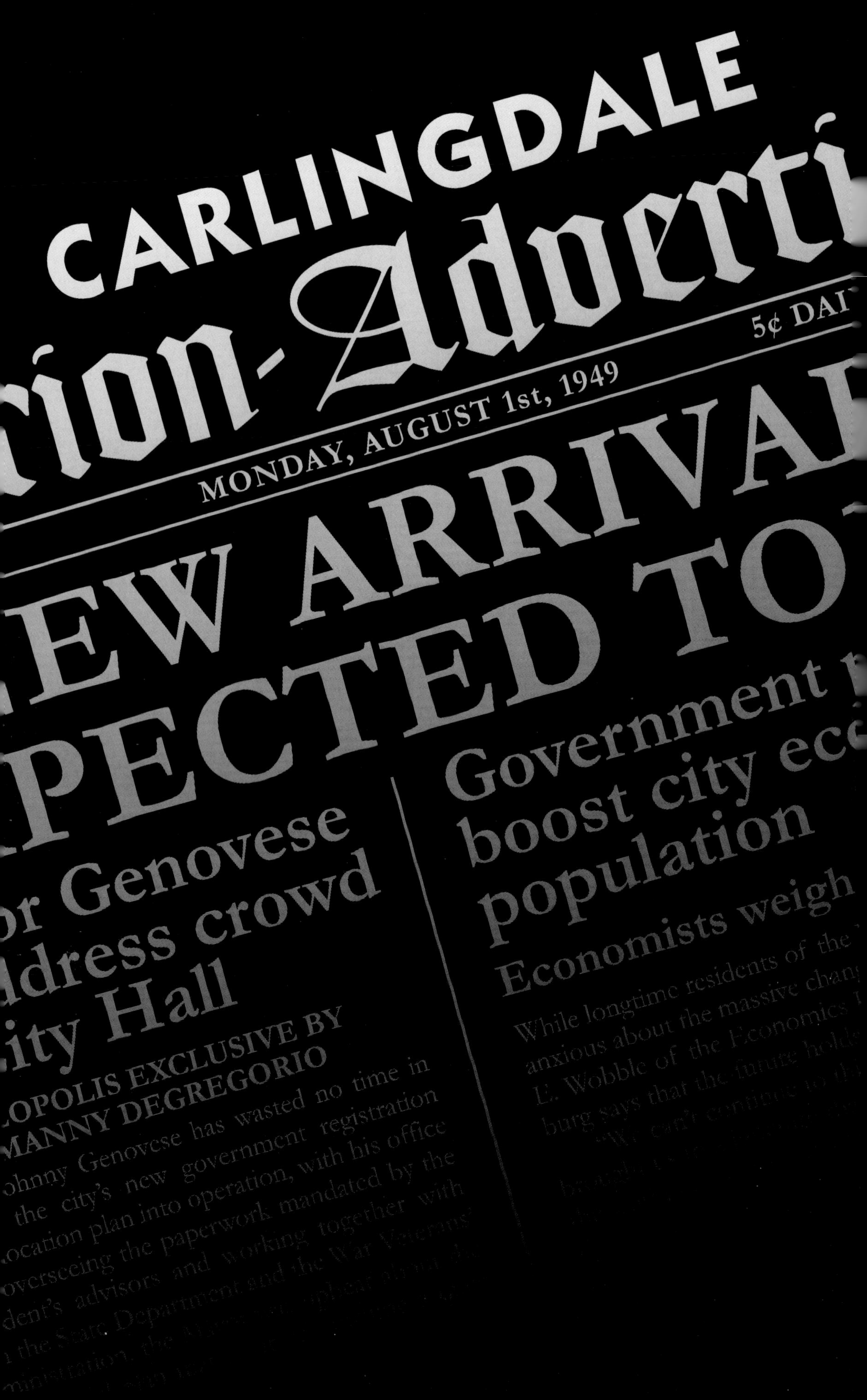
CARLINGDALE
...rion-Adverti...
5¢ DAI...
MONDAY, AUGUST 1st, 1949

...EW ARRIVAL...
...PECTED TO...

...or Genovese
...ldress crowd
...ity Hall

...LOPOLIS EXCLUSIVE BY
MANNY DEGREGORIO

...ohnny Genovese has wasted no time in
the city's new government registration
...location plan into operation, with his office
overseeing the paperwork mandated by the
...dent's advisors and working together with
the War Veterans'
...the State Department and the...
...ministration, the...

Government p...
boost city eco...
population

Economists weigh...

While longtime residents of the...
anxious about the massive chang...
E. Wobble of the Economics D...
burg says that the future holds...
"We can't continue to th...

LITTLE BOY?

LITTLE BOY, EXCUSE ME, BUT IS THIS SEAT TAKEN?

UH....NO. NO, TAKE IT, IT'S FINE.

THANK YOU. I DIDN'T KNOW. I THOUGHT YOU WERE RIDING WITH YOUR MOTHER.

I TELL YOU, SITTING DOWN. THIS IS A RELIEF.

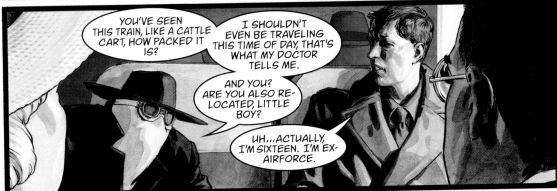

YOU'VE SEEN THIS TRAIN, LIKE A CATTLE CART, HOW PACKED IT IS?

I SHOULDN'T EVEN BE TRAVELING THIS TIME OF DAY, THAT'S WHAT MY DOCTOR TELLS ME.

AND YOU? ARE YOU ALSO RE-LOCATED, LITTLE BOY?

UH....ACTUALLY, I'M SIXTEEN. I'M EX-AIRFORCE.

AND YOU'RE SIXTEEN?

AH, WELL. THE WAR, I THINK AMERICA WAS DESPERATE, YOU KNOW?

EVEN MY PEOPLE, THEY GOT US CLEARING NAZIS OFF THE WATER-FRONT, THEY...

UH, SAY, BUDDY, EXCUSE ME? THIS'LL SOUND KINDA NUTS, I KNOW, BUT... ARE YOU A VAMPIRE?

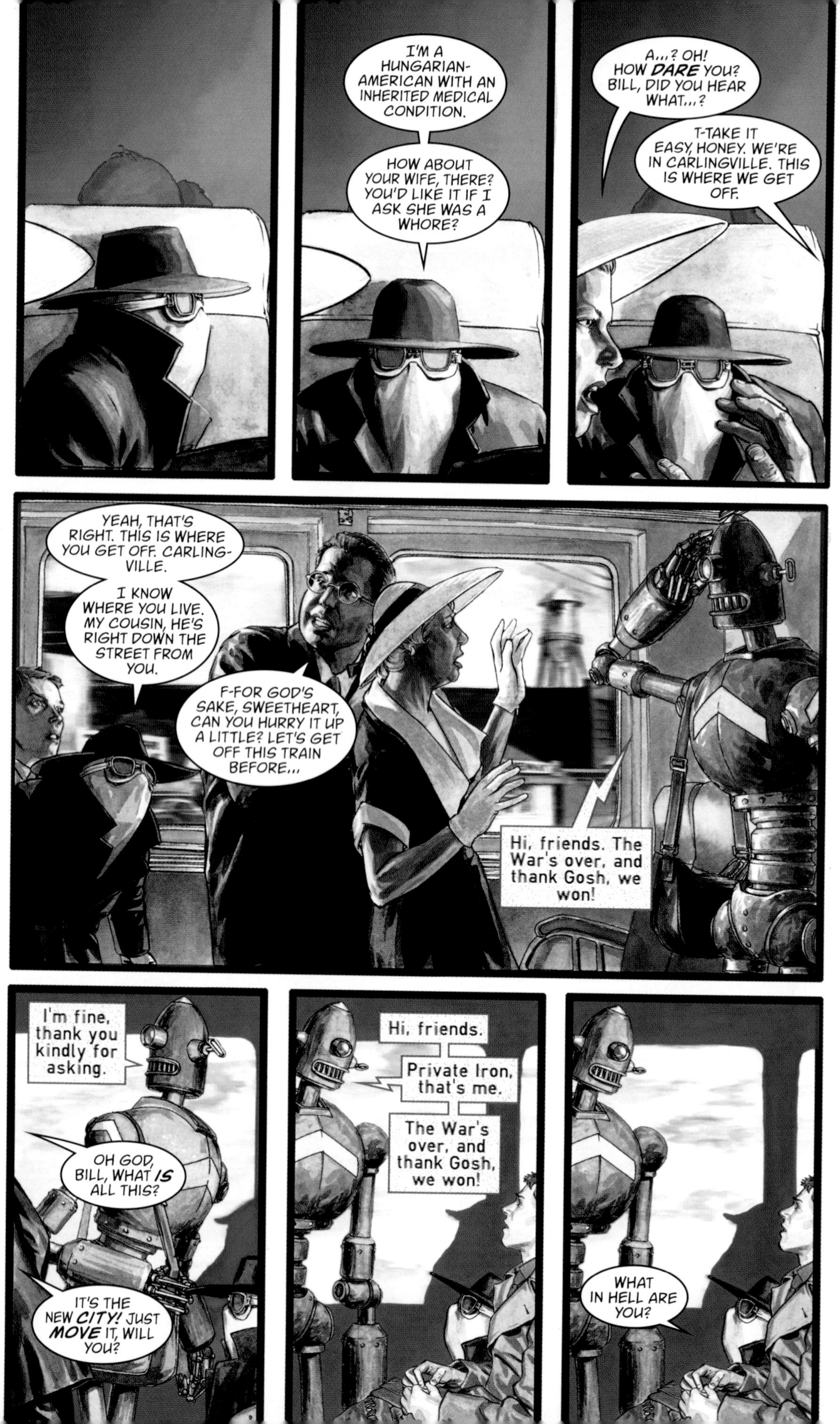

I'M A HUNGARIAN-AMERICAN WITH AN INHERITED MEDICAL CONDITION.
HOW ABOUT YOUR WIFE, THERE? YOU'D LIKE IT IF I ASK SHE WAS A WHORE?
A...? OH! HOW DARE YOU? BILL, DID YOU HEAR WHAT...?
T-TAKE IT EASY, HONEY. WE'RE IN CARLINGVILLE. THIS IS WHERE WE GET OFF.
YEAH, THAT'S RIGHT. THIS IS WHERE YOU GET OFF. CARLING-VILLE.
I KNOW WHERE YOU LIVE. MY COUSIN, HE'S RIGHT DOWN THE STREET FROM YOU.
F-FOR GOD'S SAKE, SWEETHEART, CAN YOU HURRY IT UP A LITTLE? LET'S GET OFF THIS TRAIN BEFORE...
Hi, friends. The War's over, and thank Gosh, we won!
I'm fine, thank you kindly for asking.
OH GOD, BILL, WHAT IS ALL THIS?
IT'S THE NEW CITY! JUST MOVE IT, WILL YOU?
Hi, friends.
Private Iron, that's me.
The War's over, and thank Gosh, we won!
WHAT IN HELL ARE YOU?

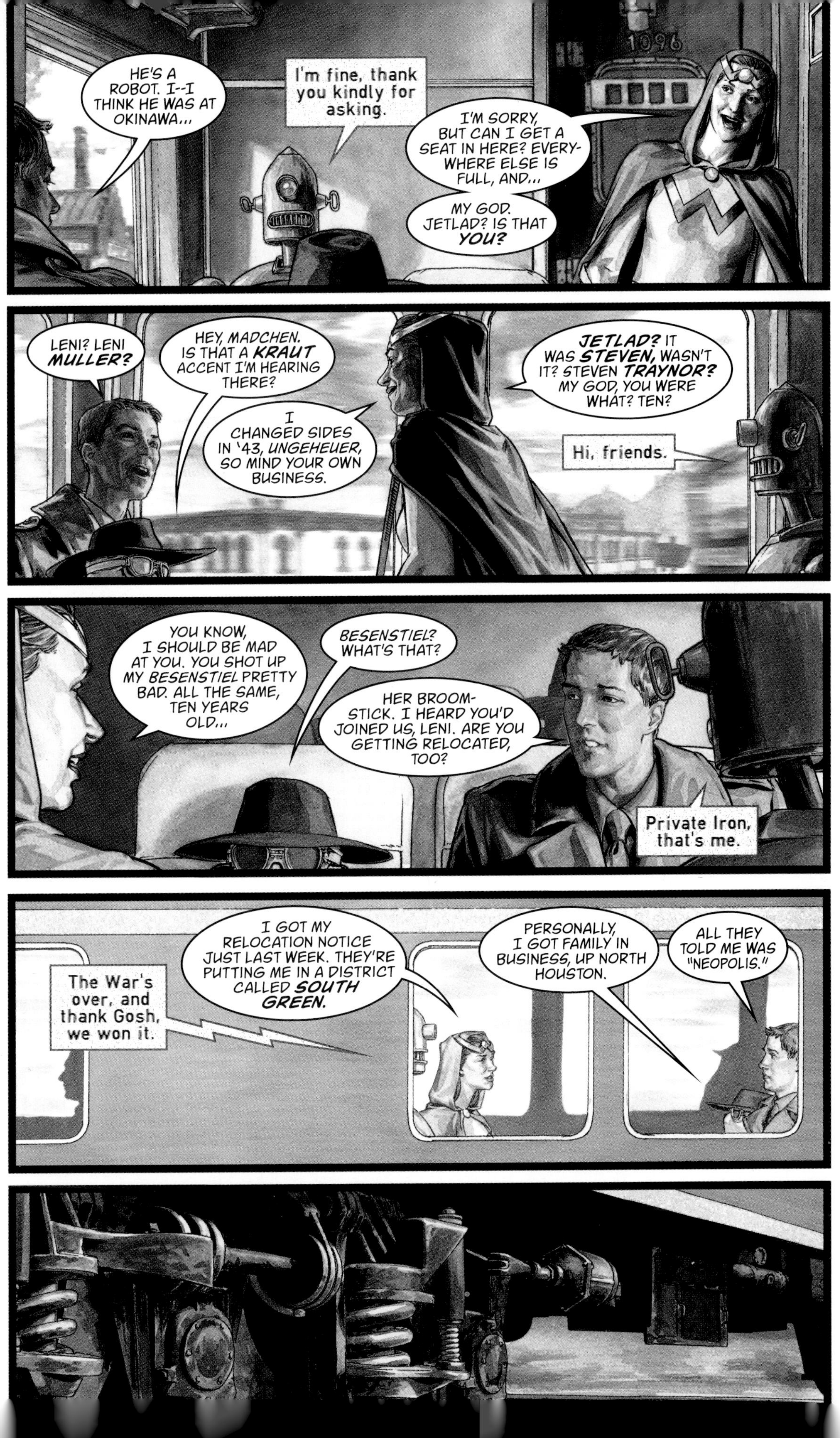

HE'S A ROBOT. I--I THINK HE WAS AT OKINAWA...
I'm fine, thank you kindly for asking.
I'M SORRY, BUT CAN I GET A SEAT IN HERE? EVERY-WHERE ELSE IS FULL, AND...
MY GOD. JETLAD? IS THAT YOU?
LENI? LENI MULLER?
HEY, MADCHEN. IS THAT A KRAUT ACCENT I'M HEARING THERE?
I CHANGED SIDES IN '43, UNGEHEUER, SO MIND YOUR OWN BUSINESS.
JETLAD? IT WAS STEVEN, WASN'T IT? STEVEN TRAYNOR? MY GOD, YOU WERE WHAT? TEN?
Hi, friends.
YOU KNOW, I SHOULD BE MAD AT YOU. YOU SHOT UP MY BESENSTIEL PRETTY BAD. ALL THE SAME, TEN YEARS OLD...
BESENSTIEL? WHAT'S THAT?
HER BROOM-STICK. I HEARD YOU'D JOINED US, LENI. ARE YOU GETTING RELOCATED, TOO?
Private Iron, that's me.
The War's over, and thank Gosh, we won it.
I GOT MY RELOCATION NOTICE JUST LAST WEEK. THEY'RE PUTTING ME IN A DISTRICT CALLED SOUTH GREEN.
PERSONALLY, I GOT FAMILY IN BUSINESS, UP NORTH HOUSTON.
ALL THEY TOLD ME WAS "NEOPOLIS."
1096

FORTY-NINERS

CHAPTER 1 WHAT IS BELIEVABLE AFTER WAR

FRAMING at
116 Fulton St
STARR
FRAME PICTURE Co

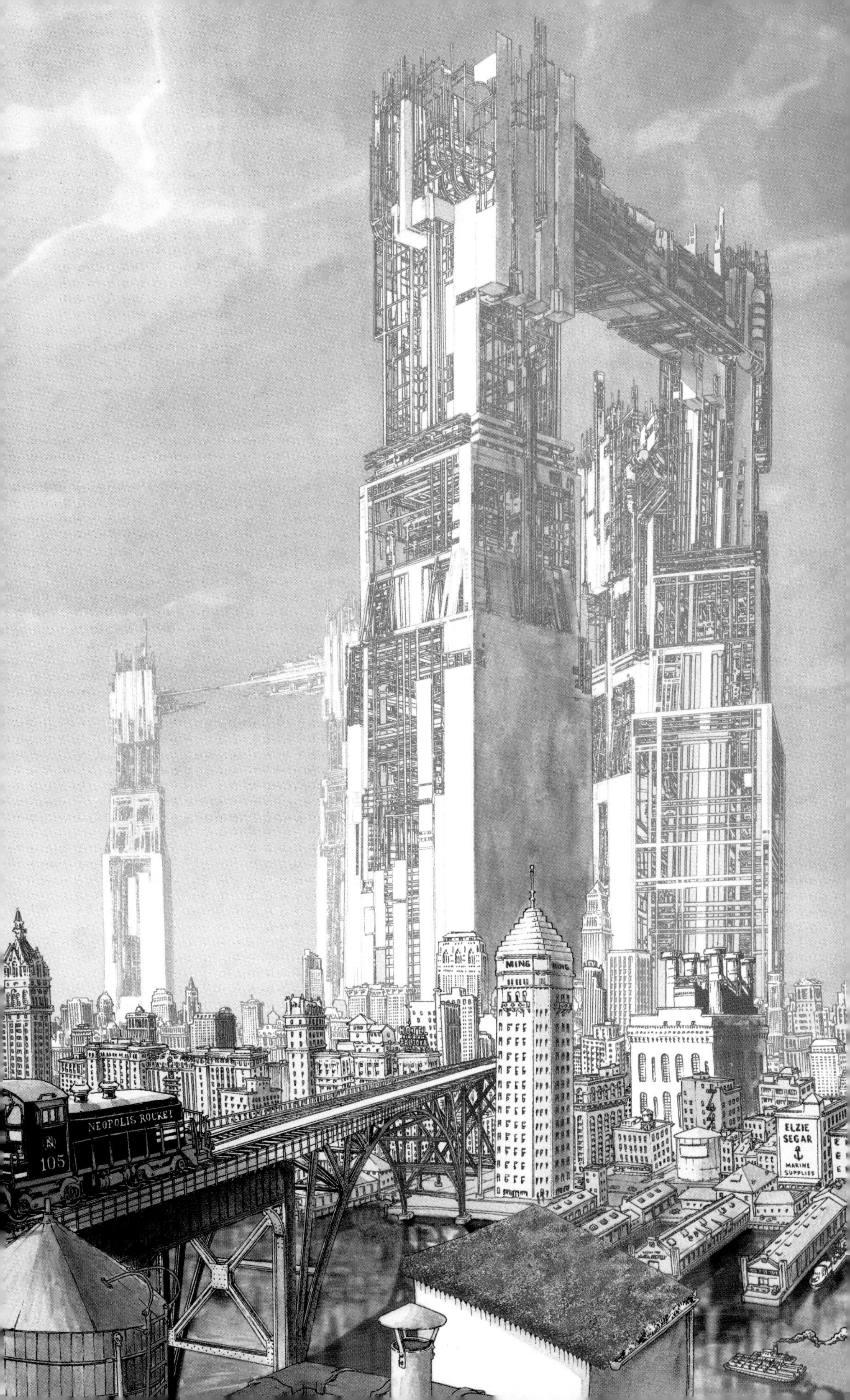
NEOPOLIS ROCKET
N
105
MING
MING
ELZIE
SEGAR
MARINE
SUPPLIES

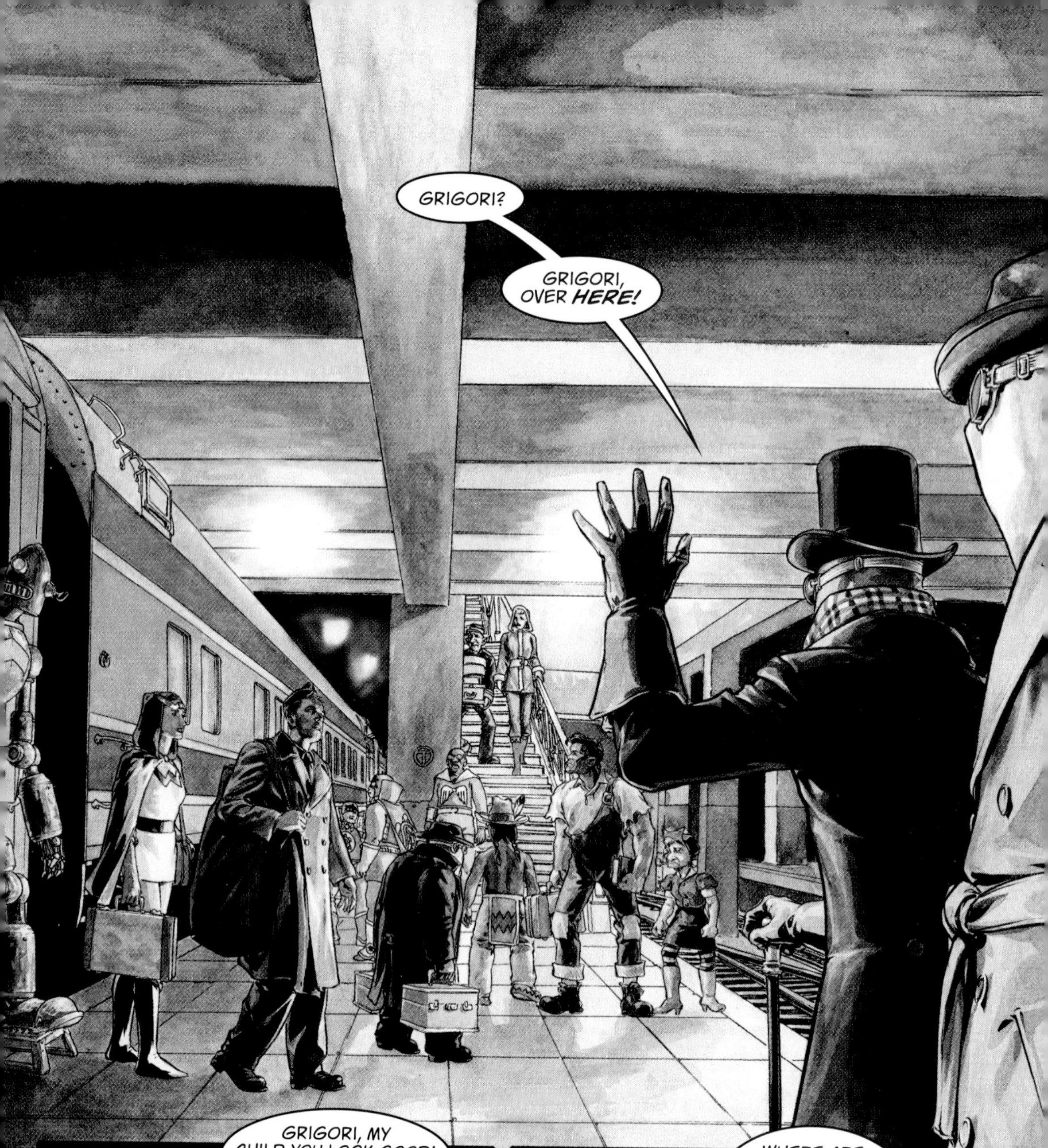
GRIGORI?
GRIGORI, OVER HERE!

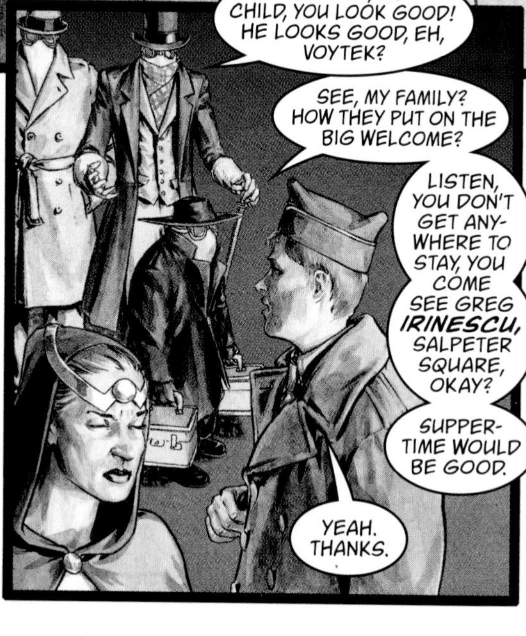
GRIGORI, MY CHILD, YOU LOOK GOOD! HE LOOKS GOOD, EH, VOYTEK?
SEE, MY FAMILY? HOW THEY PUT ON THE BIG WELCOME?
LISTEN, YOU DON'T GET ANY-WHERE TO STAY, YOU COME SEE GREG IRINESCU, SALPETER SQUARE, OKAY?
SUPPER-TIME WOULD BE GOOD.
YEAH. THANKS.

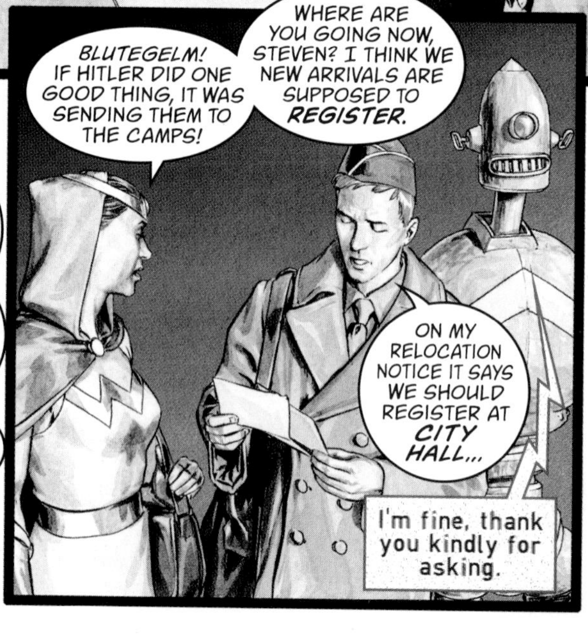
BLUTEGELM! IF HITLER DID ONE GOOD THING, IT WAS SENDING THEM TO THE CAMPS!
WHERE ARE YOU GOING NOW, STEVEN? I THINK WE NEW ARRIVALS ARE SUPPOSED TO REGISTER.
ON MY RELOCATION NOTICE IT SAYS WE SHOULD REGISTER AT CITY HALL...
I'm fine, thank you kindly for asking.

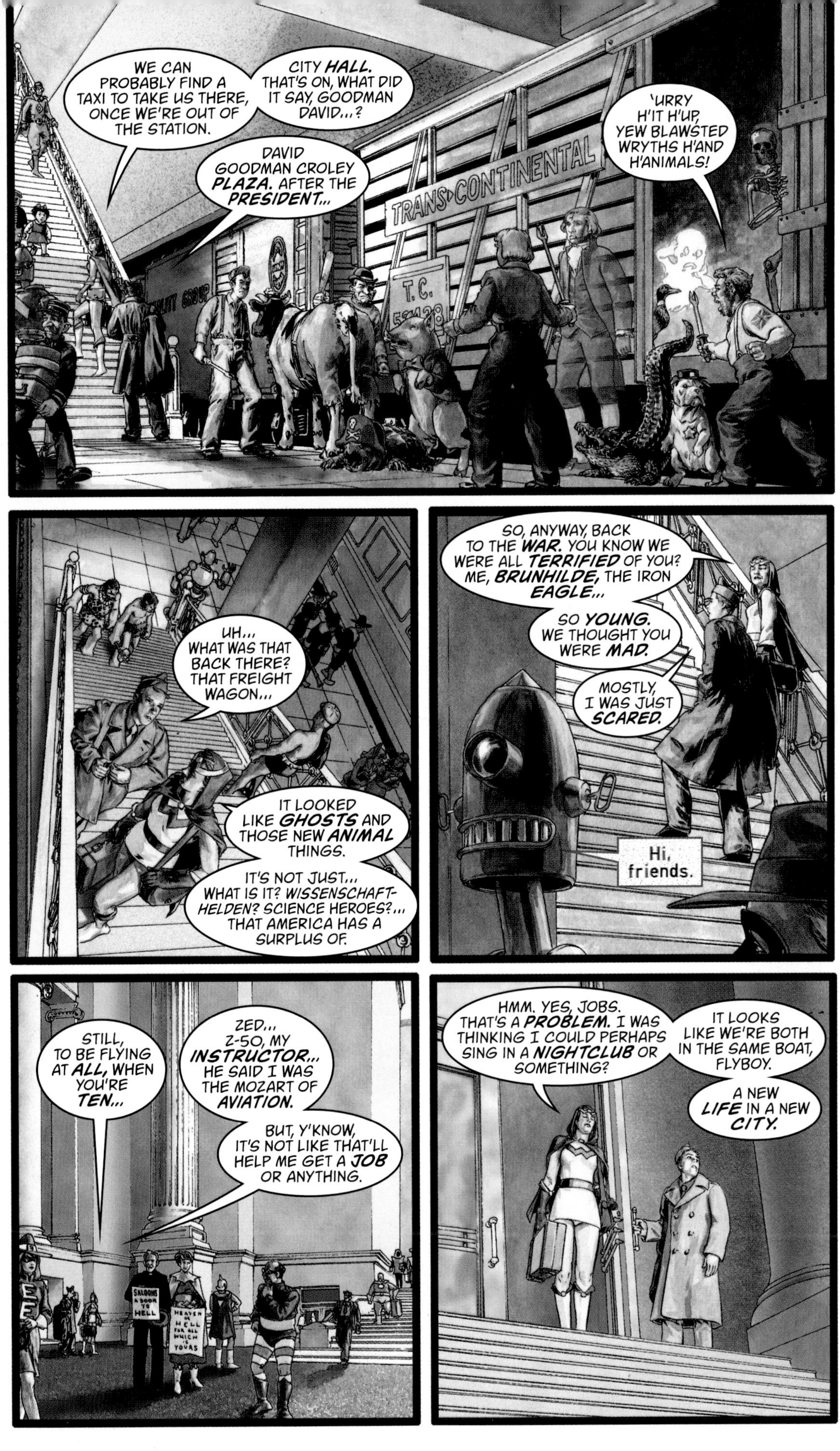
WE CAN PROBABLY FIND A TAXI TO TAKE US THERE, ONCE WE'RE OUT OF THE STATION.
CITY HALL. THAT'S ON, WHAT DID IT SAY, GOODMAN DAVID...?
DAVID GOODMAN CROLEY PLAZA. AFTER THE PRESIDENT...
TRANS·CONTINENTAL
T.C.
'URRY H'IT H'UP, YEW BLAWSTED WRYTHS H'AND H'ANIMALS!
UH... WHAT WAS THAT BACK THERE? THAT FREIGHT WAGON...
IT LOOKED LIKE GHOSTS AND THOSE NEW ANIMAL THINGS.
IT'S NOT JUST... WHAT IS IT? WISSENSCHAFT-HELDEN? SCIENCE HEROES?... THAT AMERICA HAS A SURPLUS OF.
SO, ANYWAY, BACK TO THE WAR. YOU KNOW WE WERE ALL TERRIFIED OF YOU? ME, BRUNHILDE, THE IRON EAGLE...
SO YOUNG. WE THOUGHT YOU WERE MAD.
MOSTLY, I WAS JUST SCARED.
Hi, friends.
STILL, TO BE FLYING AT ALL, WHEN YOU'RE TEN...
ZED... Z-50, MY INSTRUCTOR... HE SAID I WAS THE MOZART OF AVIATION.
BUT, Y'KNOW, IT'S NOT LIKE THAT'LL HELP ME GET A JOB OR ANYTHING.
HMM. YES, JOBS. THAT'S A PROBLEM. I WAS THINKING I COULD PERHAPS SING IN A NIGHTCLUB OR SOMETHING?
IT LOOKS LIKE WE'RE BOTH IN THE SAME BOAT, FLYBOY.
A NEW LIFE IN A NEW CITY.

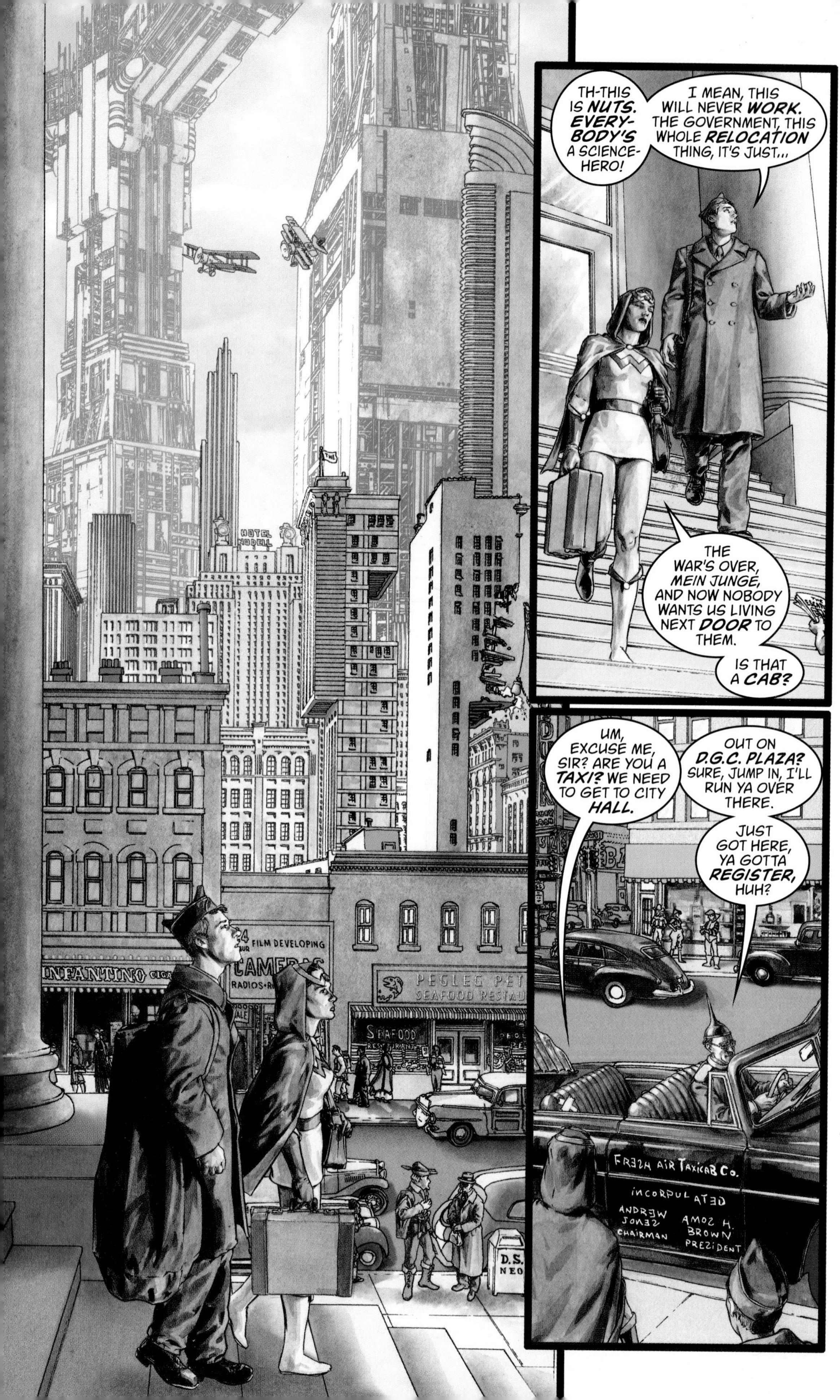

HOTEL NODELL
FILM DEVELOPING
CAMERAS
RADIOS
INFANTINO
PEGLEG PET
SEAFOOD RESTAU
SEAFOOD
RESTAURANT
TH-THIS IS *NUTS.* *EVERY-BODY'S* A SCIENCE-HERO!
I MEAN, THIS WILL NEVER *WORK.* THE GOVERNMENT, THIS WHOLE *RELOCATION* THING, IT'S JUST...
THE WAR'S OVER, *MEIN JUNGE,* AND NOW NOBODY WANTS US LIVING NEXT *DOOR* TO THEM.
IS THAT A *CAB?*
UM, EXCUSE ME, SIR? ARE YOU A *TAXI?* WE NEED TO GET TO CITY *HALL.*
OUT ON *D.G.C. PLAZA?* SURE, JUMP IN, I'LL RUN YA OVER THERE.
JUST GOT HERE, YA GOTTA *REGISTER,* HUH?
FRESH AIR TAXICAB CO.
INCORPULATED
ANDREW JONES CHAIRMAN
AMOS H. BROWN PREZIDENT

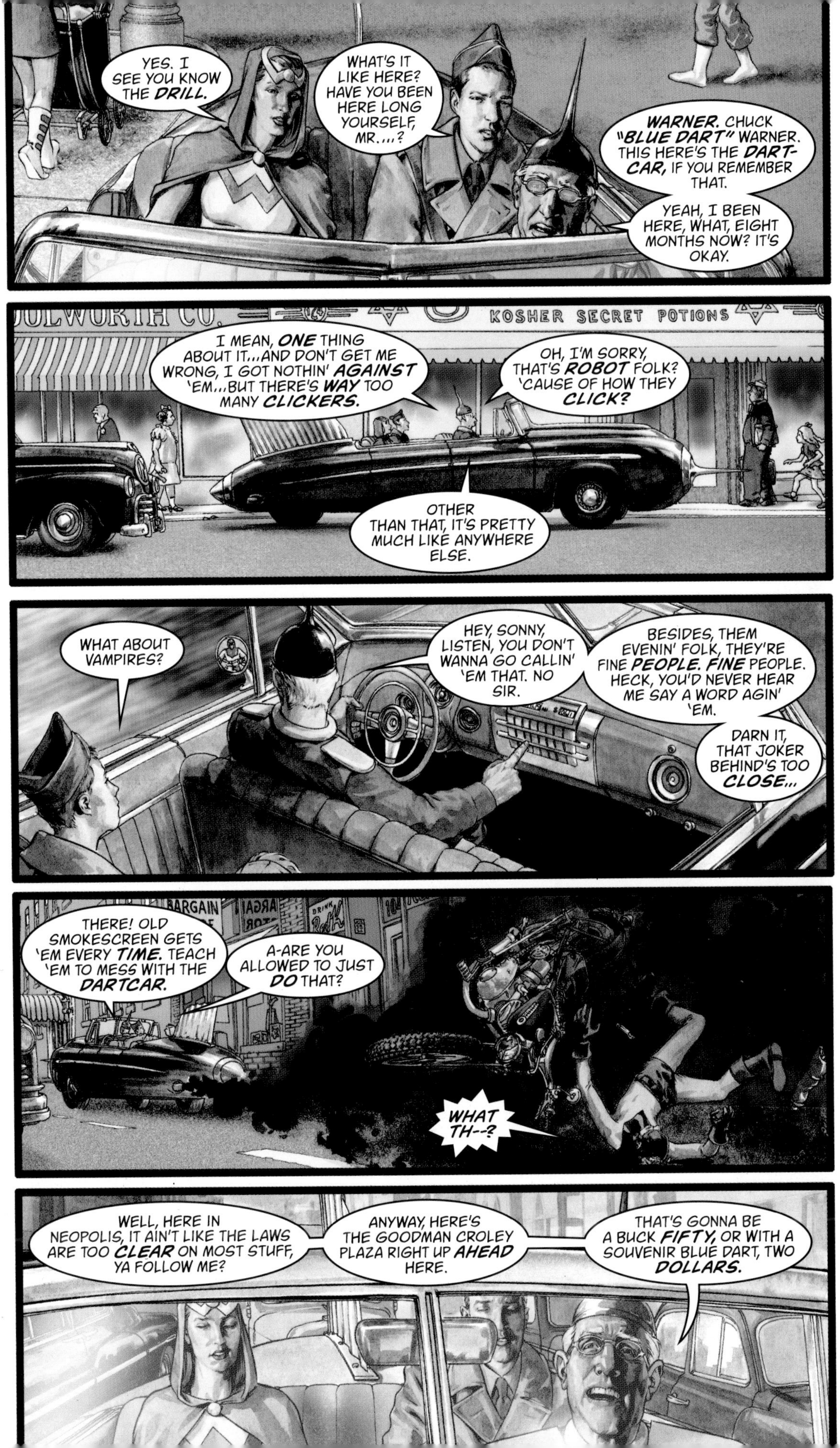
YES. I SEE YOU KNOW THE DRILL.
WHAT'S IT LIKE HERE? HAVE YOU BEEN HERE LONG YOURSELF, MR....?
WARNER. CHUCK "BLUE DART" WARNER. THIS HERE'S THE DART-CAR, IF YOU REMEMBER THAT.
YEAH, I BEEN HERE, WHAT, EIGHT MONTHS NOW? IT'S OKAY.
KOSHER SECRET POTIONS
I MEAN, ONE THING ABOUT IT...AND DON'T GET ME WRONG, I GOT NOTHIN' AGAINST 'EM...BUT THERE'S WAY TOO MANY CLICKERS.
OH, I'M SORRY, THAT'S ROBOT FOLK? 'CAUSE OF HOW THEY CLICK?
OTHER THAN THAT, IT'S PRETTY MUCH LIKE ANYWHERE ELSE.
WHAT ABOUT VAMPIRES?
HEY, SONNY, LISTEN, YOU DON'T WANNA GO CALLIN' 'EM THAT. NO SIR.
BESIDES, THEM EVENIN' FOLK, THEY'RE FINE PEOPLE. FINE PEOPLE. HECK, YOU'D NEVER HEAR ME SAY A WORD AGIN' 'EM.
DARN IT, THAT JOKER BEHIND'S TOO CLOSE...
THERE! OLD SMOKESCREEN GETS 'EM EVERY TIME. TEACH 'EM TO MESS WITH THE DARTCAR.
A-ARE YOU ALLOWED TO JUST DO THAT?
WHAT TH--?
WELL, HERE IN NEOPOLIS, IT AIN'T LIKE THE LAWS ARE TOO CLEAR ON MOST STUFF, YA FOLLOW ME?
ANYWAY, HERE'S THE GOODMAN CROLEY PLAZA RIGHT UP AHEAD HERE.
THAT'S GONNA BE A BUCK FIFTY, OR WITH A SOUVENIR BLUE DART, TWO DOLLARS.

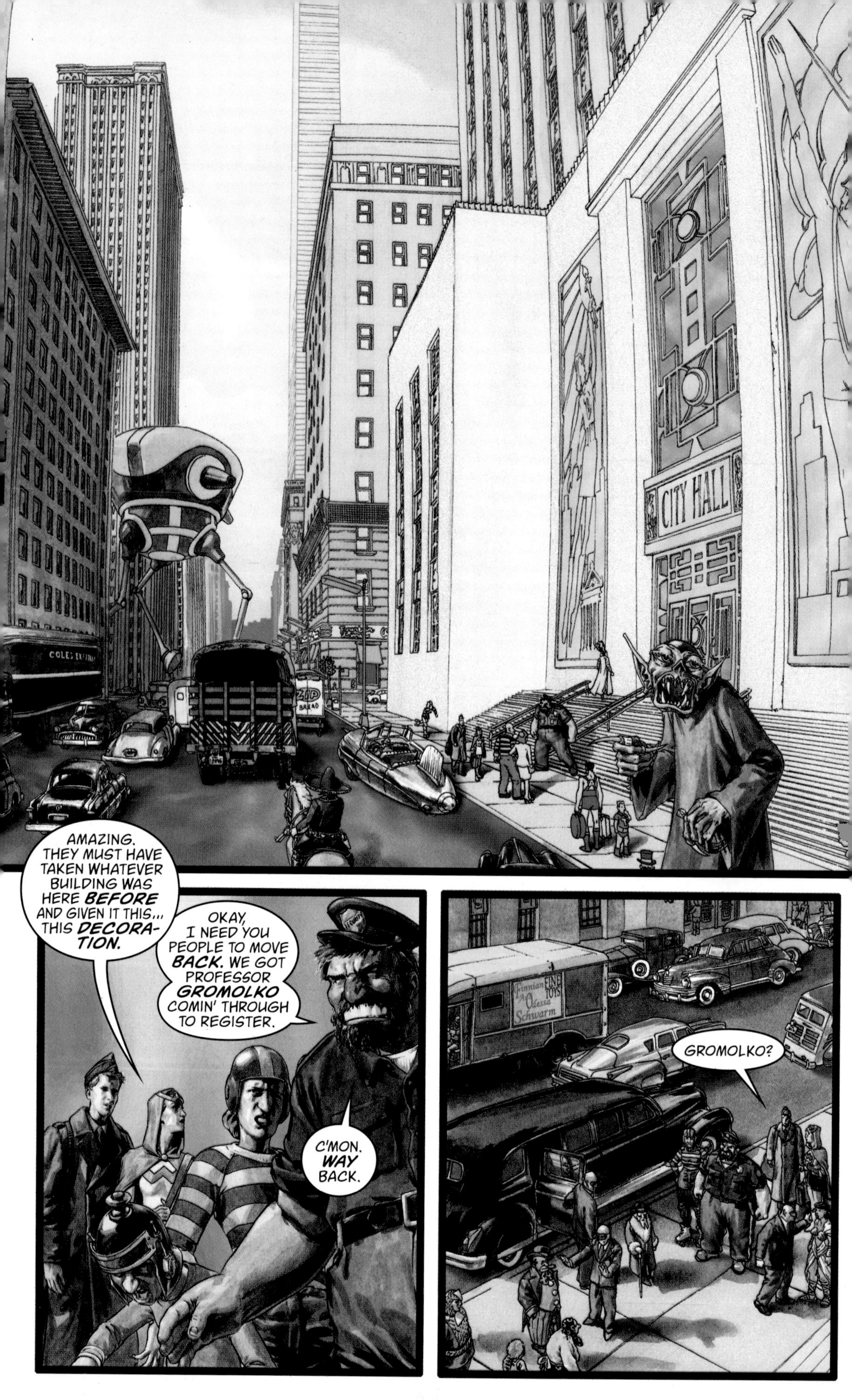
CITY HALL
COLES EXPRESS
ZIP BREAD
AMAZING. THEY MUST HAVE TAKEN WHATEVER BUILDING WAS HERE BEFORE AND GIVEN IT THIS... THIS DECORATION.
OKAY, I NEED YOU PEOPLE TO MOVE BACK. WE GOT PROFESSOR GROMOLKO COMIN' THROUGH TO REGISTER.
C'MON. WAY BACK.
Finnian FINE TOYS Odessa Schwarm
GROMOLKO?

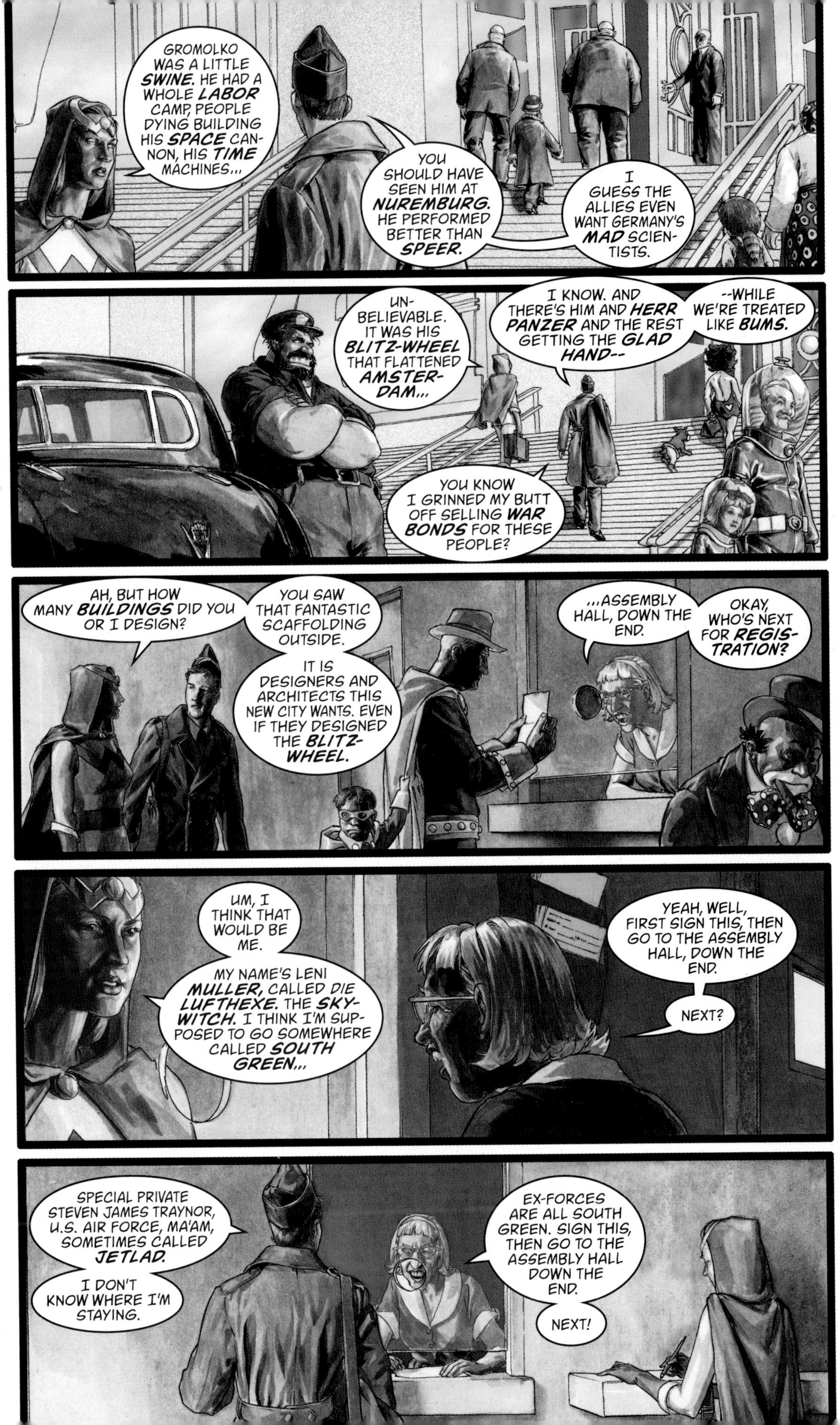
GROMOLKO WAS A LITTLE SWINE. HE HAD A WHOLE LABOR CAMP, PEOPLE DYING BUILDING HIS SPACE CANNON, HIS TIME MACHINES...
YOU SHOULD HAVE SEEN HIM AT NUREMBURG. HE PERFORMED BETTER THAN SPEER.
I GUESS THE ALLIES EVEN WANT GERMANY'S MAD SCIENTISTS.
UNBELIEVABLE. IT WAS HIS BLITZ-WHEEL THAT FLATTENED AMSTERDAM...
I KNOW. AND THERE'S HIM AND HERR PANZER AND THE REST GETTING THE GLAD HAND--
--WHILE WE'RE TREATED LIKE BUMS.
YOU KNOW I GRINNED MY BUTT OFF SELLING WAR BONDS FOR THESE PEOPLE?
AH, BUT HOW MANY BUILDINGS DID YOU OR I DESIGN?
YOU SAW THAT FANTASTIC SCAFFOLDING OUTSIDE.
IT IS DESIGNERS AND ARCHITECTS THIS NEW CITY WANTS. EVEN IF THEY DESIGNED THE BLITZ-WHEEL.
...ASSEMBLY HALL, DOWN THE END.
OKAY, WHO'S NEXT FOR REGISTRATION?
UM, I THINK THAT WOULD BE ME.
MY NAME'S LENI MULLER, CALLED DIE LUFTHEXE. THE SKY-WITCH. I THINK I'M SUPPOSED TO GO SOMEWHERE CALLED SOUTH GREEN...
YEAH, WELL, FIRST SIGN THIS, THEN GO TO THE ASSEMBLY HALL, DOWN THE END.
NEXT?
SPECIAL PRIVATE STEVEN JAMES TRAYNOR, U.S. AIR FORCE, MA'AM, SOMETIMES CALLED JETLAD.
I DON'T KNOW WHERE I'M STAYING.
EX-FORCES ARE ALL SOUTH GREEN. SIGN THIS, THEN GO TO THE ASSEMBLY HALL DOWN THE END.
NEXT!

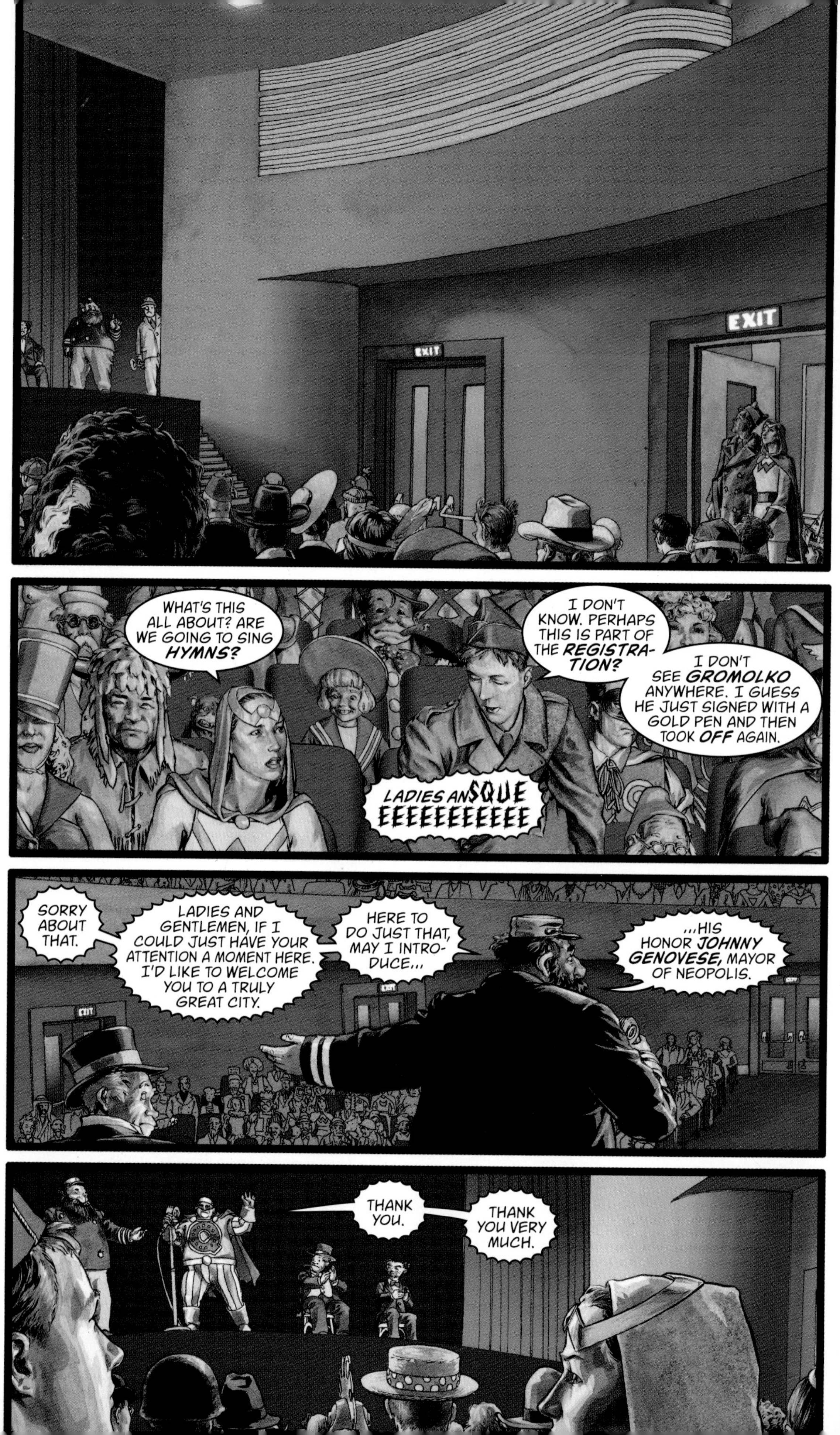
EXIT
EXIT
WHAT'S THIS ALL ABOUT? ARE WE GOING TO SING HYMNS?
I DON'T KNOW. PERHAPS THIS IS PART OF THE REGISTRATION?
I DON'T SEE GROMOLKO ANYWHERE. I GUESS HE JUST SIGNED WITH A GOLD PEN AND THEN TOOK OFF AGAIN.
LADIES ANSQUE EEEEEEEEEEE
SORRY ABOUT THAT.
LADIES AND GENTLEMEN, IF I COULD JUST HAVE YOUR ATTENTION A MOMENT HERE. I'D LIKE TO WELCOME YOU TO A TRULY GREAT CITY.
HERE TO DO JUST THAT, MAY I INTRODUCE...
...HIS HONOR JOHNNY GENOVESE, MAYOR OF NEOPOLIS.
EXIT
EXIT
THANK YOU.
THANK YOU VERY MUCH.

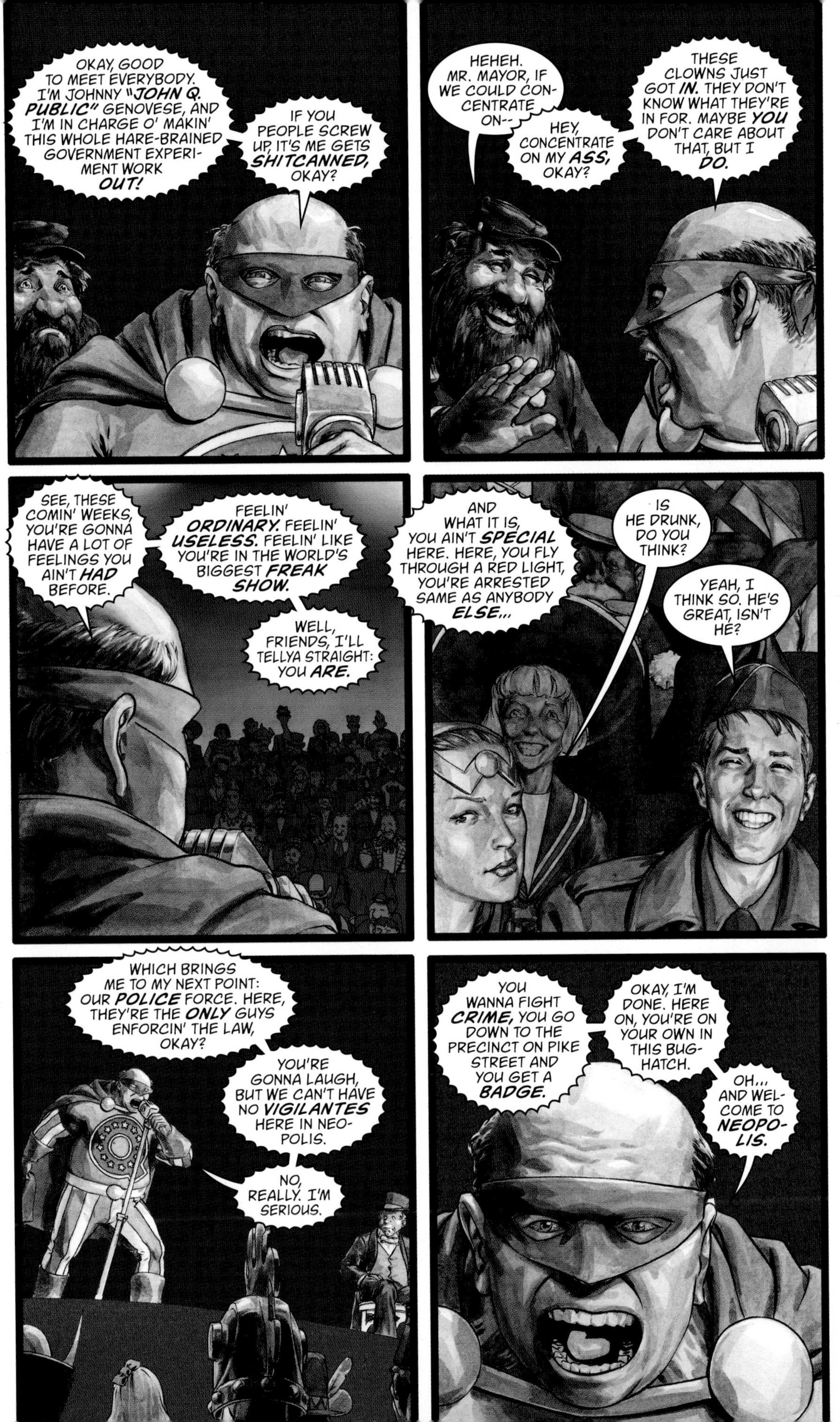
OKAY, GOOD TO MEET EVERYBODY. I'M JOHNNY "JOHN Q. PUBLIC" GENOVESE, AND I'M IN CHARGE O' MAKIN' THIS WHOLE HARE-BRAINED GOVERNMENT EXPERIMENT WORK OUT!
IF YOU PEOPLE SCREW UP, IT'S ME GETS SHITCANNED, OKAY?
HEHEH. MR. MAYOR, IF WE COULD CONCENTRATE ON--
HEY, CONCENTRATE ON MY ASS, OKAY?
THESE CLOWNS JUST GOT IN. THEY DON'T KNOW WHAT THEY'RE IN FOR. MAYBE YOU DON'T CARE ABOUT THAT, BUT I DO.
SEE, THESE COMIN' WEEKS, YOU'RE GONNA HAVE A LOT OF FEELINGS YOU AIN'T HAD BEFORE.
FEELIN' ORDINARY. FEELIN' USELESS. FEELIN' LIKE YOU'RE IN THE WORLD'S BIGGEST FREAK SHOW.
WELL, FRIENDS, I'LL TELLYA STRAIGHT: YOU ARE.
AND WHAT IT IS, YOU AIN'T SPECIAL HERE. HERE, YOU FLY THROUGH A RED LIGHT, YOU'RE ARRESTED SAME AS ANYBODY ELSE...
IS HE DRUNK, DO YOU THINK?
YEAH, I THINK SO. HE'S GREAT, ISN'T HE?
WHICH BRINGS ME TO MY NEXT POINT: OUR POLICE FORCE. HERE, THEY'RE THE ONLY GUYS ENFORCIN' THE LAW, OKAY?
YOU'RE GONNA LAUGH, BUT WE CAN'T HAVE NO VIGILANTES HERE IN NEOPOLIS.
NO, REALLY. I'M SERIOUS.
YOU WANNA FIGHT CRIME, YOU GO DOWN TO THE PRECINCT ON PIKE STREET AND YOU GET A BADGE.
OKAY, I'M DONE. HERE ON, YOU'RE ON YOUR OWN IN THIS BUG-HATCH.
OH... AND WELCOME TO NEOPOLIS.

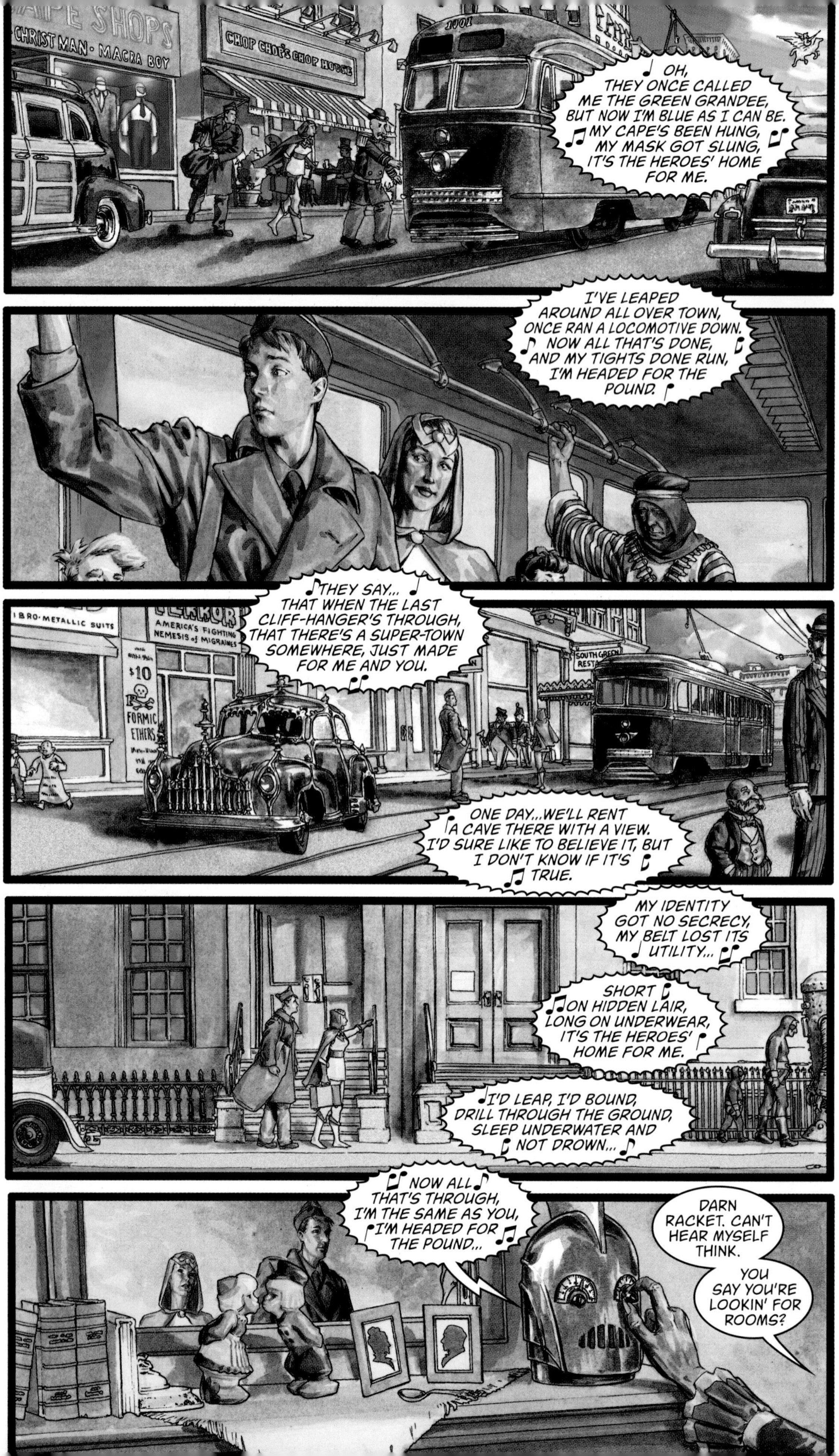
CHRIST MAN · MACRA BOY
CHOP CHOP'S CHOP HOUSE
1001
♩ OH, THEY ONCE CALLED ME THE GREEN GRANDEE, BUT NOW I'M BLUE AS I CAN BE. ♫ MY CAPE'S BEEN HUNG, MY MASK GOT SLUNG, IT'S THE HEROES' HOME FOR ME. ♫
I'VE LEAPED AROUND ALL OVER TOWN, ONCE RAN A LOCOMOTIVE DOWN. ♪ NOW ALL THAT'S DONE, AND MY TIGHTS DONE RUN, I'M HEADED FOR THE POUND. ♪
♪ THEY SAY... ♩ THAT WHEN THE LAST CLIFF-HANGER'S THROUGH, THAT THERE'S A SUPER-TOWN SOMEWHERE, JUST MADE FOR ME AND YOU. ♫
IBRO-METALLIC SUITS
AMERICA'S FIGHTING NEMESIS of MIGRAINES
$10
FORMIC ETHERS
SOUTH GREEN RESTA
ONE DAY...WE'LL RENT ♪ A CAVE THERE WITH A VIEW. I'D SURE LIKE TO BELIEVE IT, BUT I DON'T KNOW IF IT'S ♪ ♫ TRUE.
MY IDENTITY GOT NO SECRECY, MY BELT LOST ITS ♩ UTILITY... ♫
SHORT ♪ ♫ ON HIDDEN LAIR, LONG ON UNDERWEAR, IT'S THE HEROES' ♪ HOME FOR ME.
♩ I'D LEAP, I'D BOUND, DRILL THROUGH THE GROUND, SLEEP UNDERWATER AND ♪ NOT DROWN... ♪
♫ NOW ALL ♪ THAT'S THROUGH, I'M THE SAME AS YOU, ♪ I'M HEADED FOR ♫ THE POUND...
DARN RACKET. CAN'T HEAR MYSELF THINK.
YOU SAY YOU'RE LOOKIN' FOR ROOMS?

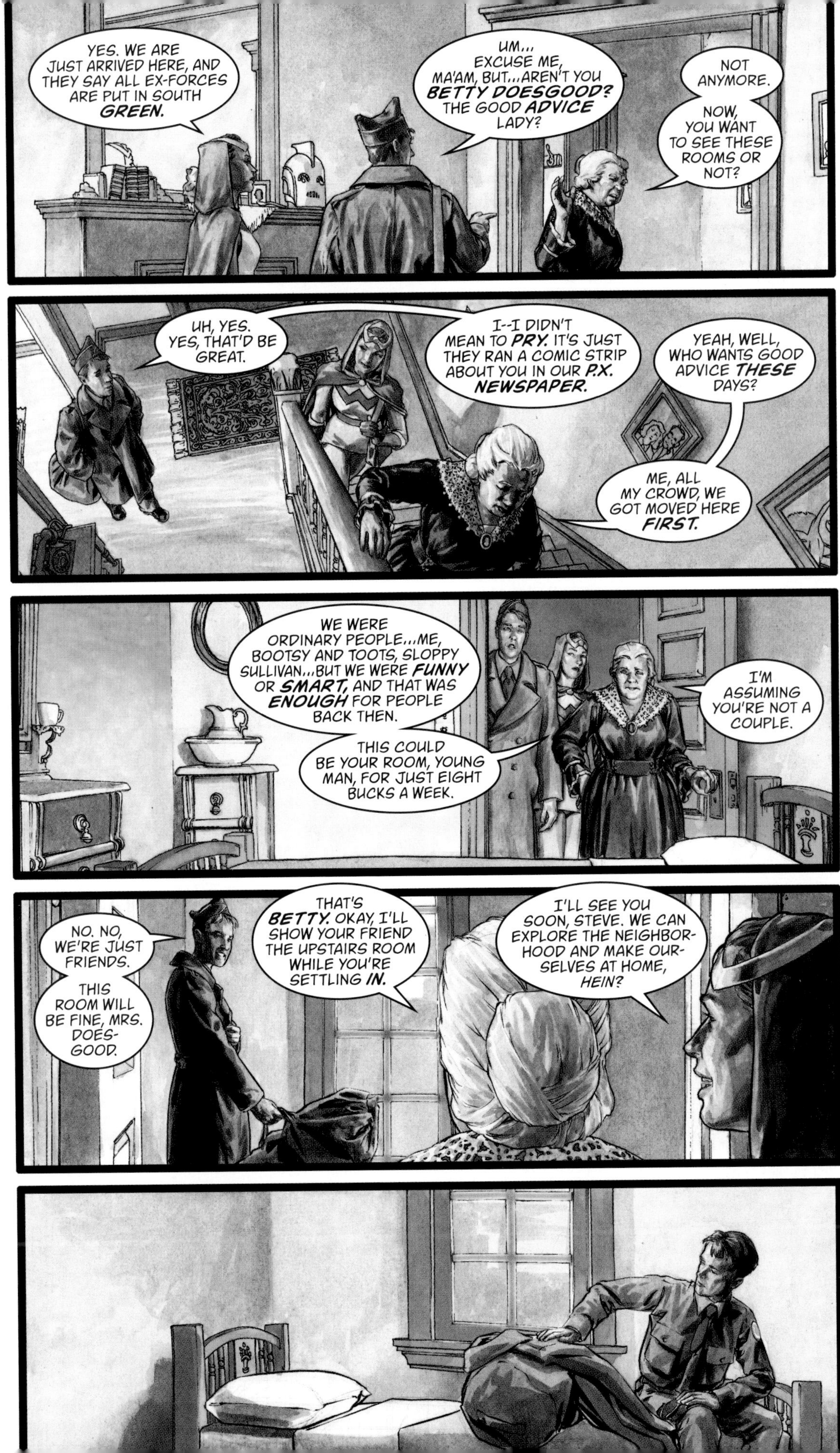
YES. WE ARE JUST ARRIVED HERE, AND THEY SAY ALL EX-FORCES ARE PUT IN SOUTH GREEN.
UM... EXCUSE ME, MA'AM, BUT...AREN'T YOU BETTY DOESGOOD? THE GOOD ADVICE LADY?
NOT ANYMORE.
NOW, YOU WANT TO SEE THESE ROOMS OR NOT?
UH, YES. YES, THAT'D BE GREAT.
I--I DIDN'T MEAN TO PRY. IT'S JUST THEY RAN A COMIC STRIP ABOUT YOU IN OUR P.X. NEWSPAPER.
YEAH, WELL, WHO WANTS GOOD ADVICE THESE DAYS?
ME, ALL MY CROWD, WE GOT MOVED HERE FIRST.
WE WERE ORDINARY PEOPLE...ME, BOOTSY AND TOOTS, SLOPPY SULLIVAN...BUT WE WERE FUNNY OR SMART, AND THAT WAS ENOUGH FOR PEOPLE BACK THEN.
THIS COULD BE YOUR ROOM, YOUNG MAN, FOR JUST EIGHT BUCKS A WEEK.
I'M ASSUMING YOU'RE NOT A COUPLE.
NO. NO, WE'RE JUST FRIENDS.
THIS ROOM WILL BE FINE, MRS. DOES-GOOD.
THAT'S BETTY. OKAY, I'LL SHOW YOUR FRIEND THE UPSTAIRS ROOM WHILE YOU'RE SETTLING IN.
I'LL SEE YOU SOON, STEVE. WE CAN EXPLORE THE NEIGHBOR-HOOD AND MAKE OUR-SELVES AT HOME, HEIN?

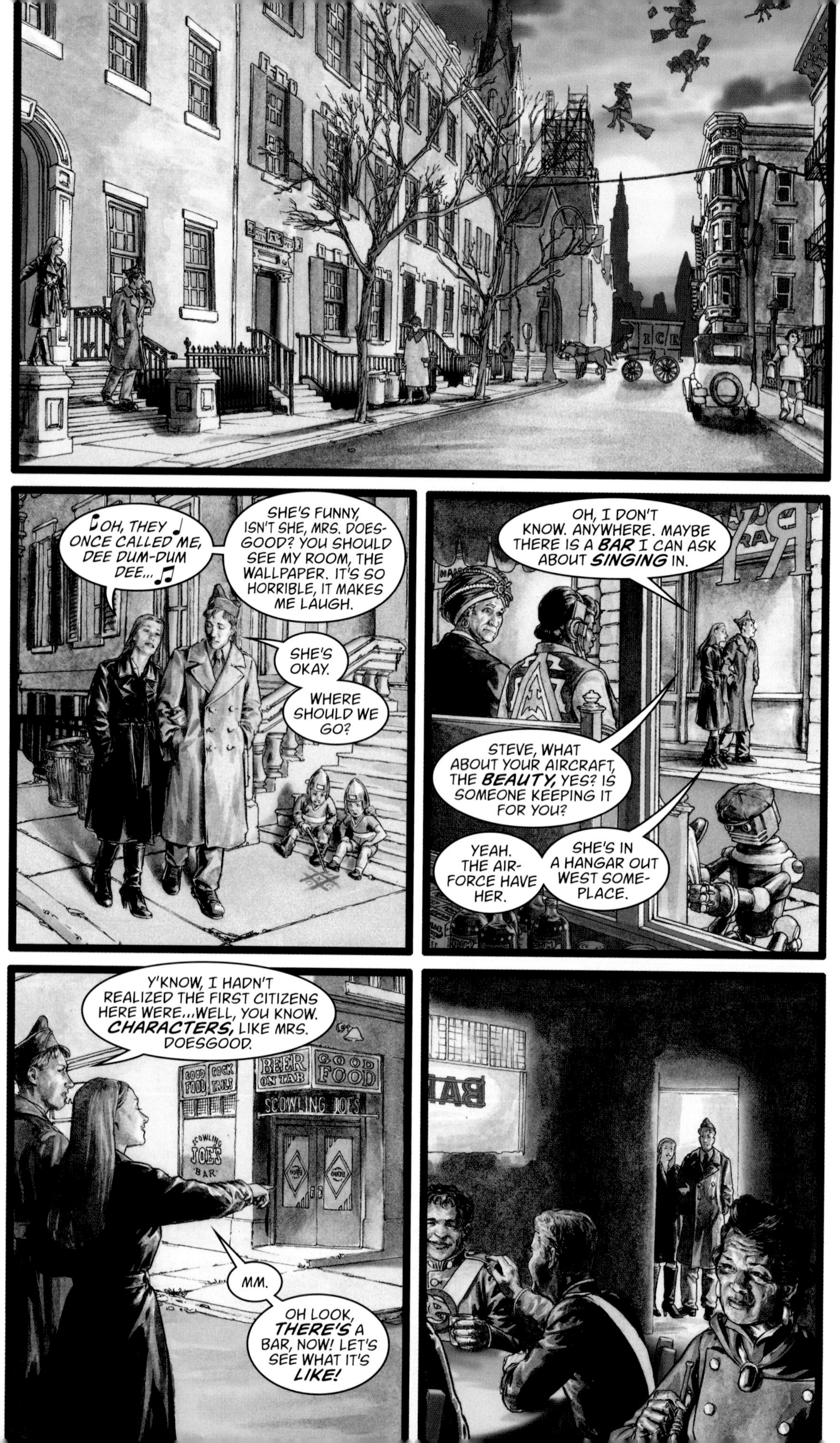

OH, THEY ONCE CALLED ME, DEE DUM-DUM DEE...
SHE'S FUNNY, ISN'T SHE, MRS. DOES-GOOD? YOU SHOULD SEE MY ROOM, THE WALLPAPER. IT'S SO HORRIBLE, IT MAKES ME LAUGH.
SHE'S OKAY.
WHERE SHOULD WE GO?
OH, I DON'T KNOW. ANYWHERE. MAYBE THERE IS A BAR I CAN ASK ABOUT SINGING IN.
STEVE, WHAT ABOUT YOUR AIRCRAFT, THE BEAUTY, YES? IS SOMEONE KEEPING IT FOR YOU?
YEAH. THE AIR-FORCE HAVE HER.
SHE'S IN A HANGAR OUT WEST SOME-PLACE.
Y'KNOW, I HADN'T REALIZED THE FIRST CITIZENS HERE WERE...WELL, YOU KNOW. CHARACTERS, LIKE MRS. DOESGOOD.
BEER ON TAB
GOOD FOOD
GOOD FOOD
COCK TAILS
SCOWLING JOE'S
SCOWLING JOE'S BAR
MM.
OH LOOK, THERE'S A BAR, NOW! LET'S SEE WHAT IT'S LIKE!

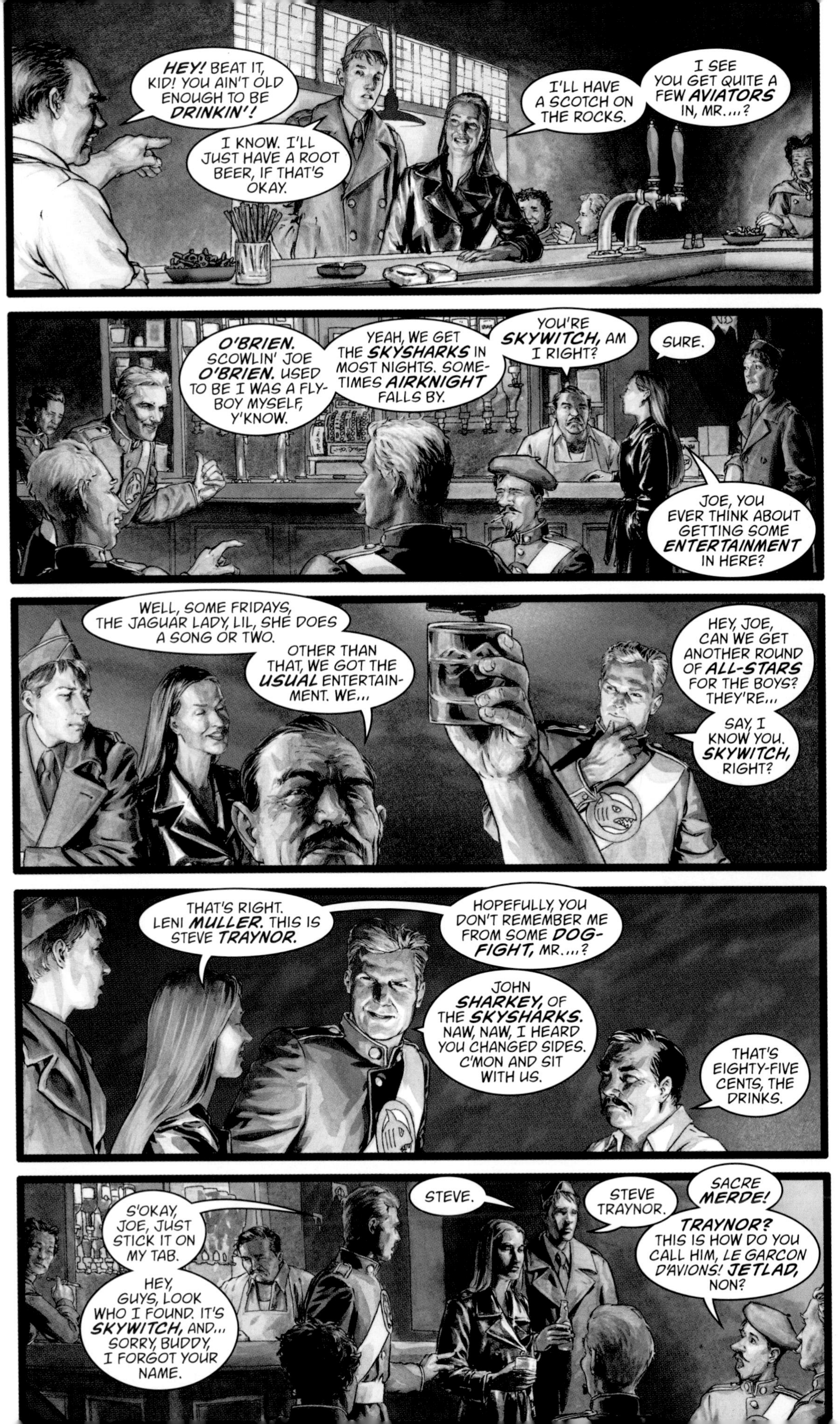
HEY! BEAT IT, KID! YOU AIN'T OLD ENOUGH TO BE DRINKIN'!
I KNOW. I'LL JUST HAVE A ROOT BEER, IF THAT'S OKAY.
I'LL HAVE A SCOTCH ON THE ROCKS.
I SEE YOU GET QUITE A FEW AVIATORS IN, MR....?
O'BRIEN. SCOWLIN' JOE O'BRIEN. USED TO BE I WAS A FLY-BOY MYSELF, Y'KNOW.
YEAH, WE GET THE SKYSHARKS IN MOST NIGHTS. SOME-TIMES AIRKNIGHT FALLS BY.
YOU'RE SKYWITCH, AM I RIGHT?
SURE.
JOE, YOU EVER THINK ABOUT GETTING SOME ENTERTAINMENT IN HERE?
WELL, SOME FRIDAYS, THE JAGUAR LADY, LIL, SHE DOES A SONG OR TWO.
OTHER THAN THAT, WE GOT THE USUAL ENTERTAIN-MENT. WE...
HEY, JOE, CAN WE GET ANOTHER ROUND OF ALL-STARS FOR THE BOYS? THEY'RE...
SAY, I KNOW YOU. SKYWITCH, RIGHT?
THAT'S RIGHT. LENI MULLER. THIS IS STEVE TRAYNOR.
HOPEFULLY, YOU DON'T REMEMBER ME FROM SOME DOG-FIGHT, MR....?
JOHN SHARKEY, OF THE SKYSHARKS. NAW, NAW, I HEARD YOU CHANGED SIDES. C'MON AND SIT WITH US.
THAT'S EIGHTY-FIVE CENTS, THE DRINKS.
S'OKAY, JOE, JUST STICK IT ON MY TAB.
HEY, GUYS, LOOK WHO I FOUND. IT'S SKYWITCH, AND... SORRY, BUDDY, I FORGOT YOUR NAME.
STEVE.
STEVE TRAYNOR.
SACRE MERDE!
TRAYNOR? THIS IS HOW DO YOU CALL HIM, LE GARCON D'AVIONS! JETLAD, NON?

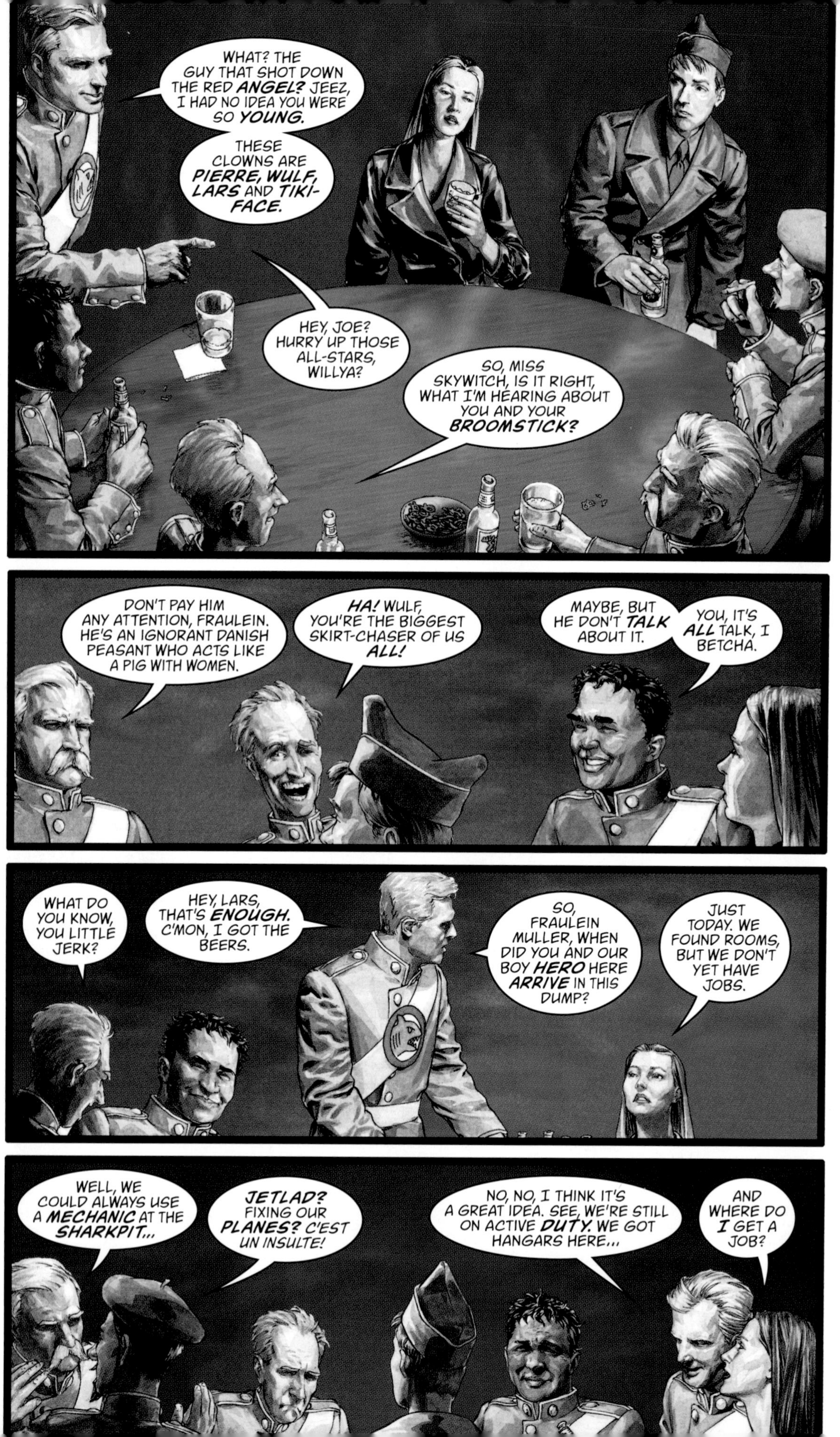
WHAT? THE GUY THAT SHOT DOWN THE RED ANGEL? JEEZ, I HAD NO IDEA YOU WERE SO YOUNG.
THESE CLOWNS ARE PIERRE, WULF, LARS AND TIKI-FACE.
HEY, JOE? HURRY UP THOSE ALL-STARS, WILLYA?
SO, MISS SKYWITCH, IS IT RIGHT, WHAT I'M HEARING ABOUT YOU AND YOUR BROOMSTICK?
DON'T PAY HIM ANY ATTENTION, FRAULEIN. HE'S AN IGNORANT DANISH PEASANT WHO ACTS LIKE A PIG WITH WOMEN.
HA! WULF, YOU'RE THE BIGGEST SKIRT-CHASER OF US ALL!
MAYBE, BUT HE DON'T TALK ABOUT IT.
YOU, IT'S ALL TALK, I BETCHA.
WHAT DO YOU KNOW, YOU LITTLE JERK?
HEY, LARS, THAT'S ENOUGH. C'MON, I GOT THE BEERS.
SO, FRAULEIN MULLER, WHEN DID YOU AND OUR BOY HERO HERE ARRIVE IN THIS DUMP?
JUST TODAY. WE FOUND ROOMS, BUT WE DON'T YET HAVE JOBS.
WELL, WE COULD ALWAYS USE A MECHANIC AT THE SHARKPIT...
JETLAD? FIXING OUR PLANES? C'EST UN INSULTE!
NO, NO, I THINK IT'S A GREAT IDEA. SEE, WE'RE STILL ON ACTIVE DUTY. WE GOT HANGARS HERE...
AND WHERE DO I GET A JOB?

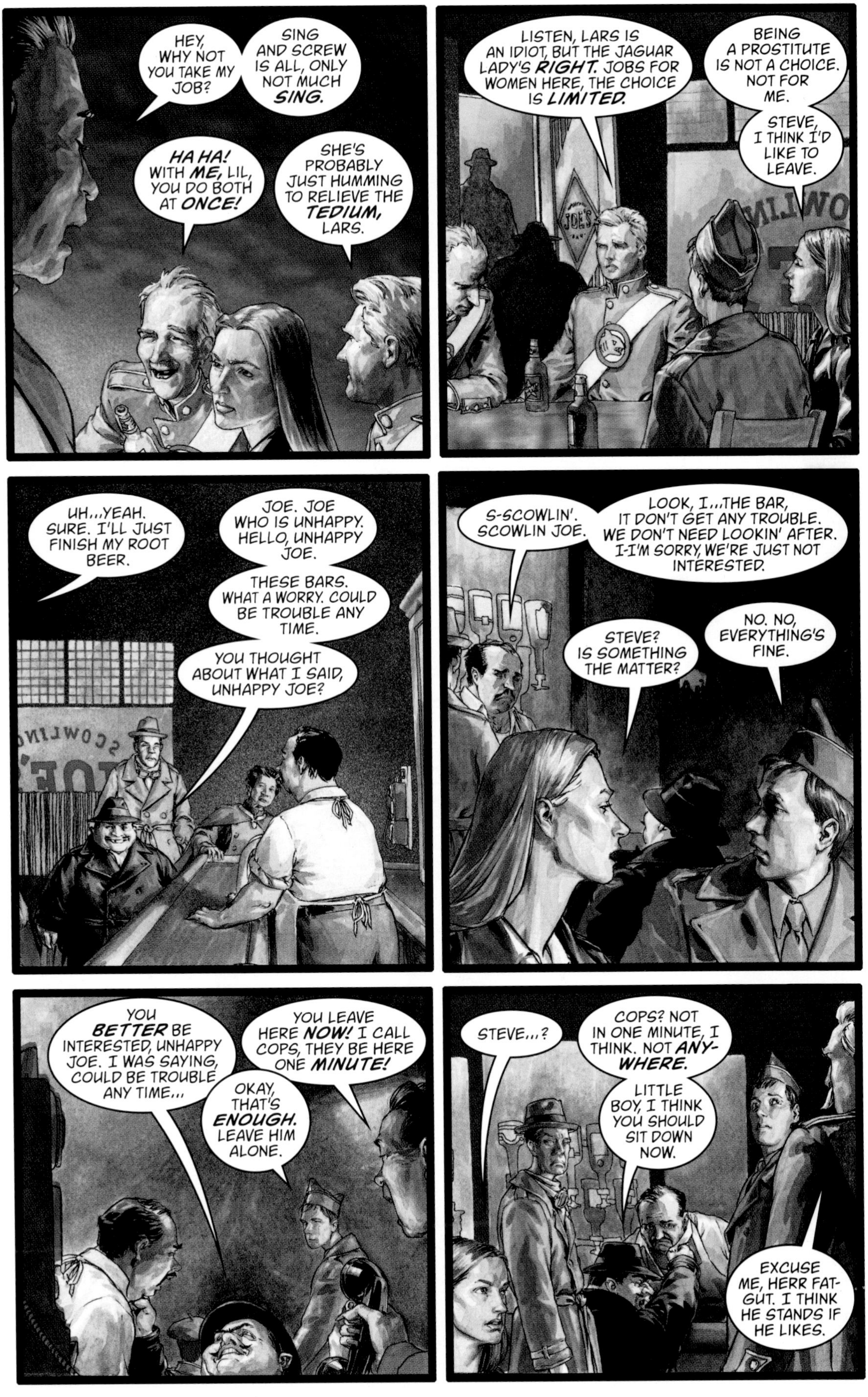
HEY, WHY NOT YOU TAKE MY JOB?
SING AND SCREW IS ALL, ONLY NOT MUCH SING.
HA HA! WITH ME, LIL, YOU DO BOTH AT ONCE!
SHE'S PROBABLY JUST HUMMING TO RELIEVE THE TEDIUM, LARS.
LISTEN, LARS IS AN IDIOT, BUT THE JAGUAR LADY'S RIGHT. JOBS FOR WOMEN HERE, THE CHOICE IS LIMITED.
BEING A PROSTITUTE IS NOT A CHOICE. NOT FOR ME.
STEVE, I THINK I'D LIKE TO LEAVE.
UH...YEAH. SURE. I'LL JUST FINISH MY ROOT BEER.
JOE. JOE WHO IS UNHAPPY. HELLO, UNHAPPY JOE.
THESE BARS. WHAT A WORRY. COULD BE TROUBLE ANY TIME.
YOU THOUGHT ABOUT WHAT I SAID, UNHAPPY JOE?
S-SCOWLIN'. SCOWLIN JOE.
LOOK, I...THE BAR, IT DON'T GET ANY TROUBLE. WE DON'T NEED LOOKIN' AFTER. I-I'M SORRY, WE'RE JUST NOT INTERESTED.
STEVE? IS SOMETHING THE MATTER?
NO. NO, EVERYTHING'S FINE.
YOU BETTER BE INTERESTED, UNHAPPY JOE. I WAS SAYING, COULD BE TROUBLE ANY TIME...
YOU LEAVE HERE NOW! I CALL COPS, THEY BE HERE ONE MINUTE!
OKAY, THAT'S ENOUGH. LEAVE HIM ALONE.
STEVE...?
COPS? NOT IN ONE MINUTE, I THINK. NOT ANY-WHERE.
LITTLE BOY, I THINK YOU SHOULD SIT DOWN NOW.
EXCUSE ME, HERR FAT-GUT. I THINK HE STANDS IF HE LIKES.

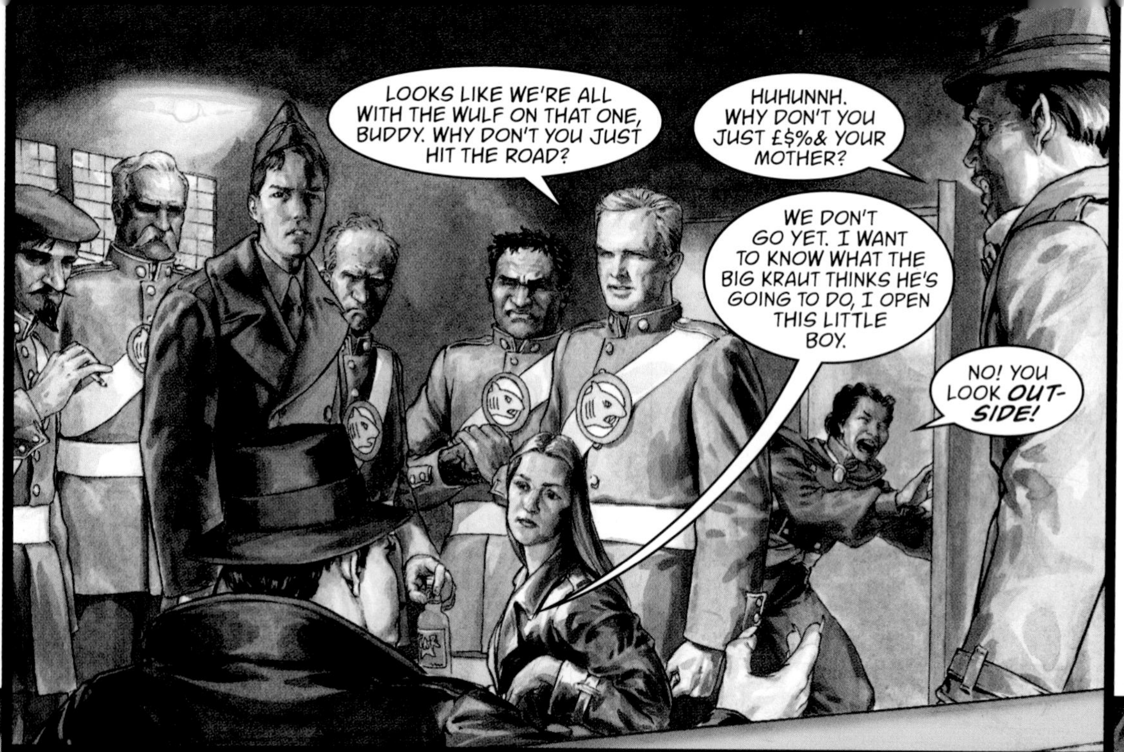
LOOKS LIKE WE'RE ALL WITH THE WULF ON THAT ONE, BUDDY. WHY DON'T YOU JUST HIT THE ROAD?
HUHUNNH. WHY DON'T YOU JUST £$%& YOUR MOTHER?
WE DON'T GO YET. I WANT TO KNOW WHAT THE BIG KRAUT THINKS HE'S GOING TO DO, I OPEN THIS LITTLE BOY.
NO! YOU LOOK OUT-SIDE!

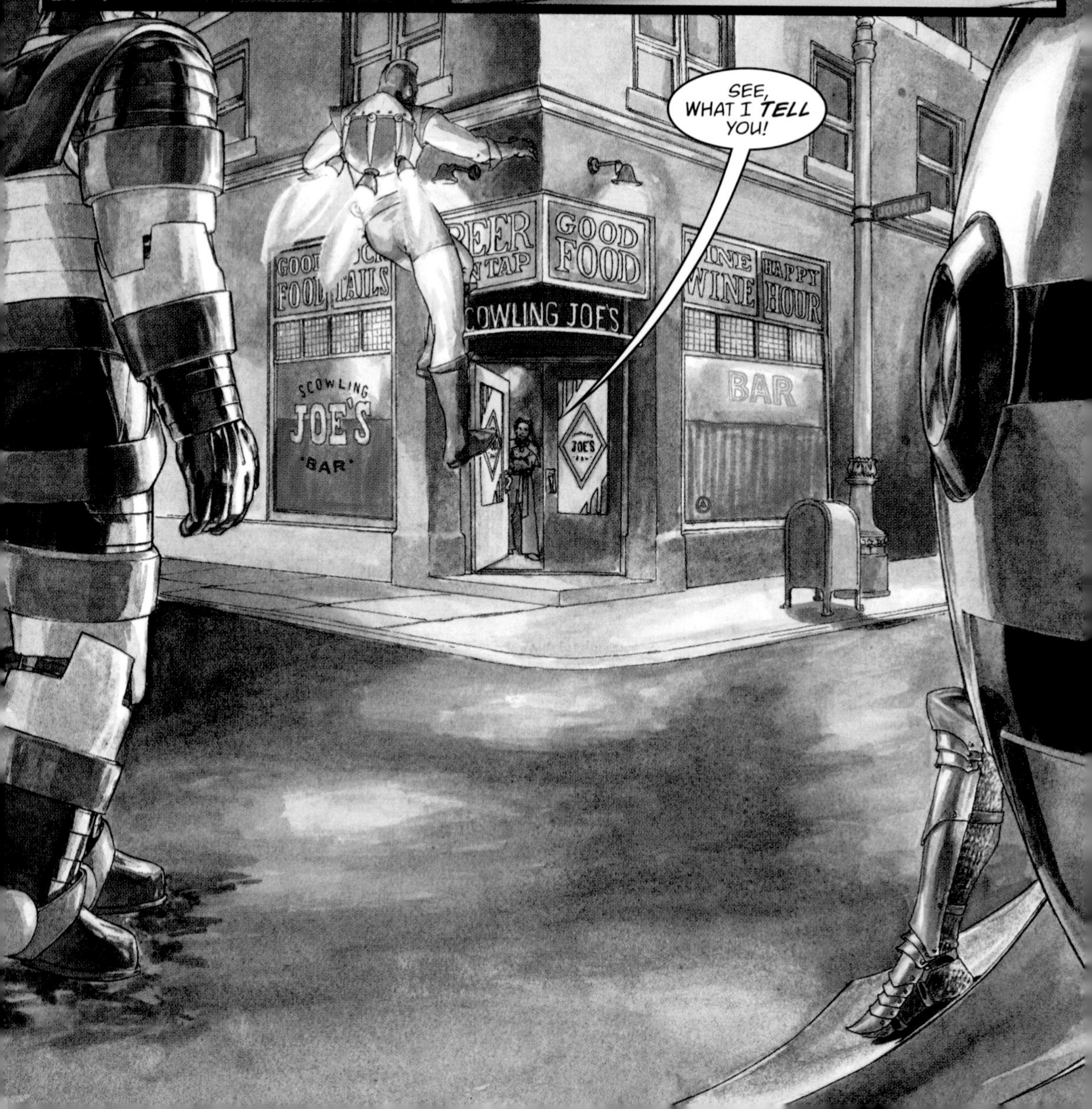
SEE, WHAT I TELL YOU!
BEER ON TAP
GOOD FOOD
WINE HAPPY HOUR
SCOWLING JOE'S
SCOWLING JOE'S BAR
JOE'S
BAR
JORDAN

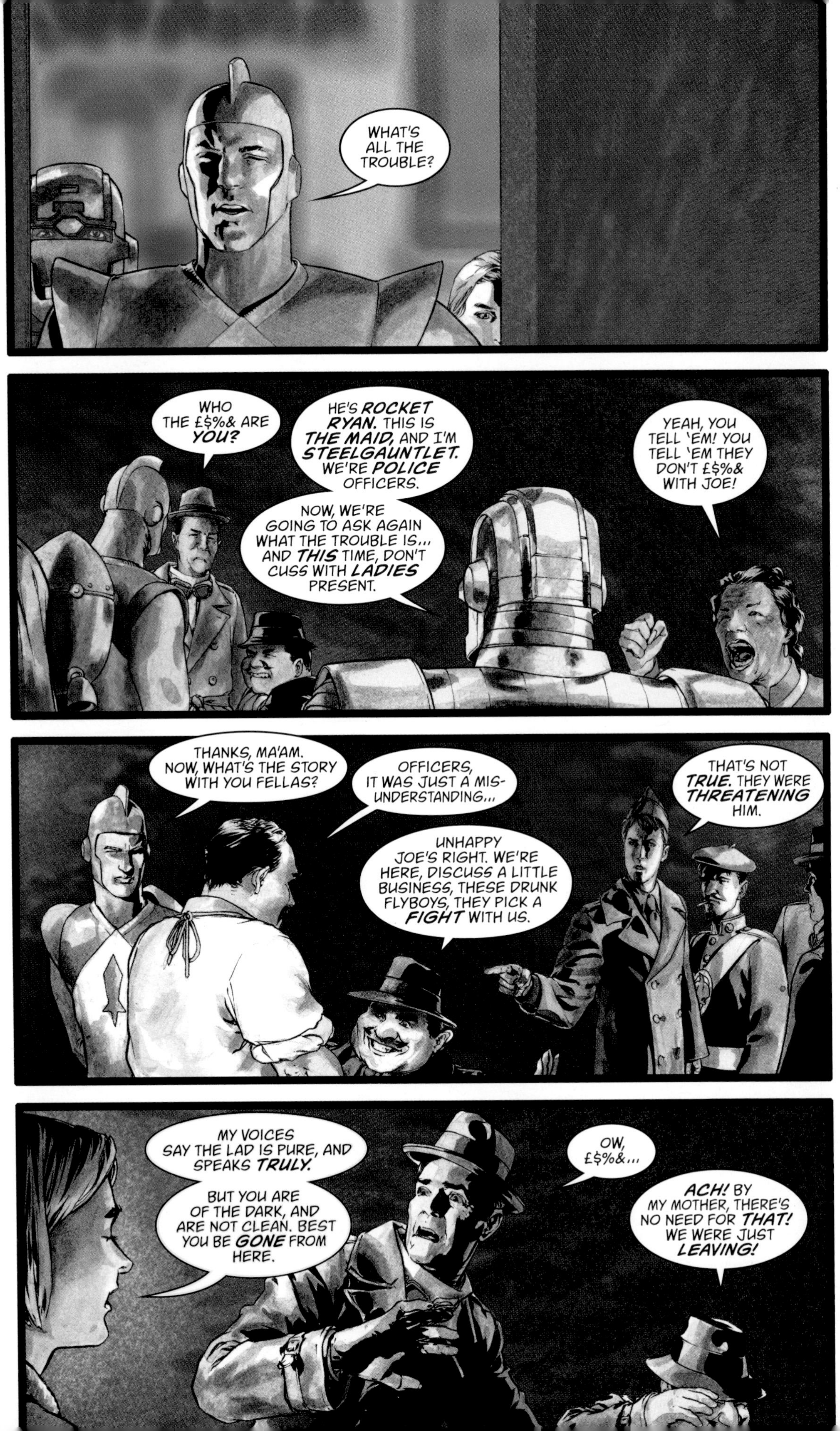

WHAT'S ALL THE TROUBLE?
WHO THE £$%& ARE YOU?
HE'S ROCKET RYAN. THIS IS THE MAID, AND I'M STEELGAUNTLET. WE'RE POLICE OFFICERS.
NOW, WE'RE GOING TO ASK AGAIN WHAT THE TROUBLE IS... AND THIS TIME, DON'T CUSS WITH LADIES PRESENT.
YEAH, YOU TELL 'EM! YOU TELL 'EM THEY DON'T £$%& WITH JOE!
THANKS, MA'AM. NOW, WHAT'S THE STORY WITH YOU FELLAS?
OFFICERS, IT WAS JUST A MIS-UNDERSTANDING...
UNHAPPY JOE'S RIGHT. WE'RE HERE, DISCUSS A LITTLE BUSINESS, THESE DRUNK FLYBOYS, THEY PICK A FIGHT WITH US.
THAT'S NOT TRUE. THEY WERE THREATENING HIM.
MY VOICES SAY THE LAD IS PURE, AND SPEAKS TRULY.
BUT YOU ARE OF THE DARK, AND ARE NOT CLEAN. BEST YOU BE GONE FROM HERE.
OW, £$%&...
ACH! BY MY MOTHER, THERE'S NO NEED FOR THAT! WE WERE JUST LEAVING!

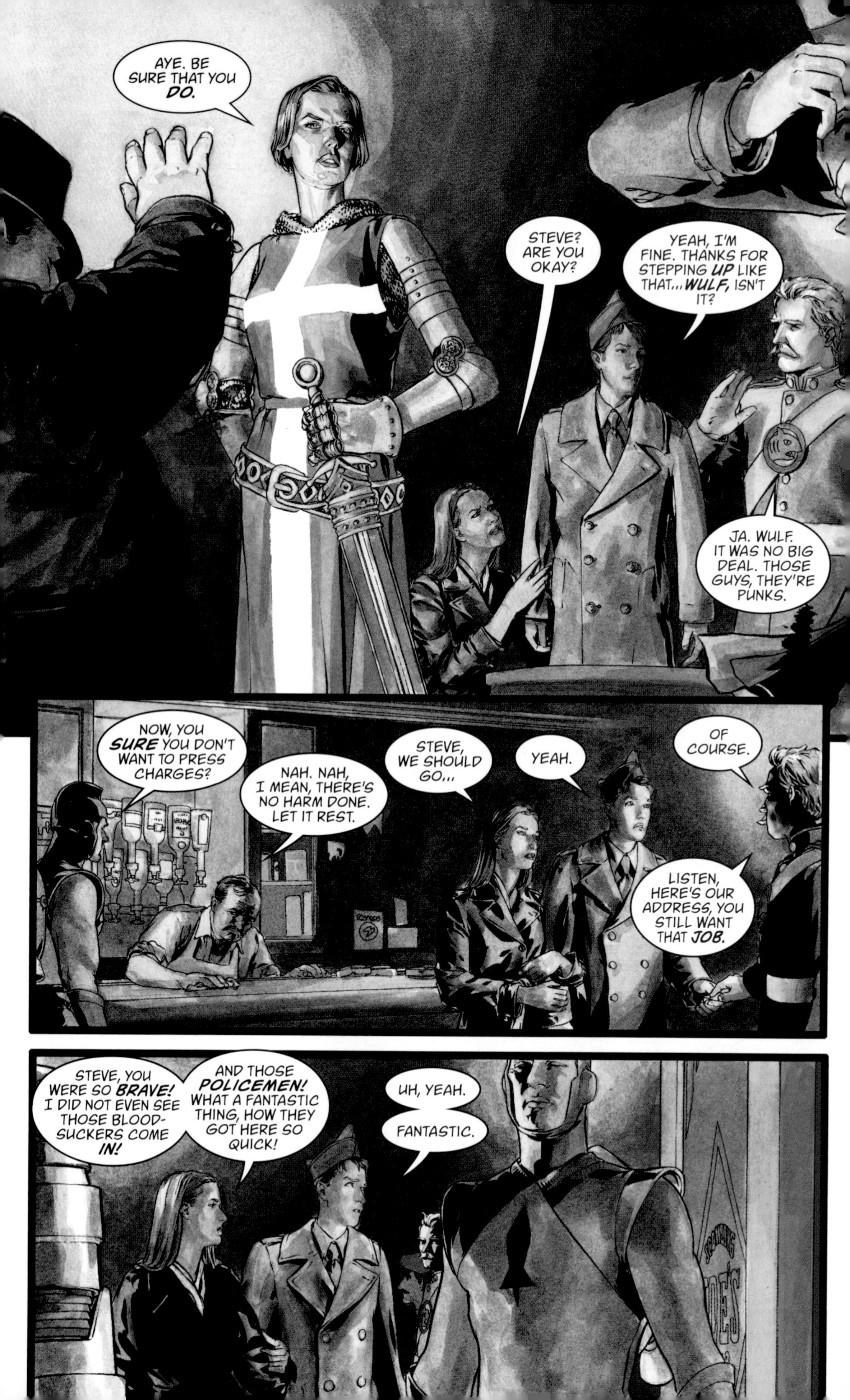
AYE. BE SURE THAT YOU DO.
STEVE? ARE YOU OKAY?
YEAH, I'M FINE. THANKS FOR STEPPING UP LIKE THAT... WULF, ISN'T IT?
JA. WULF. IT WAS NO BIG DEAL. THOSE GUYS, THEY'RE PUNKS.
NOW, YOU SURE YOU DON'T WANT TO PRESS CHARGES?
NAH. NAH, I MEAN, THERE'S NO HARM DONE. LET IT REST.
STEVE, WE SHOULD GO...
YEAH.
OF COURSE.
LISTEN, HERE'S OUR ADDRESS, YOU STILL WANT THAT JOB.
STEVE, YOU WERE SO BRAVE! I DID NOT EVEN SEE THOSE BLOOD-SUCKERS COME IN!
AND THOSE POLICEMEN! WHAT A FANTASTIC THING, HOW THEY GOT HERE SO QUICK!
UH, YEAH.
FANTASTIC.

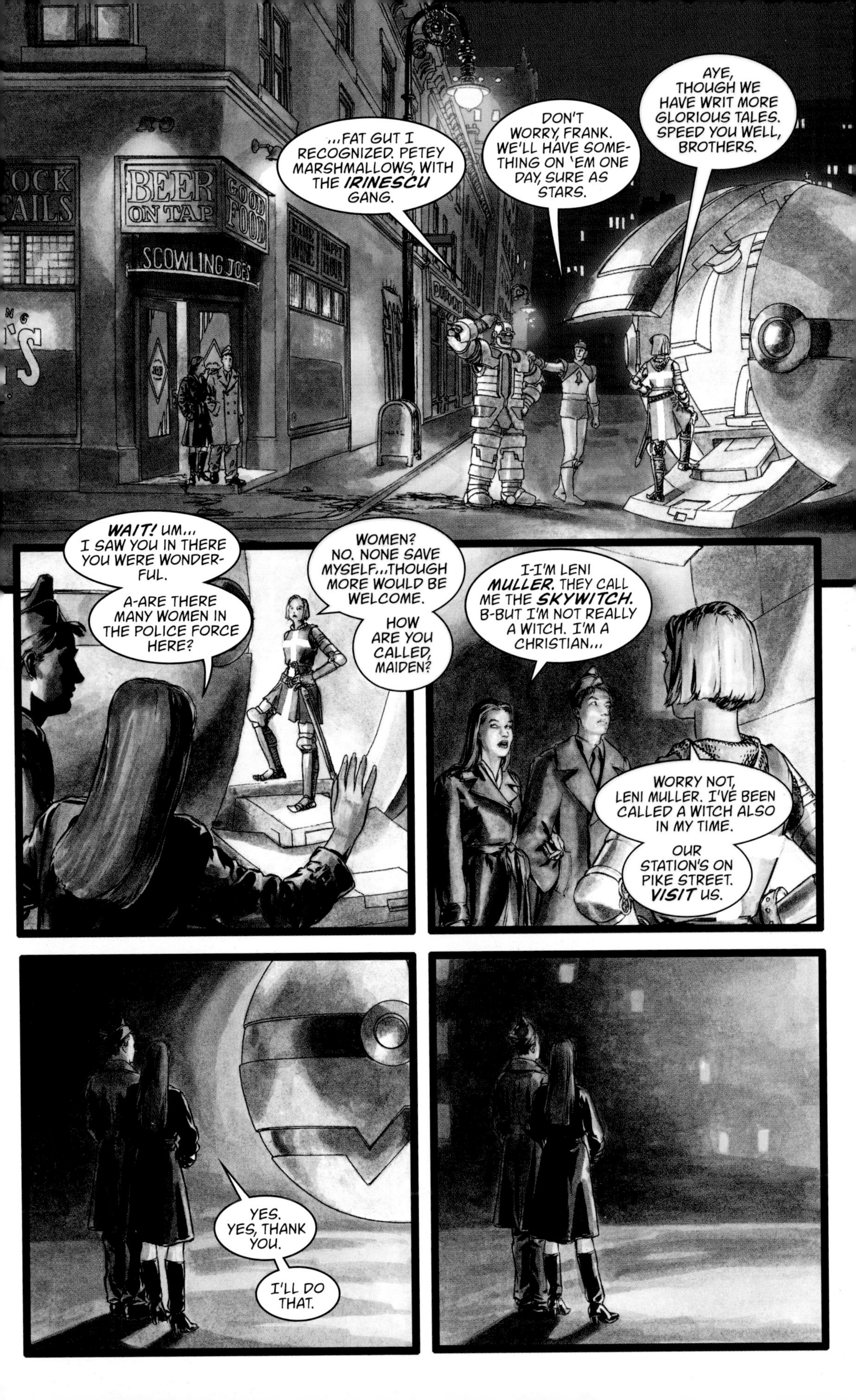
BEER ON TAP
GOOD FOOD
SCOWLING JOES
...FAT GUT I RECOGNIZED. PETEY MARSHMALLOWS, WITH THE IRINESCU GANG.
DON'T WORRY, FRANK. WE'LL HAVE SOMETHING ON 'EM ONE DAY, SURE AS STARS.
AYE, THOUGH WE HAVE WRIT MORE GLORIOUS TALES. SPEED YOU WELL, BROTHERS.
WAIT! UM... I SAW YOU IN THERE YOU WERE WONDERFUL.
A-ARE THERE MANY WOMEN IN THE POLICE FORCE HERE?
WOMEN? NO. NONE SAVE MYSELF...THOUGH MORE WOULD BE WELCOME.
HOW ARE YOU CALLED, MAIDEN?
I-I'M LENI MULLER. THEY CALL ME THE SKYWITCH. B-BUT I'M NOT REALLY A WITCH. I'M A CHRISTIAN...
WORRY NOT, LENI MULLER. I'VE BEEN CALLED A WITCH ALSO IN MY TIME.
OUR STATION'S ON PIKE STREET. VISIT US.
YES. YES, THANK YOU.
I'LL DO THAT.

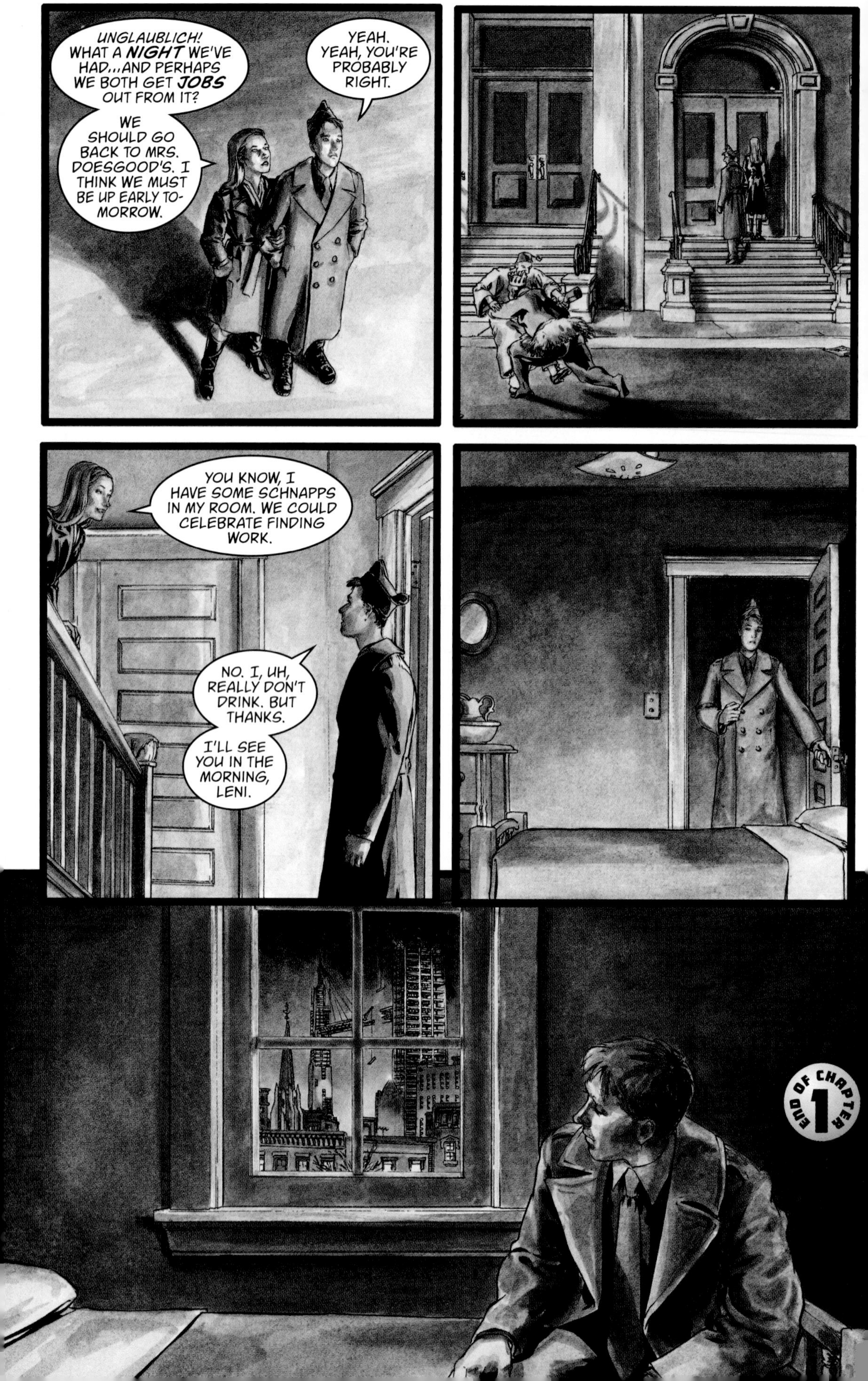
UNGLAUBLICH! WHAT A NIGHT WE'VE HAD...AND PERHAPS WE BOTH GET JOBS OUT FROM IT?
YEAH. YEAH, YOU'RE PROBABLY RIGHT.
WE SHOULD GO BACK TO MRS. DOESGOOD'S. I THINK WE MUST BE UP EARLY TO-MORROW.
YOU KNOW, I HAVE SOME SCHNAPPS IN MY ROOM. WE COULD CELEBRATE FINDING WORK.
NO. I, UH, REALLY DON'T DRINK. BUT THANKS.
I'LL SEE YOU IN THE MORNING, LENI.
END OF CHAPTER 1

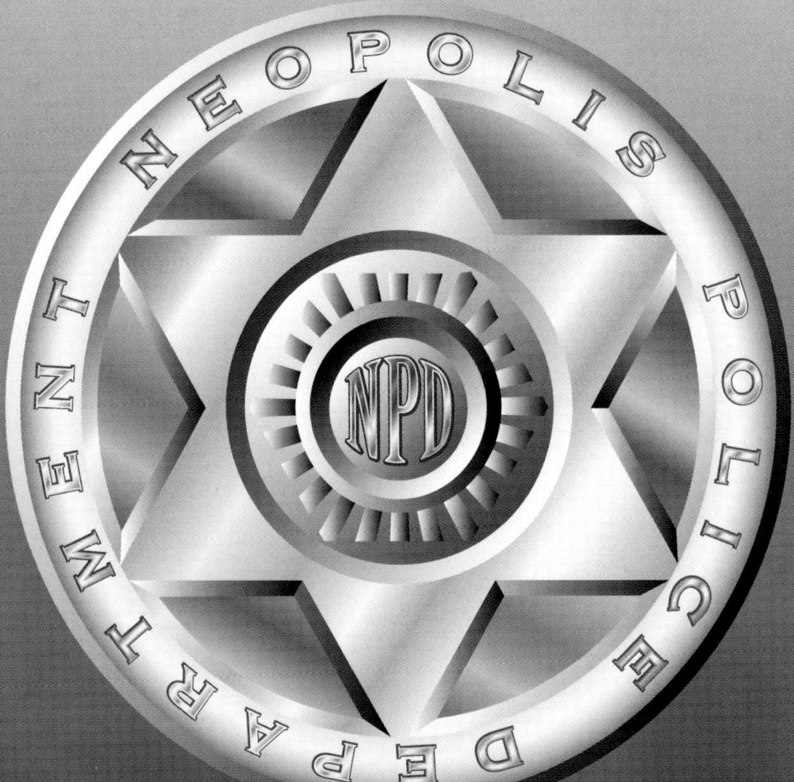
NEOPOLIS POLICE DEPARTMENT
NPD

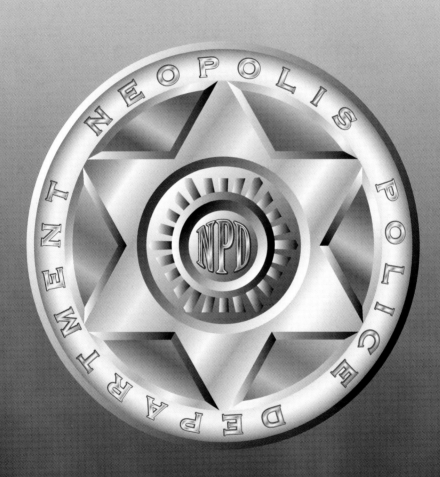

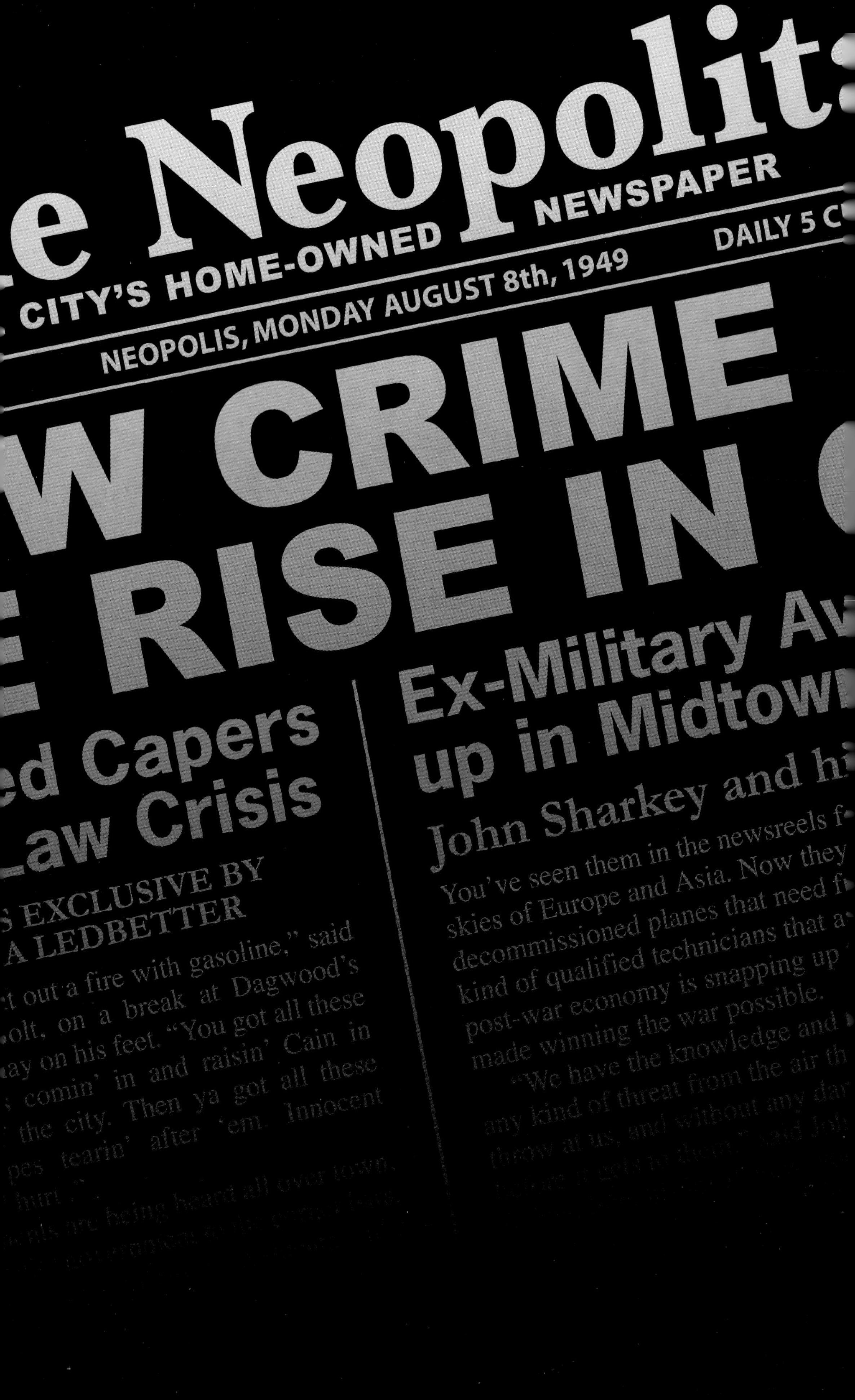

e Neopolit

CITY'S HOME-OWNED NEWSPAPER

DAILY 5 C

NEOPOLIS, MONDAY AUGUST 8th, 1949

W CRIME
E RISE IN

ed Capers
Law Crisis

EXCLUSIVE BY
A LEDBETTER

t out a fire with gasoline," said
olt, on a break at Dagwood's
ay on his feet. "You got all these
comin' in and raisin' Cain in
the city. Then ya got all these
pes tearin' after 'em. Innocent
hurt
als are being heard all over town.

Ex-Military Av
up in Midtow

John Sharkey and hi

You've seen them in the newsreels f
skies of Europe and Asia. Now they
decommissioned planes that need f
kind of qualified technicians that a
post-war economy is snapping up
made winning the war possible.
"We have the knowledge and
any kind of threat from the air th
throw at us, and without any dan
before it gets to them," said Joh

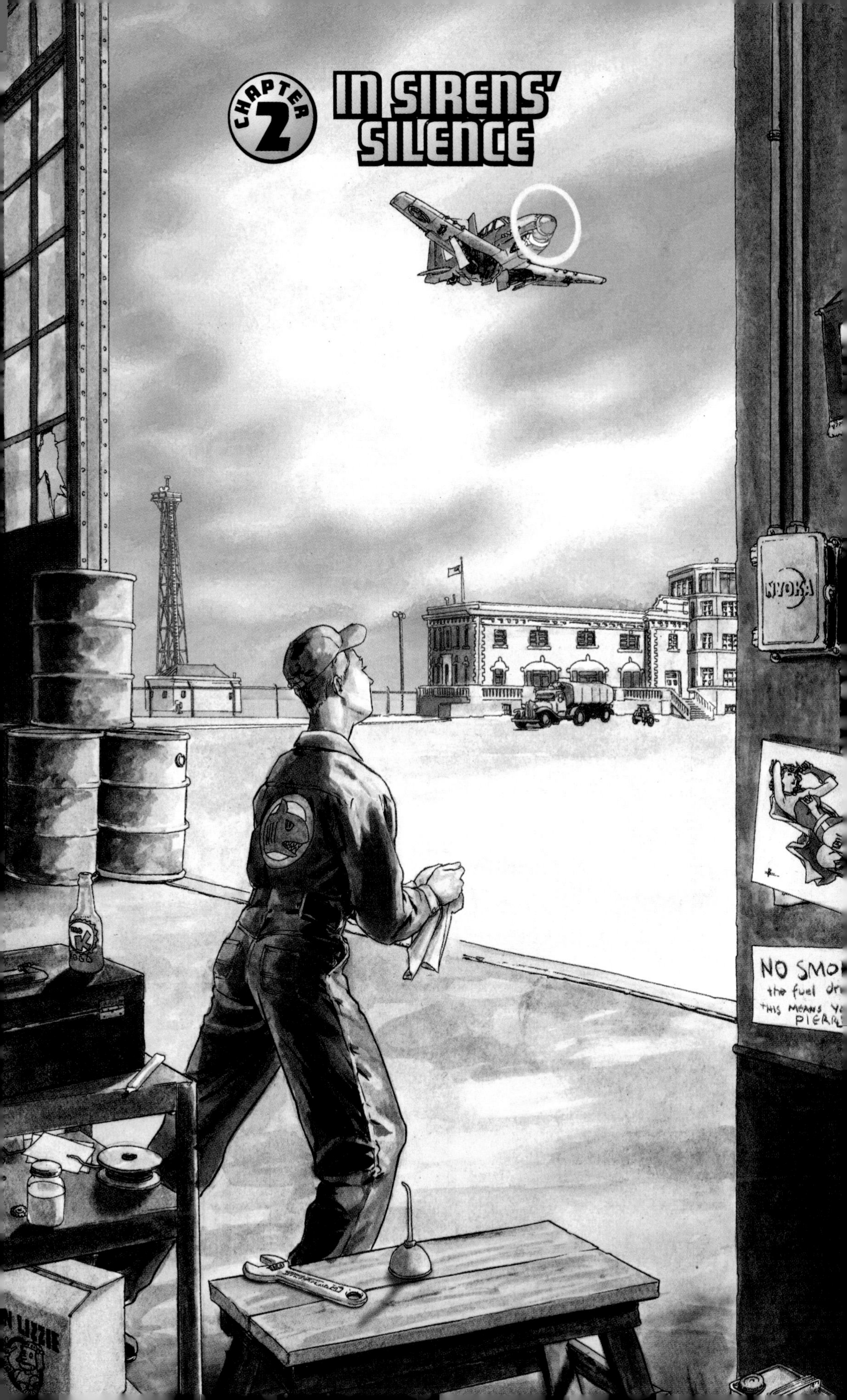
CHAPTER 2
IN SIRENS' SILENCE
NYOKA
LIZZIE

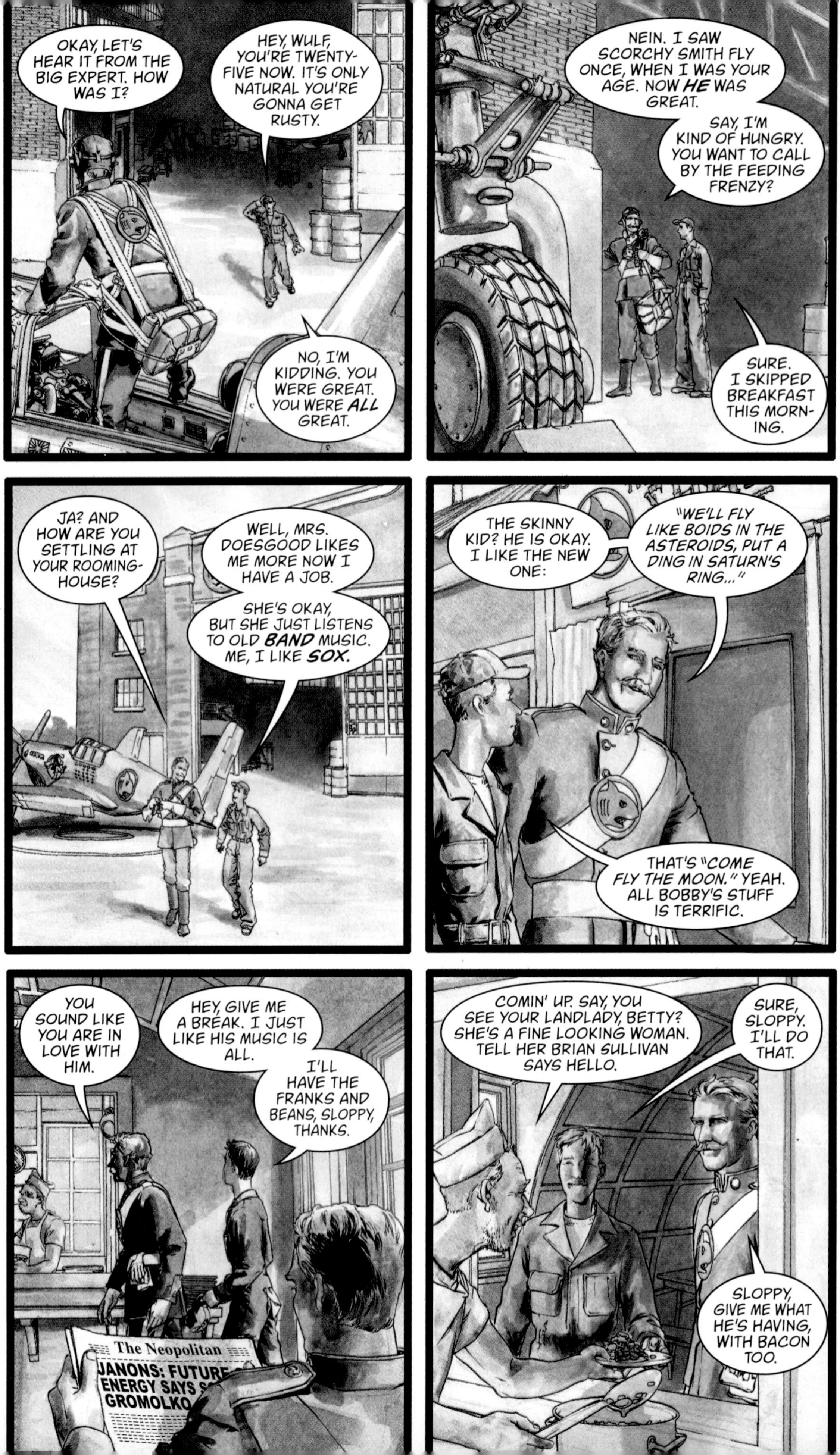
OKAY, LET'S HEAR IT FROM THE BIG EXPERT. HOW WAS I?
HEY, WULF, YOU'RE TWENTY-FIVE NOW. IT'S ONLY NATURAL YOU'RE GONNA GET RUSTY.
NO, I'M KIDDING. YOU WERE GREAT. YOU WERE *ALL* GREAT.
NEIN. I SAW SCORCHY SMITH FLY ONCE, WHEN I WAS YOUR AGE. NOW *HE* WAS GREAT.
SAY, I'M KIND OF HUNGRY. YOU WANT TO CALL BY THE FEEDING FRENZY?
SURE. I SKIPPED BREAKFAST THIS MORN-ING.
JA? AND HOW ARE YOU SETTLING AT YOUR ROOMING-HOUSE?
WELL, MRS. DOESGOOD LIKES ME MORE NOW I HAVE A JOB.
SHE'S OKAY, BUT SHE JUST LISTENS TO OLD *BAND* MUSIC. ME, I LIKE *SOX.*
THE SKINNY KID? HE IS OKAY. I LIKE THE NEW ONE:
"WE'LL FLY LIKE BOIDS IN THE ASTEROIDS, PUT A DING IN SATURN'S RING..."
THAT'S *"COME FLY THE MOON."* YEAH. ALL BOBBY'S STUFF IS TERRIFIC.
YOU SOUND LIKE YOU ARE IN LOVE WITH HIM.
HEY, GIVE ME A BREAK. I JUST LIKE HIS MUSIC IS ALL.
I'LL HAVE THE FRANKS AND BEANS, SLOPPY, THANKS.
The Neopolitan
JANONS: FUTURE
ENERGY SAYS
GROMOLKO
COMIN' UP. SAY, YOU SEE YOUR LANDLADY, BETTY? SHE'S A FINE LOOKING WOMAN. TELL HER BRIAN SULLIVAN SAYS HELLO.
SURE, SLOPPY. I'LL DO THAT.
SLOPPY, GIVE ME WHAT HE'S HAVING, WITH BACON TOO.

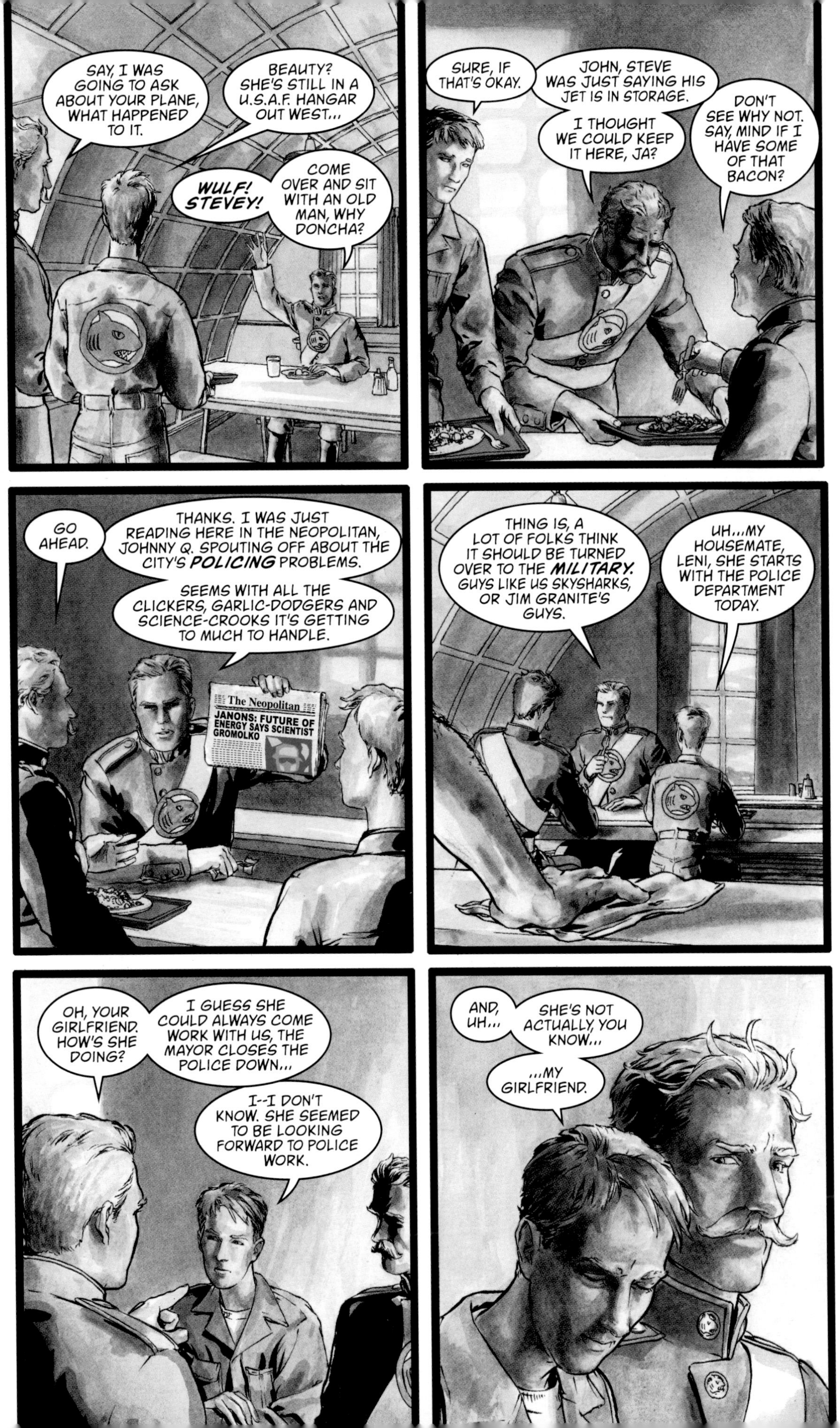
SAY, I WAS GOING TO ASK ABOUT YOUR PLANE, WHAT HAPPENED TO IT.
BEAUTY? SHE'S STILL IN A U.S.A.F. HANGAR OUT WEST...
WULF! STEVEY!
COME OVER AND SIT WITH AN OLD MAN, WHY DONCHA?
SURE, IF THAT'S OKAY.
JOHN, STEVE WAS JUST SAYING HIS JET IS IN STORAGE.
I THOUGHT WE COULD KEEP IT HERE, JA?
DON'T SEE WHY NOT. SAY, MIND IF I HAVE SOME OF THAT BACON?
GO AHEAD.
THANKS. I WAS JUST READING HERE IN THE NEOPOLITAN, JOHNNY Q. SPOUTING OFF ABOUT THE CITY'S POLICING PROBLEMS.
SEEMS WITH ALL THE CLICKERS, GARLIC-DODGERS AND SCIENCE-CROOKS IT'S GETTING TO MUCH TO HANDLE.
The Neopolitan
JANONS: FUTURE OF ENERGY SAYS SCIENTIST GROMOLKO
THING IS, A LOT OF FOLKS THINK IT SHOULD BE TURNED OVER TO THE MILITARY. GUYS LIKE US SKYSHARKS, OR JIM GRANITE'S GUYS.
UH...MY HOUSEMATE, LENI, SHE STARTS WITH THE POLICE DEPARTMENT TODAY.
OH, YOUR GIRLFRIEND. HOW'S SHE DOING?
I GUESS SHE COULD ALWAYS COME WORK WITH US, THE MAYOR CLOSES THE POLICE DOWN...
I--I DON'T KNOW. SHE SEEMED TO BE LOOKING FORWARD TO POLICE WORK.
AND, UH...
SHE'S NOT ACTUALLY, YOU KNOW...
...MY GIRLFRIEND.

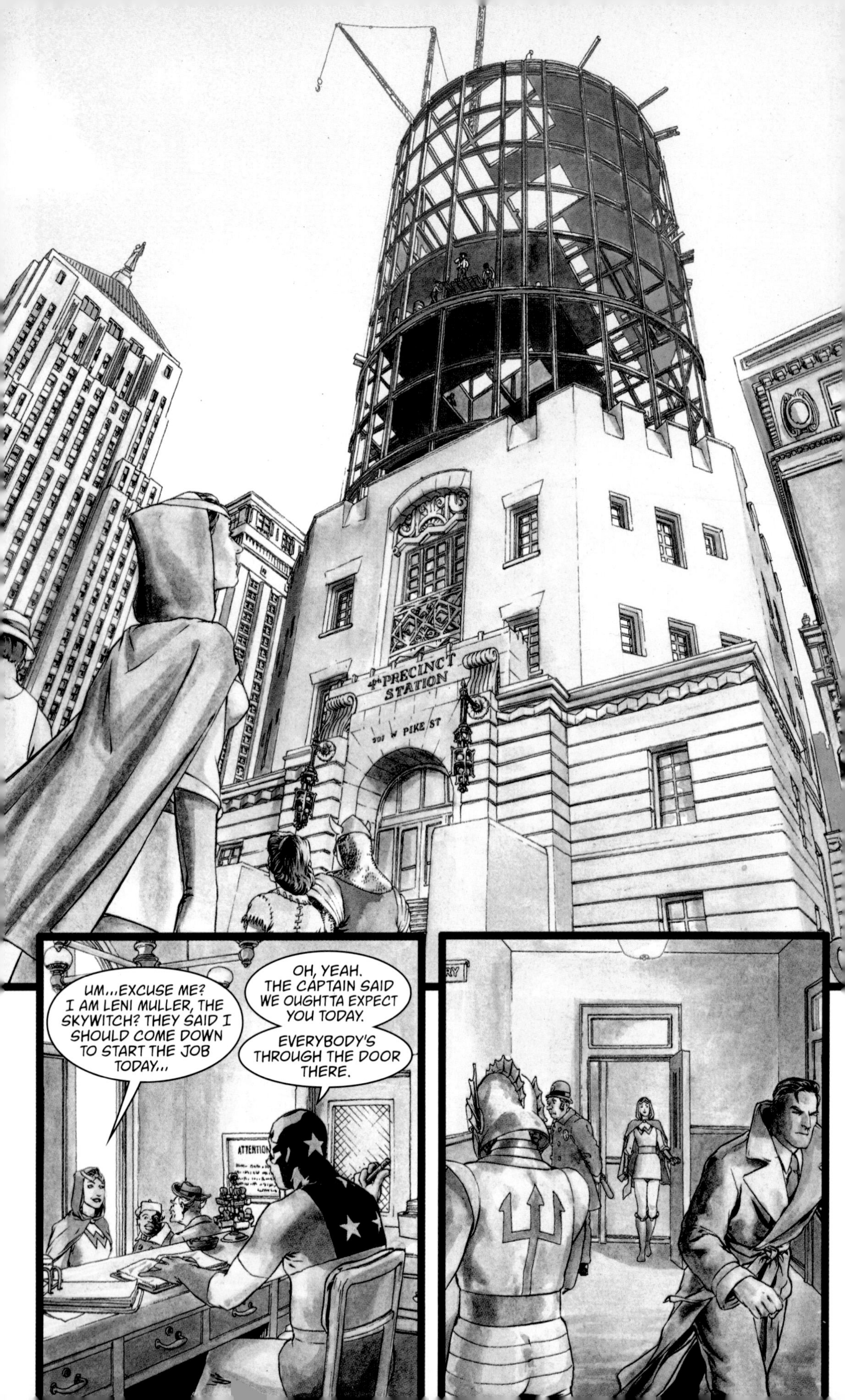

4th PRECINCT STATION
W PIKE ST
UM...EXCUSE ME? I AM LENI MULLER, THE SKYWITCH? THEY SAID I SHOULD COME DOWN TO START THE JOB TODAY...
OH, YEAH. THE CAPTAIN SAID WE OUGHTTA EXPECT YOU TODAY.
EVERYBODY'S THROUGH THE DOOR THERE.
ATTENTION

...SO LET ME ASK YOU AGAIN, TIN-DICK: HOW MANY OTHER BURGLARIES YOU DO? TWO? THREE?

I'M FINE, THANK YOU KINDLY FOR ASKING.

LOOK, JUST ANSWER OFFICER PURE'S QUESTION, OKAY?

YEAH. Y'KNOW, MY NEIGHBOR, THEM NEW TELEVISION SETS? SHE GOT ONE.

WHEN THE SOUND GOES, OR THERE'S SNOW, SHE WHACKS IT!

UH...ADAM, BETTER LEAVE OFF WITH THAT. CAN I HELP YOU, LADY?

HI, FRIENDS.

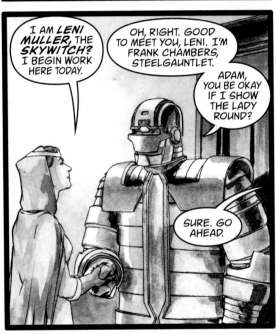

I AM LENI MULLER, THE SKYWITCH? I BEGIN WORK HERE TODAY.

OH, RIGHT. GOOD TO MEET YOU, LENI. I'M FRANK CHAMBERS, STEELGAUNTLET.

ADAM, YOU BE OKAY IF I SHOW THE LADY ROUND?

SURE. GO AHEAD.

HI, FRIENDS.

HI, HI, HI, HI...

THAT ROBOT THAT YOUR FRIEND WAS...QUESTIONING. I THINK I MET HIM WHEN I ARRIVED IN THIS CITY.

WELL, BEST YOU'RE NOT TOO FRIENDLY. CLICKERS ARE NOTHING BUT TROUBLE.

HERE. CAPTAIN'S OFFICE IS THIS WAY.

...SAYING, MAX, IS THAT YOU SHOULD PLAY DOWN THE *TIME-TWINS.* JUST DROP THEIR BANNER FROM YOUR *LOGO* IS ALL.

CREEPING *COMETS,* DOC! DOES THIS GO FOR *ALL* SIDE-KICKS NOW?

UH... CAPTAIN? SORRY TO *INTER-RUPT...*

THAT'S OKAY, FRANK. COME ON IN. ME AND OFFICER RYAN WERE ALL THROUGH.

AH. THIS MUST BE FRAULEIN *MULLER.*

THAT'S RIGHT, SIR. HI, MAX. HOW'S IT GOING?

NOWHERE. FAST. I'LL SEE YOU LATER.

DON'T MIND HIM. HE THINKS NEOPOLIS IS READY FOR 25TH CENTURY VALUES, AND I *DON'T.*

SO YOU'RE THE *SKYWITCH.* WELCOME ABOARD, OFFICER MULLER.

I'M *ZARAN ORVAL.* THEY CALL ME DOCTOR *OMEGA.*

NICE MEETING YOU, CAPTAIN.

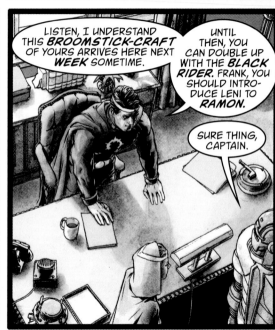

LISTEN, I UNDERSTAND THIS *BROOMSTICK-CRAFT* OF YOURS ARRIVES HERE NEXT *WEEK* SOMETIME.

UNTIL THEN, YOU CAN DOUBLE UP WITH THE *BLACK RIDER.* FRANK, YOU SHOULD INTRO-DUCE LENI TO *RAMON.*

SURE THING, CAPTAIN.

GOOD. LENI, I'M NOT GOING TO PRETEND POLICING NEOPOLIS IS *EASY,* BUT IF YOU HAVE ANY PROBLEMS, YOU COME STRAIGHT TO *ME,* OKAY?

COME ON. I'LL TAKE YOU TO *RAMON.*

YES, SIR. THANK YOU, SIR.

HE SEEMS LIKE A FAIR MAN.

YEAH, THE DOC'S OKAY. YOU KNOW HE'S FROM OUTER *SPACE?* HIS WORLD'S *SUN* COLLAPSED INTO SOMETHING CALLED AN *OMEGA POINT,* OR SO I HEAR.

WHAT'S THIS *BROOMSTICK* HE MENTIONED?

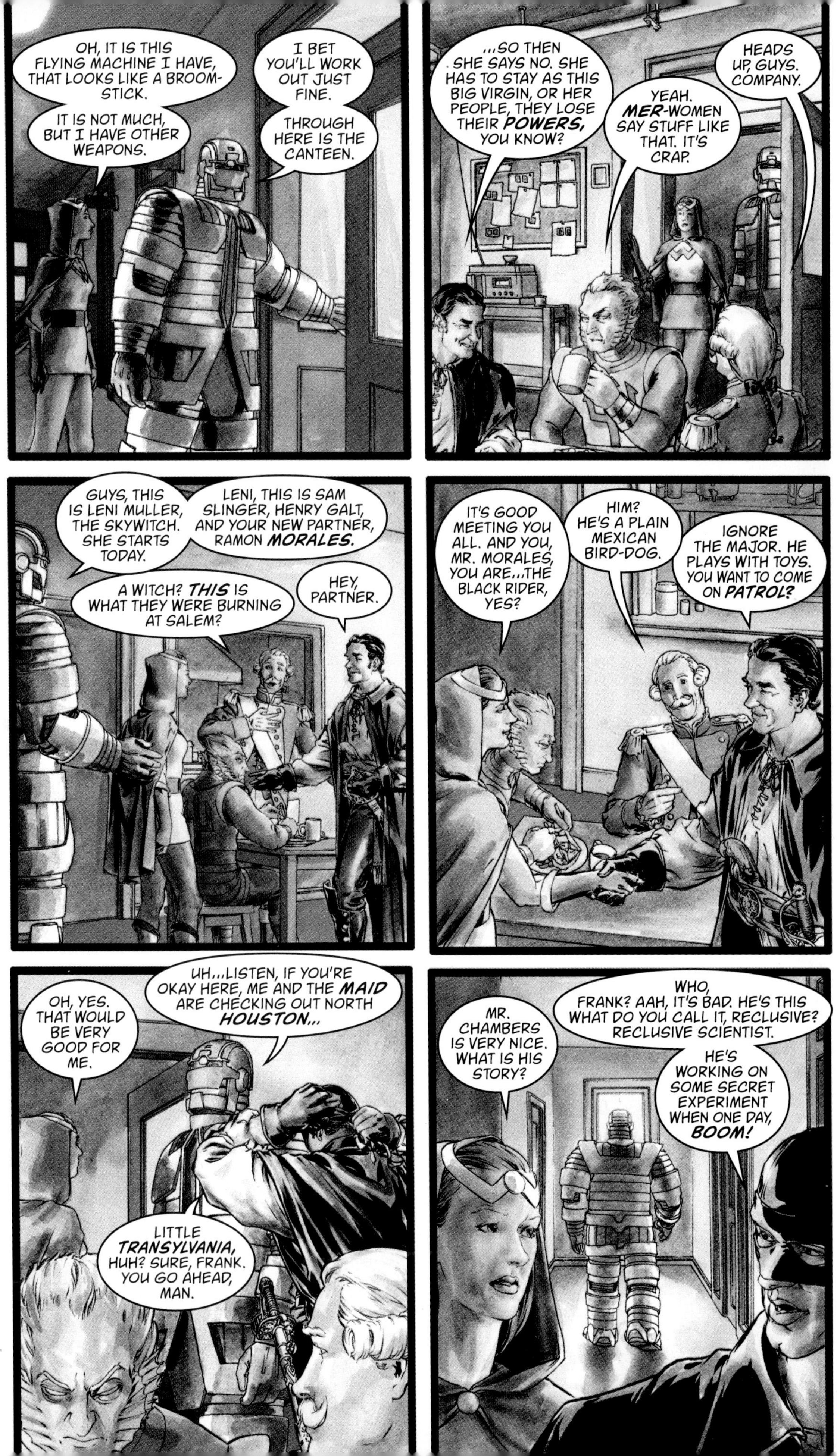
OH, IT IS THIS FLYING MACHINE I HAVE, THAT LOOKS LIKE A BROOM-STICK.
IT IS NOT MUCH, BUT I HAVE OTHER WEAPONS.
I BET YOU'LL WORK OUT JUST FINE.
THROUGH HERE IS THE CANTEEN.
...SO THEN SHE SAYS NO. SHE HAS TO STAY AS THIS BIG VIRGIN, OR HER PEOPLE, THEY LOSE THEIR POWERS, YOU KNOW?
YEAH. MER-WOMEN SAY STUFF LIKE THAT. IT'S CRAP.
HEADS UP, GUYS. COMPANY.
GUYS, THIS IS LENI MULLER, THE SKYWITCH. SHE STARTS TODAY.
LENI, THIS IS SAM SLINGER, HENRY GALT, AND YOUR NEW PARTNER, RAMON MORALES.
A WITCH? THIS IS WHAT THEY WERE BURNING AT SALEM?
HEY, PARTNER.
IT'S GOOD MEETING YOU ALL. AND YOU, MR. MORALES, YOU ARE...THE BLACK RIDER, YES?
HIM? HE'S A PLAIN MEXICAN BIRD-DOG.
IGNORE THE MAJOR. HE PLAYS WITH TOYS. YOU WANT TO COME ON PATROL?
OH, YES. THAT WOULD BE VERY GOOD FOR ME.
UH...LISTEN, IF YOU'RE OKAY HERE, ME AND THE MAID ARE CHECKING OUT NORTH HOUSTON...
LITTLE TRANSYLVANIA, HUH? SURE, FRANK. YOU GO AHEAD, MAN.
MR. CHAMBERS IS VERY NICE. WHAT IS HIS STORY?
WHO, FRANK? AAH, IT'S BAD. HE'S THIS WHAT DO YOU CALL IT, RECLUSIVE? RECLUSIVE SCIENTIST.
HE'S WORKING ON SOME SECRET EXPERIMENT WHEN ONE DAY, BOOM!

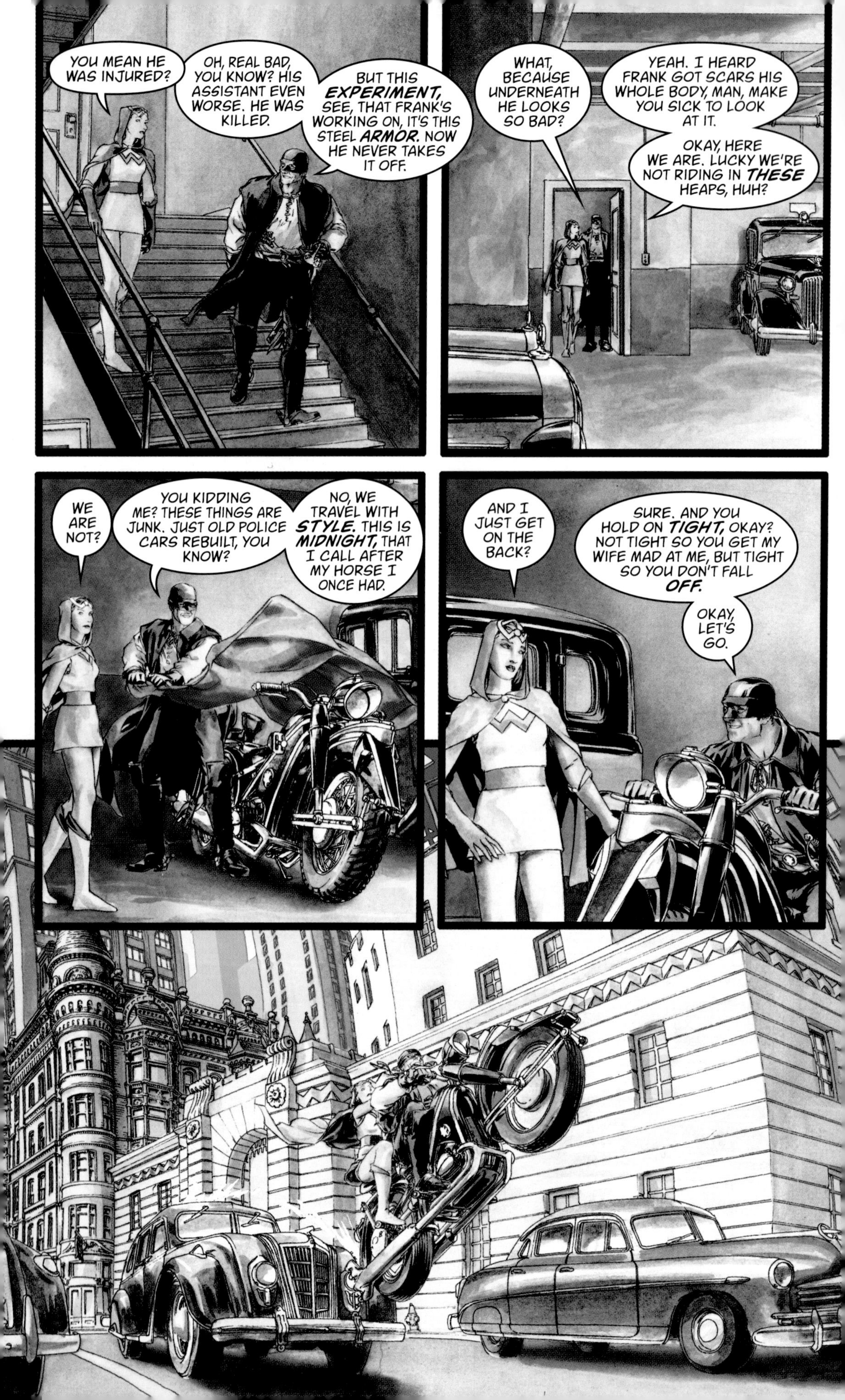
YOU MEAN HE WAS INJURED?
OH, REAL BAD, YOU KNOW? HIS ASSISTANT EVEN WORSE. HE WAS KILLED.
BUT THIS EXPERIMENT, SEE, THAT FRANK'S WORKING ON, IT'S THIS STEEL ARMOR. NOW HE NEVER TAKES IT OFF.
WHAT, BECAUSE UNDERNEATH HE LOOKS SO BAD?
YEAH. I HEARD FRANK GOT SCARS HIS WHOLE BODY, MAN, MAKE YOU SICK TO LOOK AT IT.
OKAY, HERE WE ARE. LUCKY WE'RE NOT RIDING IN THESE HEAPS, HUH?
WE ARE NOT?
YOU KIDDING ME? THESE THINGS ARE JUNK. JUST OLD POLICE CARS REBUILT, YOU KNOW?
NO, WE TRAVEL WITH STYLE. THIS IS MIDNIGHT, THAT I CALL AFTER MY HORSE I ONCE HAD.
AND I JUST GET ON THE BACK?
SURE. AND YOU HOLD ON TIGHT, OKAY? NOT TIGHT SO YOU GET MY WIFE MAD AT ME, BUT TIGHT SO YOU DON'T FALL OFF.
OKAY, LET'S GO.

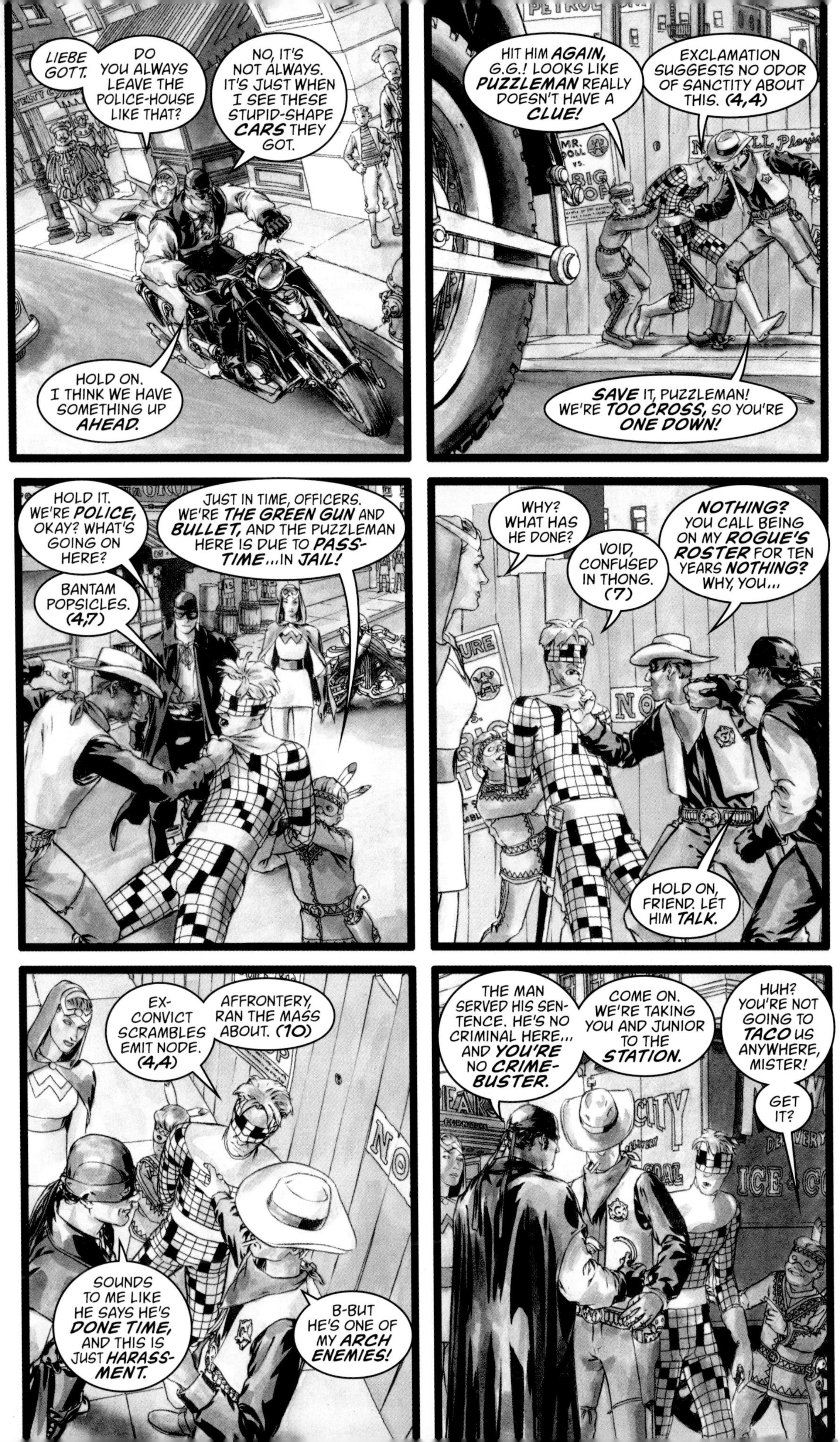

LIEBE GOTT.
DO YOU ALWAYS LEAVE THE POLICE-HOUSE LIKE THAT?
NO, IT'S NOT ALWAYS. IT'S JUST WHEN I SEE THESE STUPID-SHAPE CARS THEY GOT.
HOLD ON. I THINK WE HAVE SOMETHING UP AHEAD.
HIT HIM AGAIN, G.G.! LOOKS LIKE PUZZLEMAN REALLY DOESN'T HAVE A CLUE!
EXCLAMATION SUGGESTS NO ODOR OF SANCTITY ABOUT THIS. (4,4)
SAVE IT, PUZZLEMAN! WE'RE TOO CROSS, SO YOU'RE ONE DOWN!
HOLD IT. WE'RE POLICE, OKAY? WHAT'S GOING ON HERE?
BANTAM POPSICLES. (4,7)
JUST IN TIME, OFFICERS. WE'RE THE GREEN GUN AND BULLET, AND THE PUZZLEMAN HERE IS DUE TO PASS-TIME...IN JAIL!
WHY? WHAT HAS HE DONE?
VOID, CONFUSED IN THONG. (7)
NOTHING? YOU CALL BEING ON MY ROGUE'S ROSTER FOR TEN YEARS NOTHING? WHY, YOU...
HOLD ON, FRIEND. LET HIM TALK.
EX-CONVICT SCRAMBLES EMIT NODE. (4,4)
AFFRONTERY, RAN THE MASS ABOUT. (10)
SOUNDS TO ME LIKE HE SAYS HE'S DONE TIME, AND THIS IS JUST HARASS-MENT.
B-BUT HE'S ONE OF MY ARCH ENEMIES!
THE MAN SERVED HIS SEN-TENCE. HE'S NO CRIMINAL HERE... AND YOU'RE NO CRIME-BUSTER.
COME ON. WE'RE TAKING YOU AND JUNIOR TO THE STATION.
HUH? YOU'RE NOT GOING TO TACO US ANYWHERE, MISTER!
GET IT?

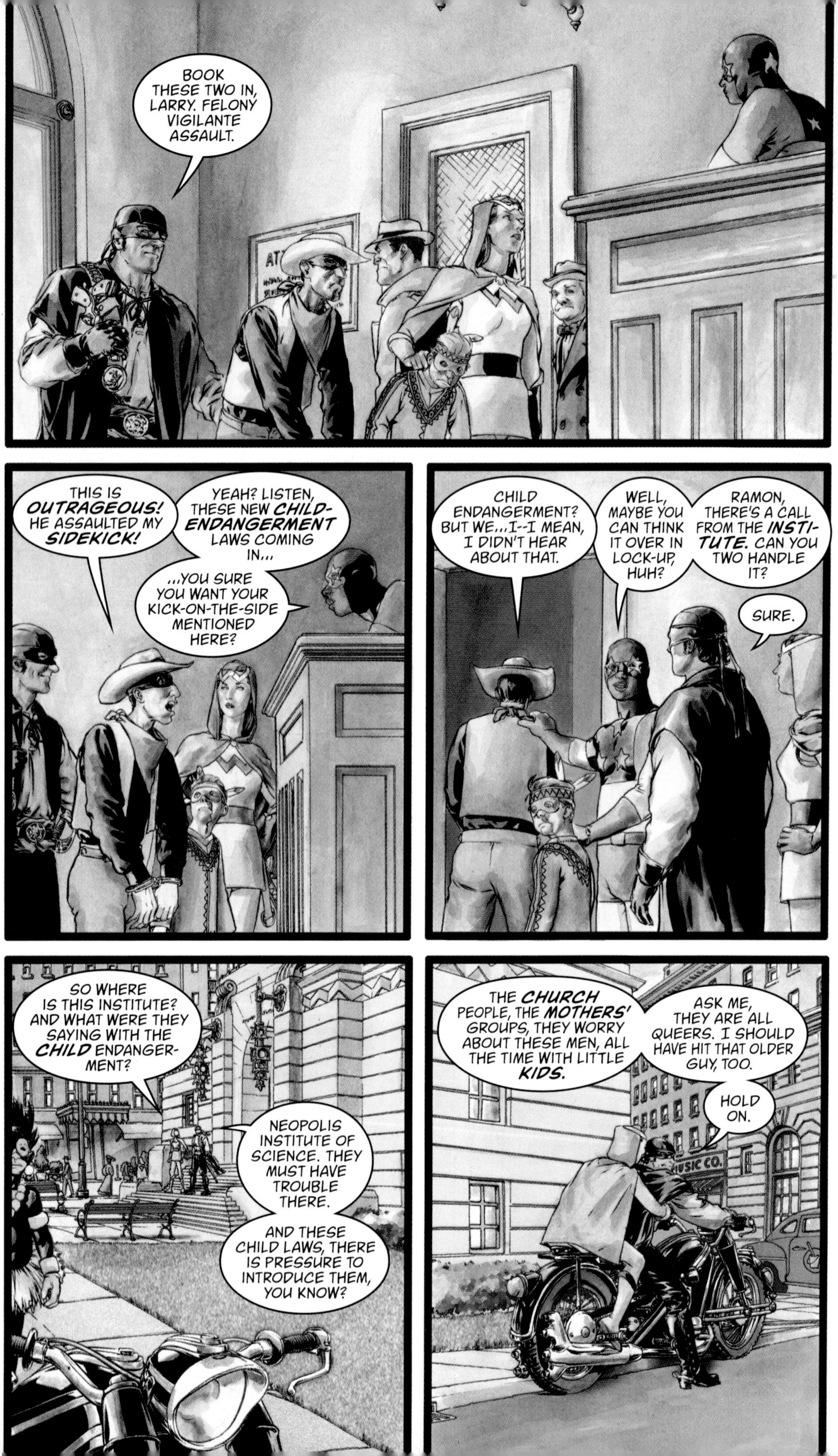
BOOK THESE TWO IN, LARRY. FELONY VIGILANTE ASSAULT.
THIS IS OUTRAGEOUS! HE ASSAULTED MY SIDEKICK!
YEAH? LISTEN, THESE NEW CHILD-ENDANGERMENT LAWS COMING IN...
...YOU SURE YOU WANT YOUR KICK-ON-THE-SIDE MENTIONED HERE?
CHILD ENDANGERMENT? BUT WE...I--I MEAN, I DIDN'T HEAR ABOUT THAT.
WELL, MAYBE YOU CAN THINK IT OVER IN LOCK-UP, HUH?
RAMON, THERE'S A CALL FROM THE INSTITUTE. CAN YOU TWO HANDLE IT?
SURE.
SO WHERE IS THIS INSTITUTE? AND WHAT WERE THEY SAYING WITH THE CHILD ENDANGERMENT?
NEOPOLIS INSTITUTE OF SCIENCE. THEY MUST HAVE TROUBLE THERE.
AND THESE CHILD LAWS, THERE IS PRESSURE TO INTRODUCE THEM, YOU KNOW?
THE CHURCH PEOPLE, THE MOTHERS' GROUPS, THEY WORRY ABOUT THESE MEN, ALL THE TIME WITH LITTLE KIDS.
ASK ME, THEY ARE ALL QUEERS. I SHOULD HAVE HIT THAT OLDER GUY, TOO.
HOLD ON.
MUSIC CO.

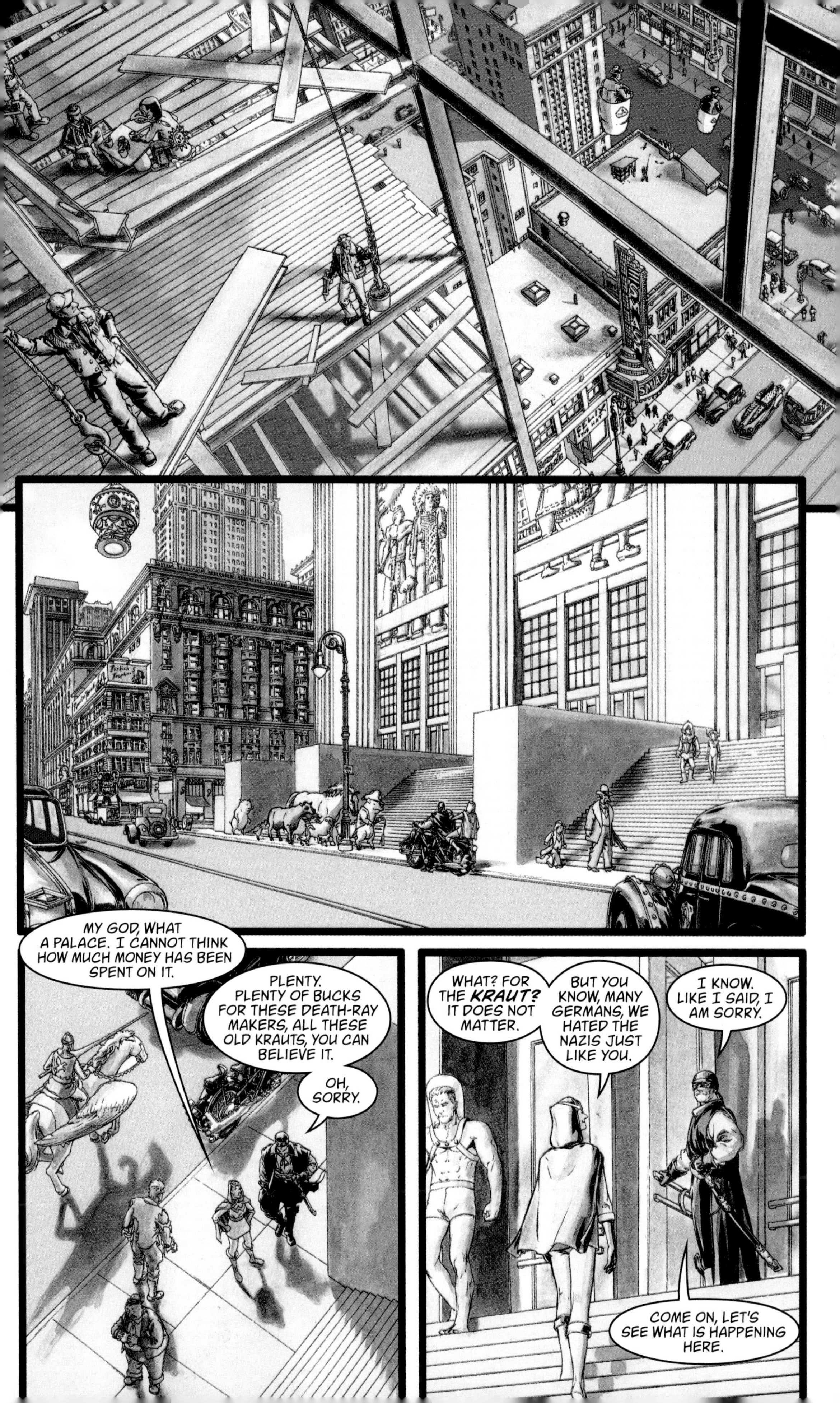
MY GOD, WHAT A PALACE. I CANNOT THINK HOW MUCH MONEY HAS BEEN SPENT ON IT.
PLENTY. PLENTY OF BUCKS FOR THESE DEATH-RAY MAKERS, ALL THESE OLD KRAUTS, YOU CAN BELIEVE IT.
OH, SORRY.
WHAT? FOR THE ***KRAUT?*** IT DOES NOT MATTER.
BUT YOU KNOW, MANY GERMANS, WE HATED THE NAZIS JUST LIKE YOU.
I KNOW. LIKE I SAID, I AM SORRY.
COME ON, LET'S SEE WHAT IS HAPPENING HERE.

NEOPOLIS POLICE DEPARTMENT.

SO WHAT IS THAT WE GOT HERE?

ROCKWELL FRANKLIN, *THE EAGLE'S VOICE.* I'M LIAISON AT THE INSTITUTE.

I'M AFRAID WHAT WE *GOT* IS A DEAD BODY. ONE OF OUR SCIENTIFIC ADVISORS.

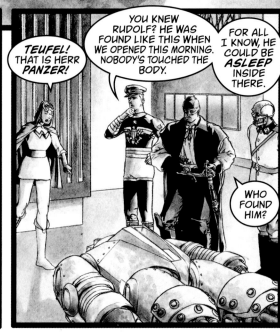

TEUFEL! THAT IS HERR *PANZER!*

YOU KNEW RUDOLF? HE WAS FOUND LIKE THIS WHEN WE OPENED THIS MORNING. NOBODY'S TOUCHED THE BODY.

FOR ALL I KNOW, HE COULD BE *ASLEEP* INSIDE THERE.

WHO FOUND HIM?

THAT WAS ME. I AM DR. KONRAD DIETRICH, SOMETIMES CALLED *DIE EISEN MASKE.*

WHEN I UN-LOCKED EARLIER, TO CONTINUE OUR *JANON* PROJECT, RUDOLF WAS HERE.

RAMON, PANZER WAS IMPORTANT. THIS IS *DELICATE,* I THINK.

MAYBE. BUT BEFORE ANYBODY PHONES J. EDGAR HOOVER...

...WE BETTER MAKE SURE THIS MAN'S DEAD.

YOU HEARD WHAT "THE EAGLE'S VOICE" HERE SAID. HE COULD BE *ASLEEP.*

IF I CAN GET THIS HELMET-LOCK...

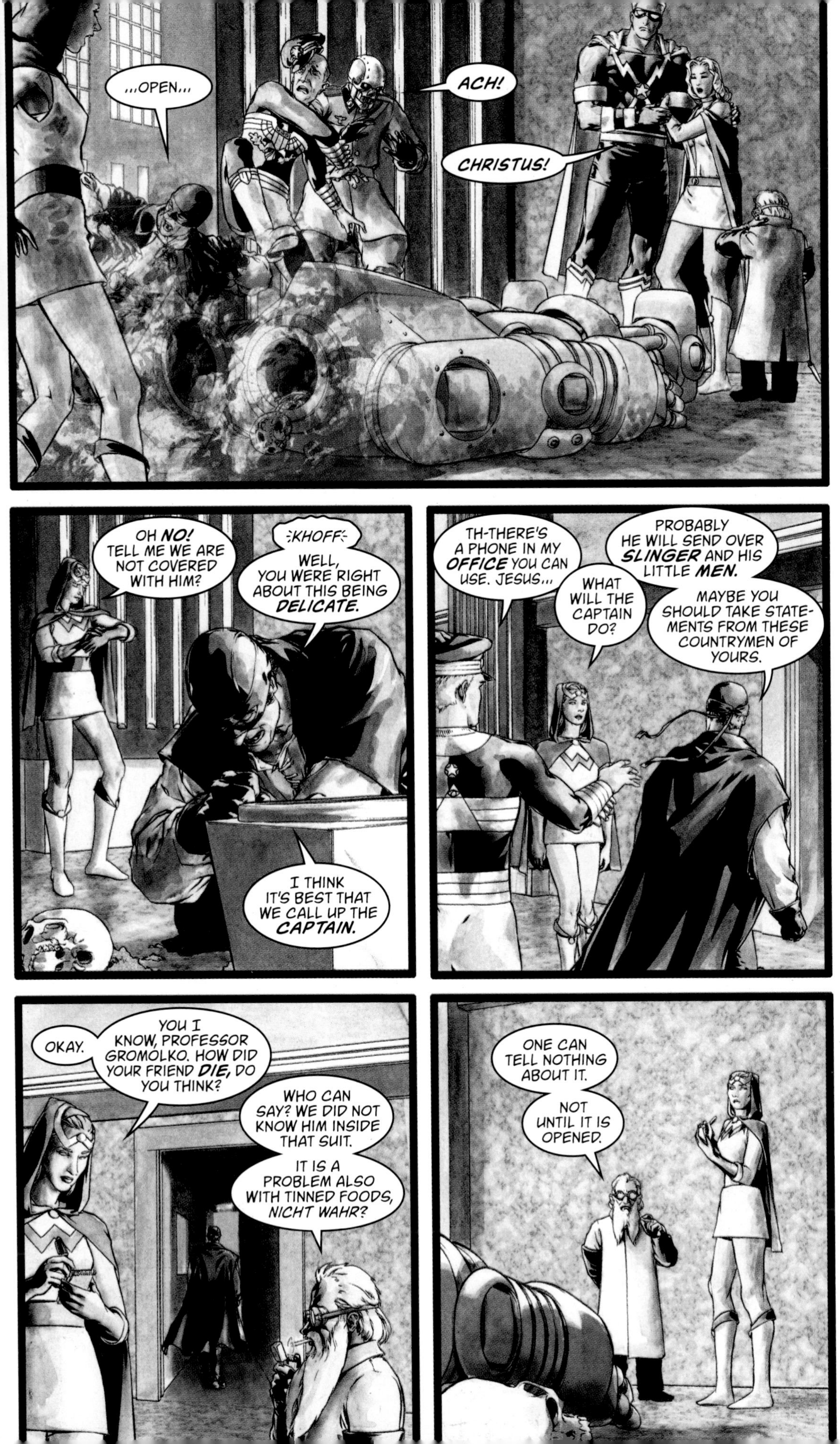

...OPEN...
ACH!
CHRISTUS!
OH NO! TELL ME WE ARE NOT COVERED WITH HIM?
-KHOFF-
WELL, YOU WERE RIGHT ABOUT THIS BEING DELICATE.
I THINK IT'S BEST THAT WE CALL UP THE CAPTAIN.
TH-THERE'S A PHONE IN MY OFFICE YOU CAN USE. JESUS...
WHAT WILL THE CAPTAIN DO?
PROBABLY HE WILL SEND OVER SLINGER AND HIS LITTLE MEN.
MAYBE YOU SHOULD TAKE STATE-MENTS FROM THESE COUNTRYMEN OF YOURS.
OKAY.
YOU I KNOW, PROFESSOR GROMOLKO. HOW DID YOUR FRIEND DIE, DO YOU THINK?
WHO CAN SAY? WE DID NOT KNOW HIM INSIDE THAT SUIT.
IT IS A PROBLEM ALSO WITH TINNED FOODS, NICHT WAHR?
ONE CAN TELL NOTHING ABOUT IT.
NOT UNTIL IT IS OPENED.

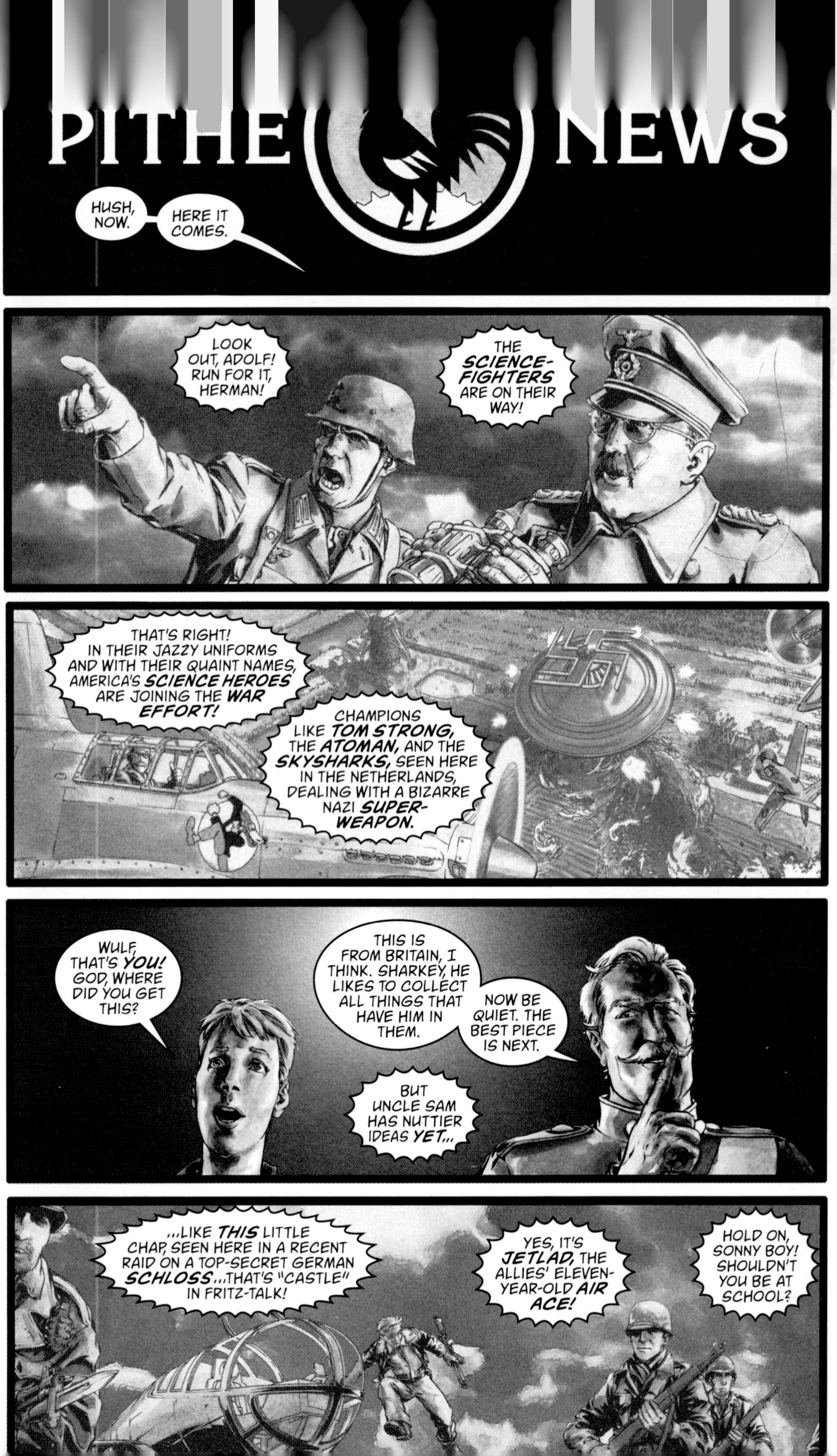
PITHE NEWS
HUSH, NOW.
HERE IT COMES.
LOOK OUT, ADOLF! RUN FOR IT, HERMAN!
THE SCIENCE-FIGHTERS ARE ON THEIR WAY!
THAT'S RIGHT! IN THEIR JAZZY UNIFORMS AND WITH THEIR QUAINT NAMES, AMERICA'S SCIENCE HEROES ARE JOINING THE WAR EFFORT!
CHAMPIONS LIKE TOM STRONG, THE ATOMAN, AND THE SKYSHARKS, SEEN HERE IN THE NETHERLANDS, DEALING WITH A BIZARRE NAZI SUPER-WEAPON.
WULF, THAT'S YOU! GOD, WHERE DID YOU GET THIS?
THIS IS FROM BRITAIN, I THINK. SHARKEY, HE LIKES TO COLLECT ALL THINGS THAT HAVE HIM IN THEM.
NOW BE QUIET. THE BEST PIECE IS NEXT.
BUT UNCLE SAM HAS NUTTIER IDEAS YET...
...LIKE THIS LITTLE CHAP, SEEN HERE IN A RECENT RAID ON A TOP-SECRET GERMAN SCHLOSS...THAT'S "CASTLE" IN FRITZ-TALK!
YES, IT'S JETLAD, THE ALLIES' ELEVEN-YEAR-OLD AIR ACE!
HOLD ON, SONNY BOY! SHOULDN'T YOU BE AT SCHOOL?

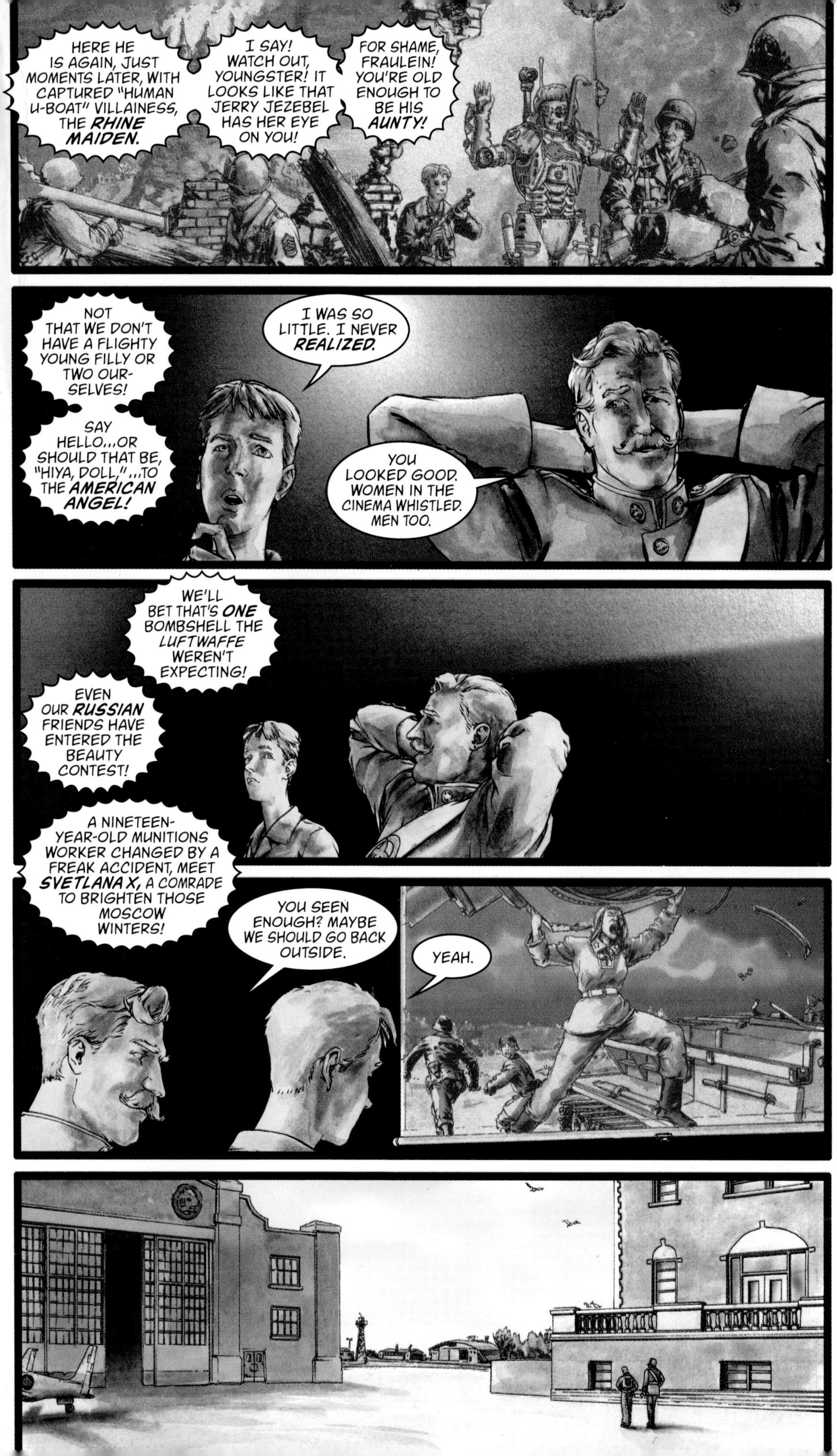
HERE HE IS AGAIN, JUST MOMENTS LATER, WITH CAPTURED "HUMAN U-BOAT" VILLAINESS, THE ***RHINE MAIDEN.***
I SAY! WATCH OUT, YOUNGSTER! IT LOOKS LIKE THAT JERRY JEZEBEL HAS HER EYE ON YOU!
FOR SHAME, FRAULEIN! YOU'RE OLD ENOUGH TO BE HIS ***AUNTY!***
NOT THAT WE DON'T HAVE A FLIGHTY YOUNG FILLY OR TWO OURSELVES!
I WAS SO LITTLE. I NEVER ***REALIZED.***
SAY HELLO...OR SHOULD THAT BE, "HIYA, DOLL,"...TO THE ***AMERICAN ANGEL!***
YOU LOOKED GOOD. WOMEN IN THE CINEMA WHISTLED. MEN TOO.
WE'LL BET THAT'S ***ONE*** BOMBSHELL THE *LUFTWAFFE* WEREN'T EXPECTING!
EVEN OUR ***RUSSIAN*** FRIENDS HAVE ENTERED THE BEAUTY CONTEST!
A NINETEEN-YEAR-OLD MUNITIONS WORKER CHANGED BY A FREAK ACCIDENT, MEET ***SVETLANA X,*** A COMRADE TO BRIGHTEN THOSE MOSCOW WINTERS!
YOU SEEN ENOUGH? MAYBE WE SHOULD GO BACK OUTSIDE.
YEAH.

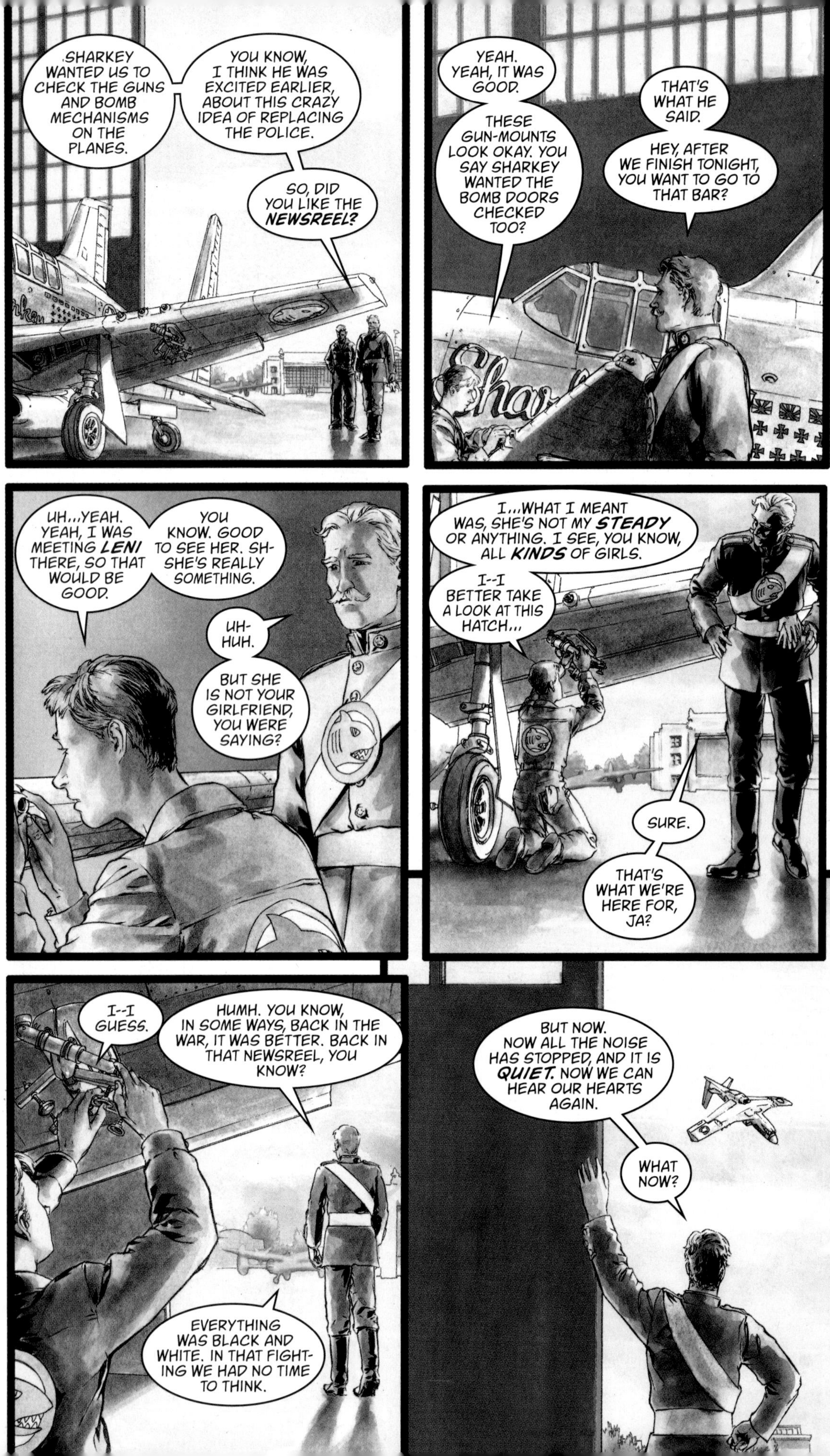
SHARKEY WANTED US TO CHECK THE GUNS AND BOMB MECHANISMS ON THE PLANES.
YOU KNOW, I THINK HE WAS EXCITED EARLIER, ABOUT THIS CRAZY IDEA OF REPLACING THE POLICE.
SO, DID YOU LIKE THE ***NEWSREEL?***
YEAH. YEAH, IT WAS GOOD.
THESE GUN-MOUNTS LOOK OKAY. YOU SAY SHARKEY WANTED THE BOMB DOORS CHECKED TOO?
THAT'S WHAT HE SAID.
HEY, AFTER WE FINISH TONIGHT, YOU WANT TO GO TO THAT BAR?
UH...YEAH. YEAH, I WAS MEETING ***LENI*** THERE, SO THAT WOULD BE GOOD.
YOU KNOW. GOOD TO SEE HER. SH-SHE'S REALLY SOMETHING.
UH-HUH.
BUT SHE IS NOT YOUR GIRLFRIEND, YOU WERE SAYING?
I...WHAT I MEANT WAS, SHE'S NOT MY ***STEADY*** OR ANYTHING. I SEE, YOU KNOW, ALL ***KINDS*** OF GIRLS.
I--I BETTER TAKE A LOOK AT THIS HATCH...
SURE.
THAT'S WHAT WE'RE HERE FOR, JA?
I--I GUESS.
HUMH. YOU KNOW, IN SOME WAYS, BACK IN THE WAR, IT WAS BETTER. BACK IN THAT NEWSREEL, YOU KNOW?
EVERYTHING WAS BLACK AND WHITE. IN THAT FIGHTING WE HAD NO TIME TO THINK.
BUT NOW. NOW ALL THE NOISE HAS STOPPED, AND IT IS ***QUIET.*** NOW WE CAN HEAR OUR HEARTS AGAIN.
WHAT NOW?

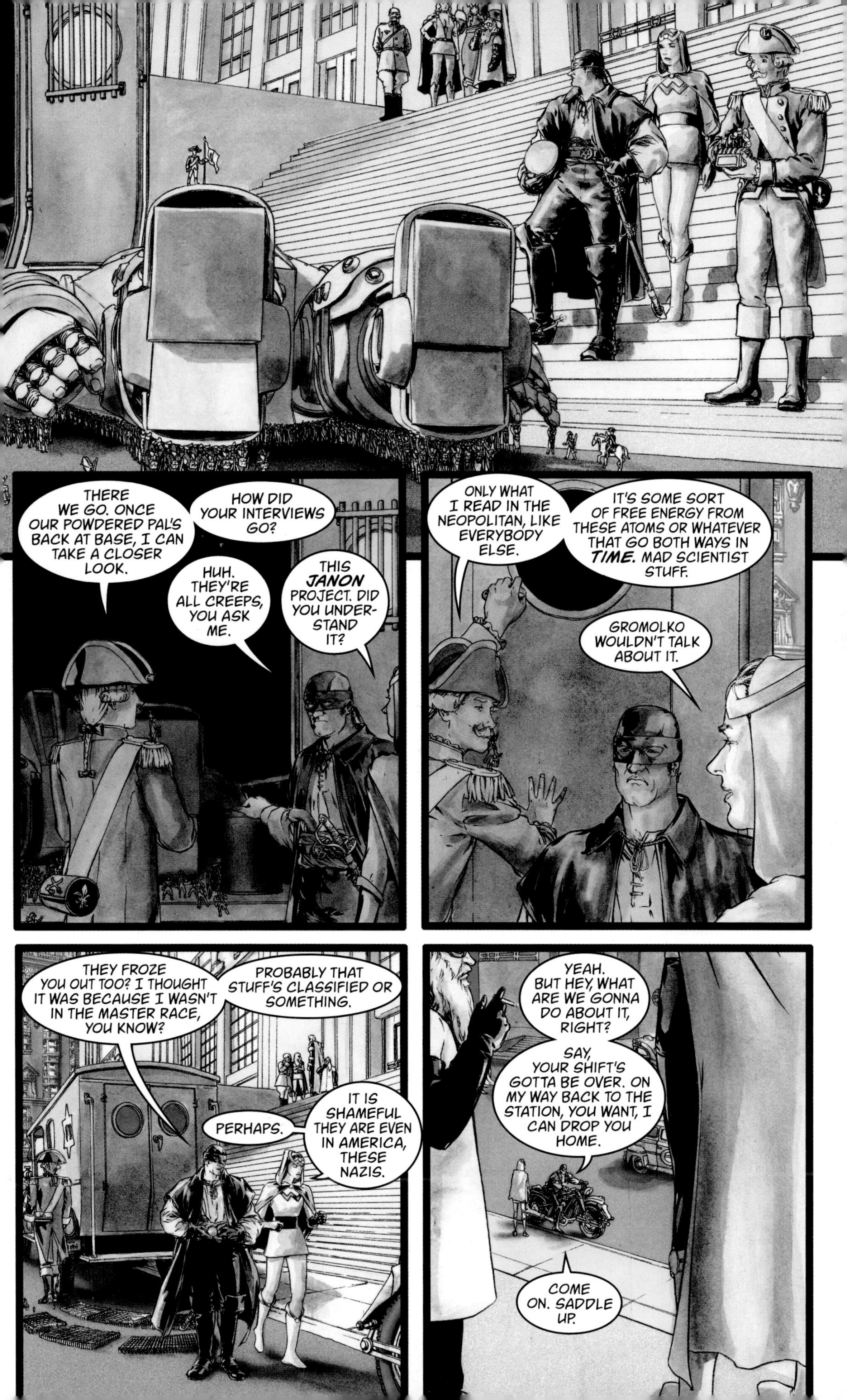
THERE WE GO. ONCE OUR POWDERED PAL'S BACK AT BASE, I CAN TAKE A CLOSER LOOK.
HOW DID YOUR INTERVIEWS GO?
HUH. THEY'RE ALL CREEPS, YOU ASK ME.
THIS JANON PROJECT. DID YOU UNDER-STAND IT?
ONLY WHAT I READ IN THE NEOPOLITAN, LIKE EVERYBODY ELSE.
IT'S SOME SORT OF FREE ENERGY FROM THESE ATOMS OR WHATEVER THAT GO BOTH WAYS IN TIME. MAD SCIENTIST STUFF.
GROMOLKO WOULDN'T TALK ABOUT IT.
THEY FROZE YOU OUT TOO? I THOUGHT IT WAS BECAUSE I WASN'T IN THE MASTER RACE, YOU KNOW?
PROBABLY THAT STUFF'S CLASSIFIED OR SOMETHING.
PERHAPS.
IT IS SHAMEFUL THEY ARE EVEN IN AMERICA, THESE NAZIS.
YEAH. BUT HEY, WHAT ARE WE GONNA DO ABOUT IT, RIGHT?
SAY, YOUR SHIFT'S GOTTA BE OVER. ON MY WAY BACK TO THE STATION, YOU WANT, I CAN DROP YOU HOME.
COME ON. SADDLE UP.

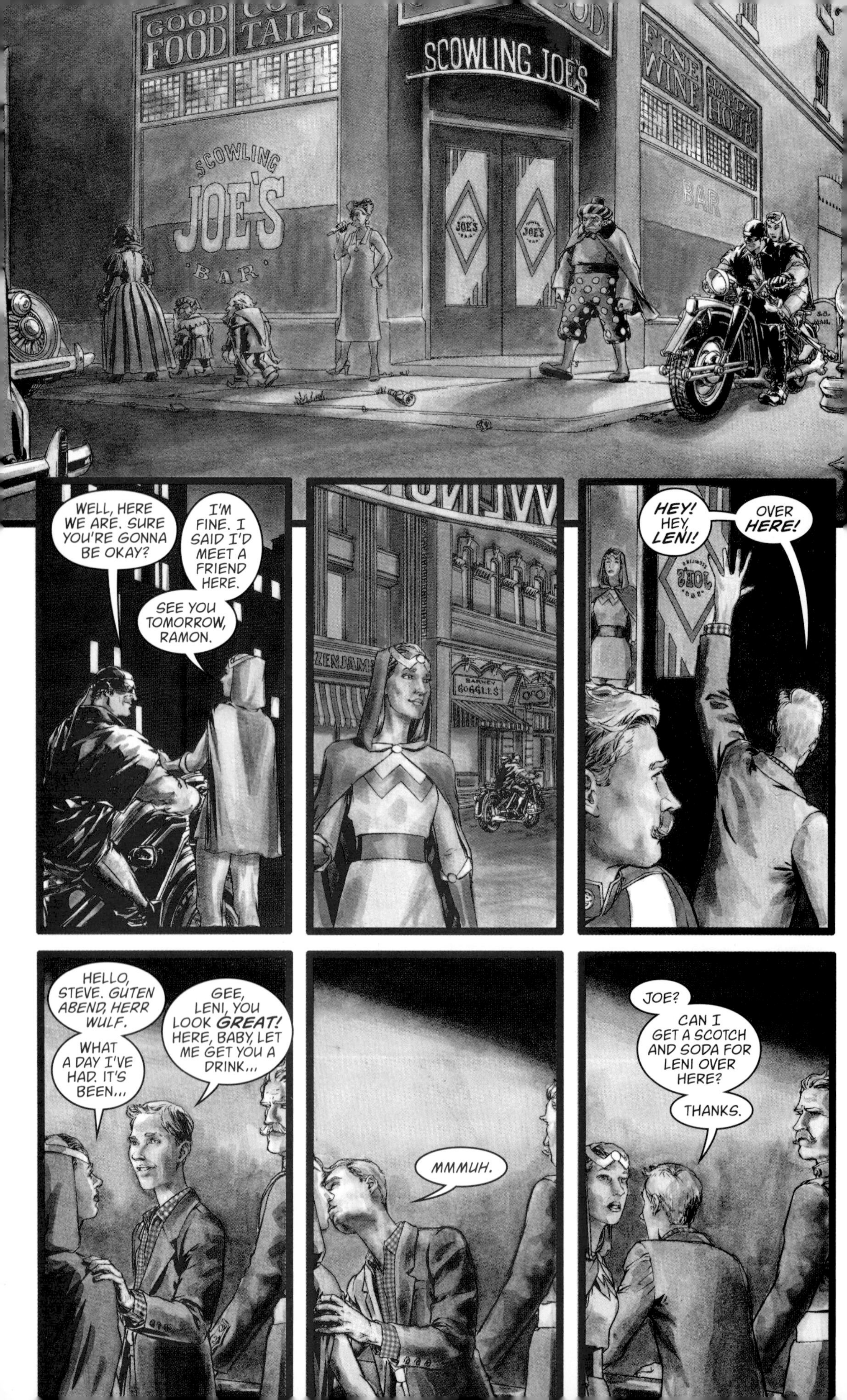
GOOD FOOD
SCOWLING JOE'S
FINE WINE
HAPPY HOUR
SCOWLING JOE'S BAR
BAR
WELL, HERE WE ARE. SURE YOU'RE GONNA BE OKAY?
I'M FINE. I SAID I'D MEET A FRIEND HERE.
SEE YOU TOMORROW, RAMON.
BARNEY GOGGLES
HEY! HEY, LENI!
OVER HERE!
HELLO, STEVE. GUTEN ABEND, HERR WULF.
WHAT A DAY I'VE HAD. IT'S BEEN...
GEE, LENI, YOU LOOK GREAT! HERE, BABY, LET ME GET YOU A DRINK...
MMMUH.
JOE?
CAN I GET A SCOTCH AND SODA FOR LENI OVER HERE?
THANKS.

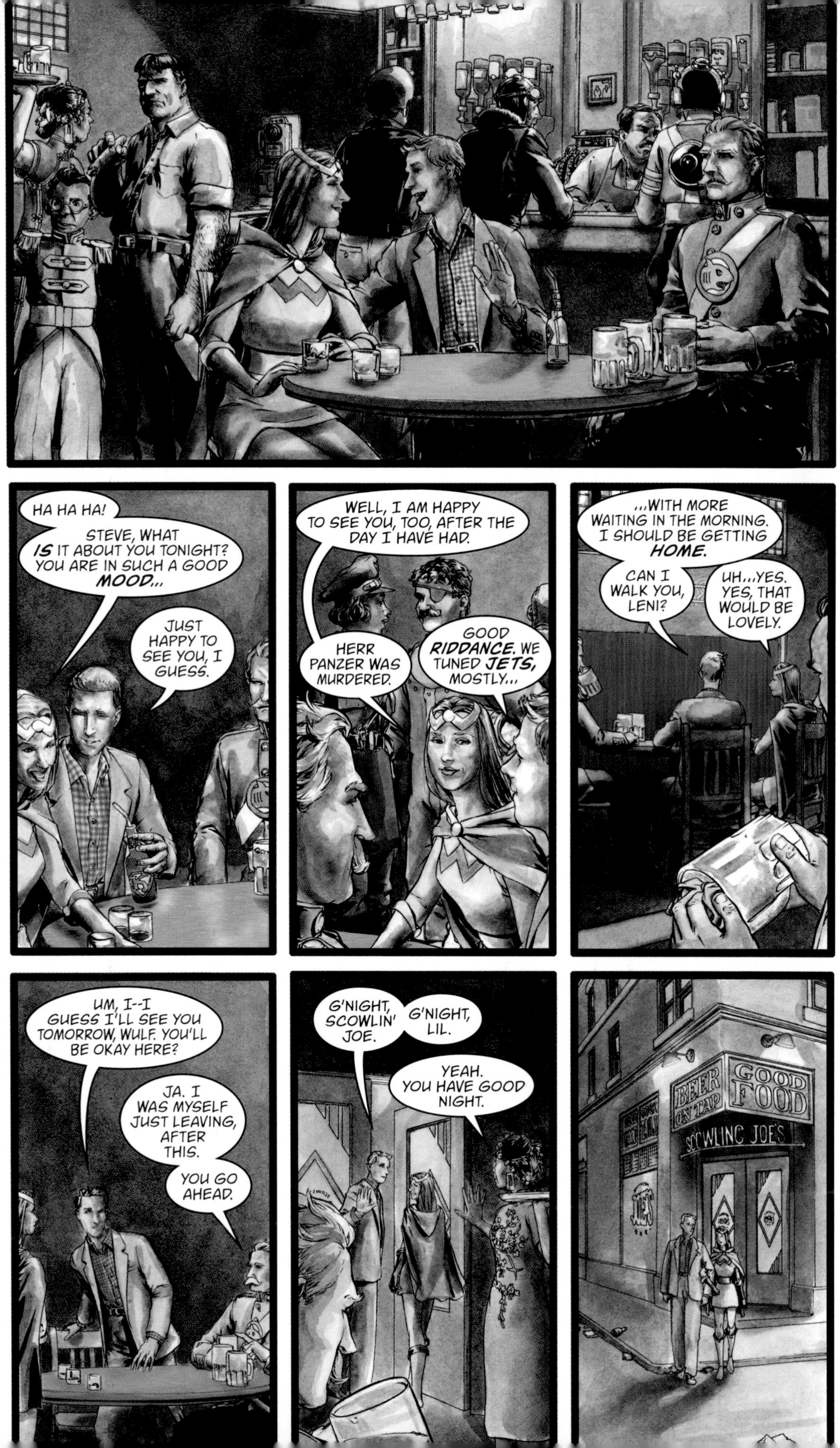
HA HA HA!
STEVE, WHAT IS IT ABOUT YOU TONIGHT? YOU ARE IN SUCH A GOOD MOOD...
JUST HAPPY TO SEE YOU, I GUESS.
WELL, I AM HAPPY TO SEE YOU, TOO, AFTER THE DAY I HAVE HAD.
HERR PANZER WAS MURDERED.
GOOD RIDDANCE. WE TUNED JETS, MOSTLY...
...WITH MORE WAITING IN THE MORNING. I SHOULD BE GETTING HOME.
CAN I WALK YOU, LENI?
UH...YES. YES, THAT WOULD BE LOVELY.
UM, I--I GUESS I'LL SEE YOU TOMORROW, WULF. YOU'LL BE OKAY HERE?
JA. I WAS MYSELF JUST LEAVING, AFTER THIS.
YOU GO AHEAD.
G'NIGHT, SCOWLIN' JOE.
G'NIGHT, LIL.
YEAH. YOU HAVE GOOD NIGHT.
BEER ON TAP
GOOD FOOD
SCOWLING JOE'S

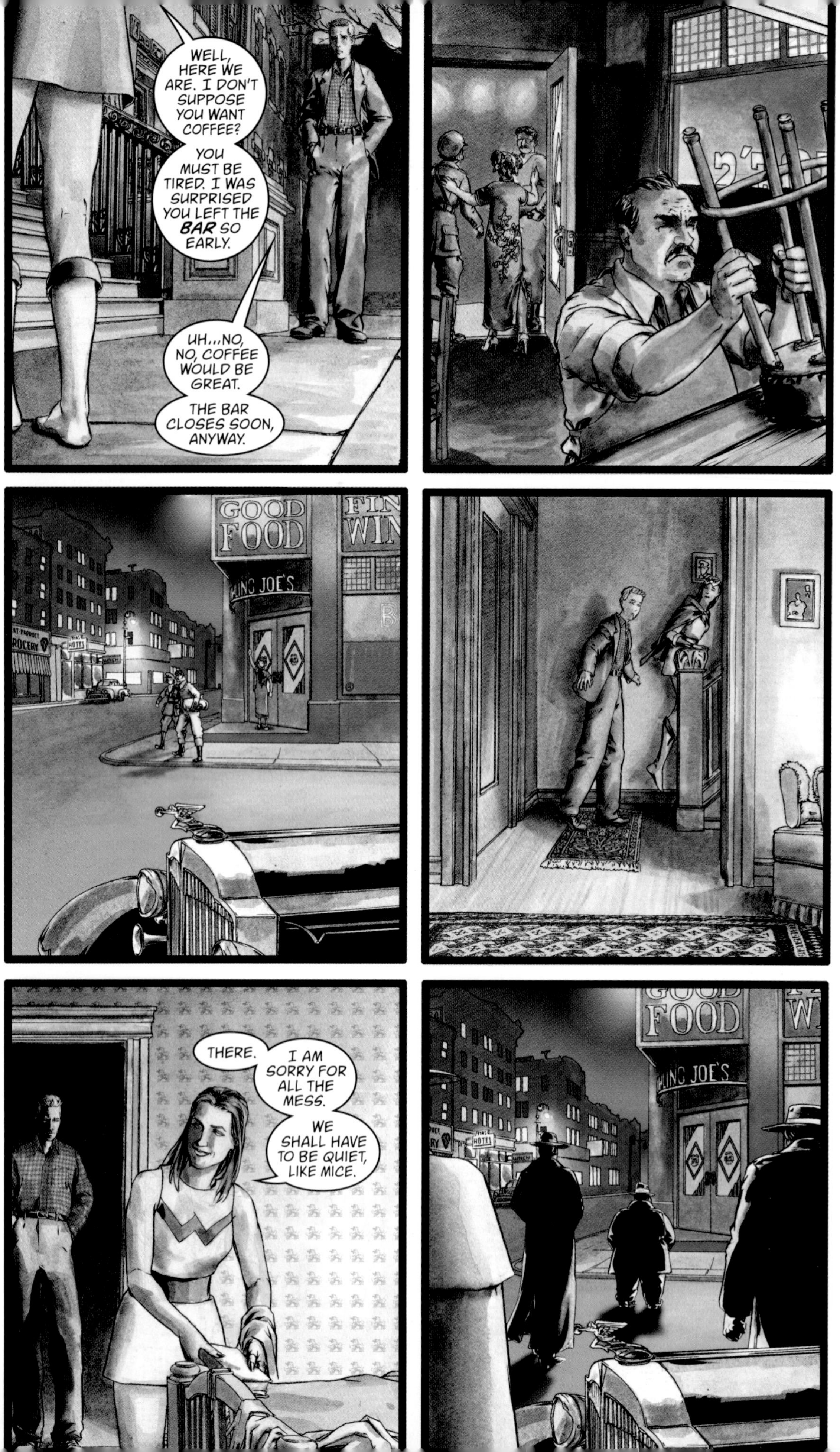
WELL, HERE WE ARE. I DON'T SUPPOSE YOU WANT COFFEE?
YOU MUST BE TIRED. I WAS SURPRISED YOU LEFT THE BAR SO EARLY.
UH...NO, NO, COFFEE WOULD BE GREAT.
THE BAR CLOSES SOON, ANYWAY.
GOOD FOOD
THERE.
I AM SORRY FOR ALL THE MESS.
WE SHALL HAVE TO BE QUIET, LIKE MICE.
FOOD

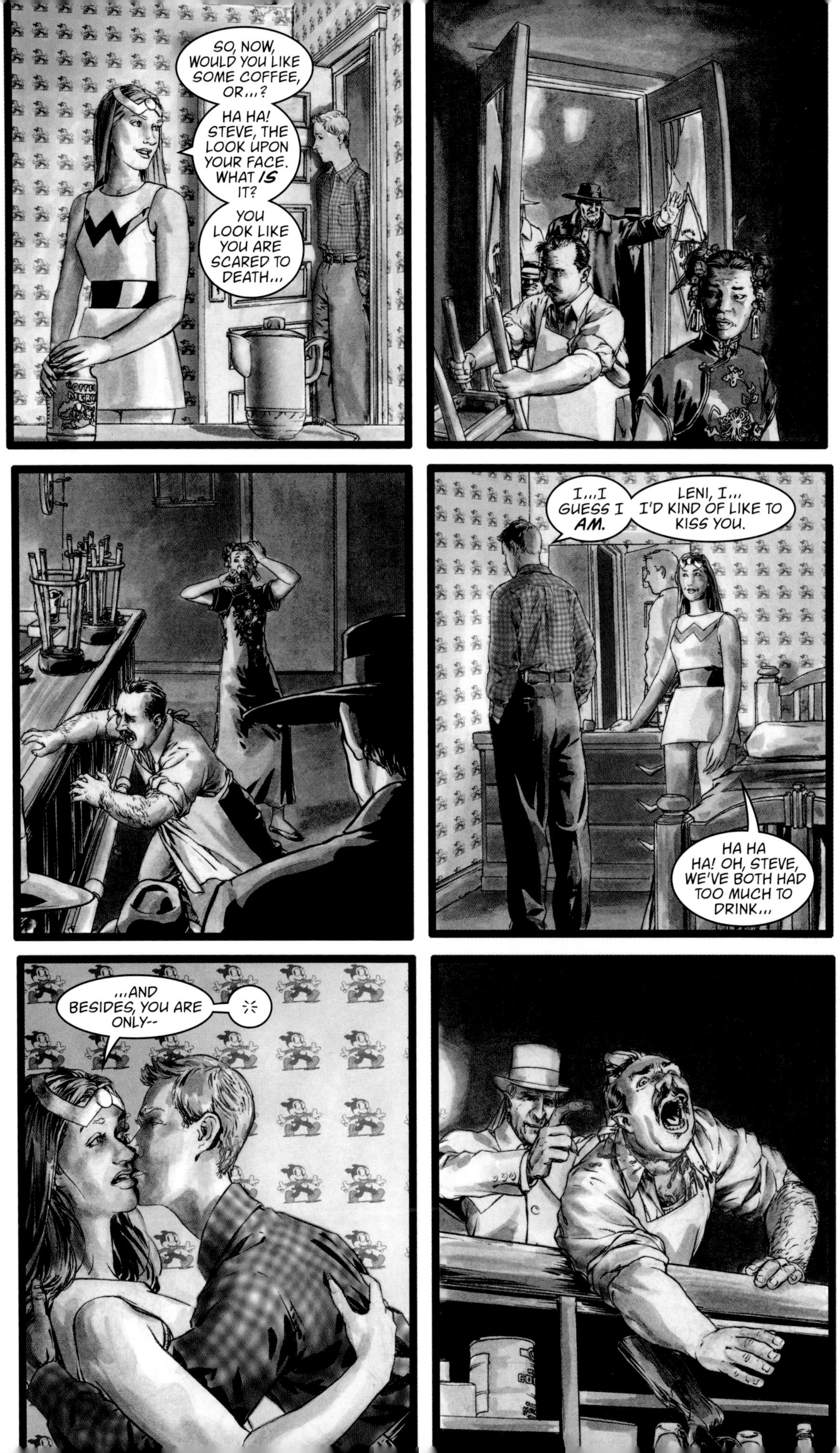
SO, NOW, WOULD YOU LIKE SOME COFFEE, OR...?
HA HA! STEVE, THE LOOK UPON YOUR FACE. WHAT *IS* IT?
YOU LOOK LIKE YOU ARE SCARED TO DEATH...
I...I GUESS I *AM.*
LENI, I... I'D KIND OF LIKE TO KISS YOU.
HA HA HA! OH, STEVE, WE'VE BOTH HAD TOO MUCH TO DRINK...
...AND BESIDES, YOU ARE ONLY--

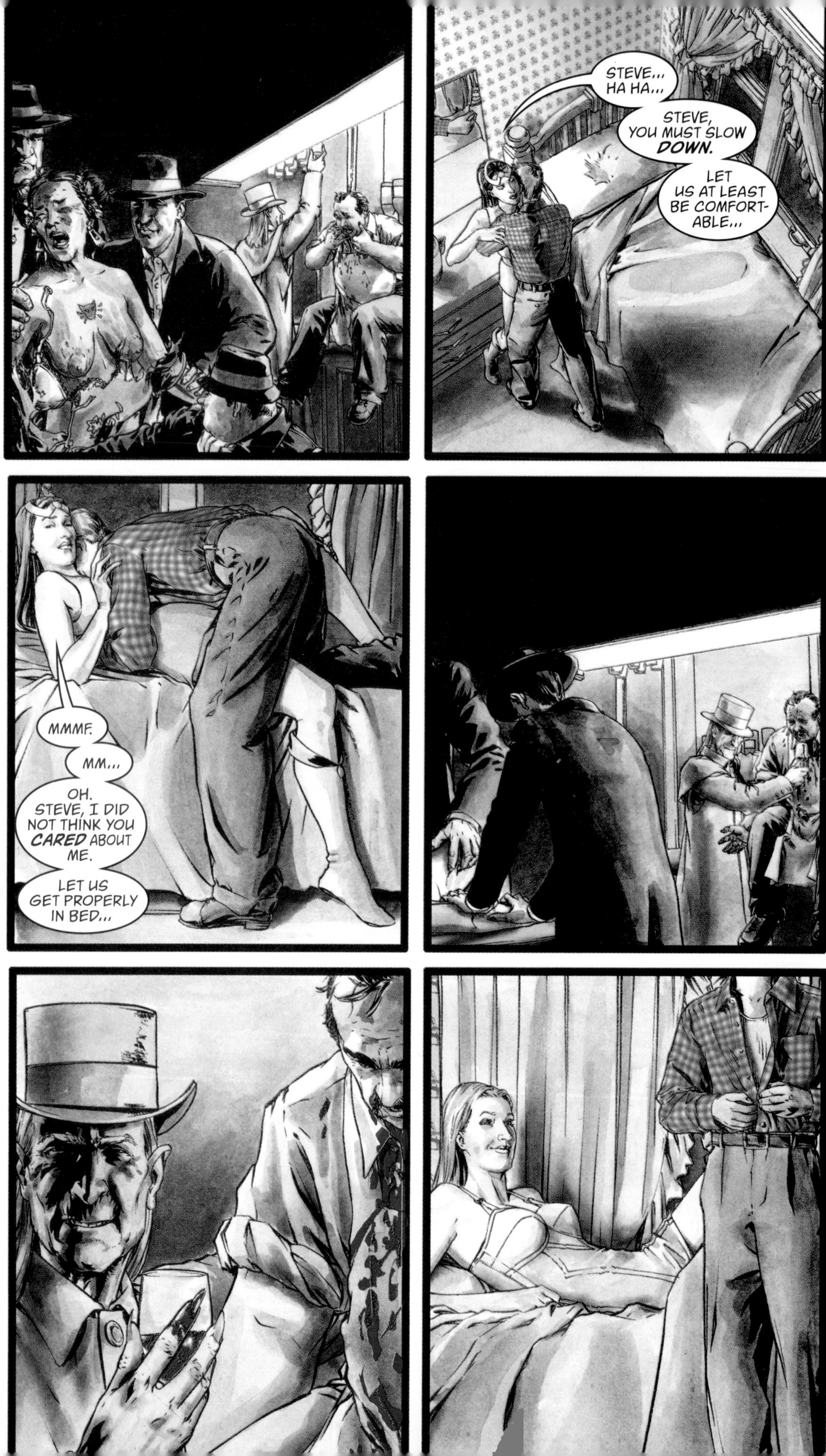
STEVE... HA HA...
STEVE, YOU MUST SLOW DOWN.
LET US AT LEAST BE COMFORT-ABLE...
MMMF.
MM...
OH. STEVE, I DID NOT THINK YOU CARED ABOUT ME.
LET US GET PROPERLY IN BED...

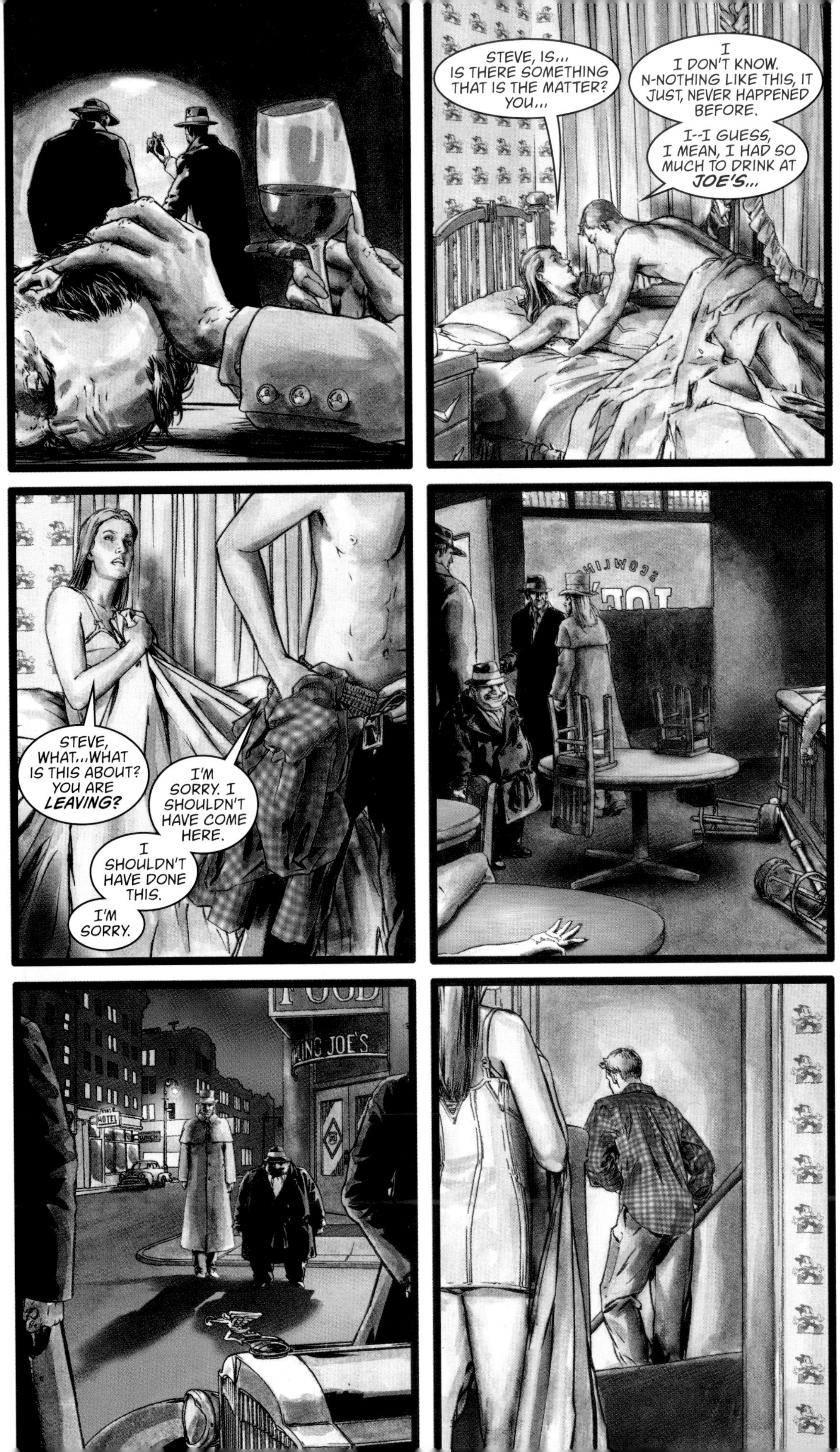

STEVE, IS... IS THERE SOMETHING THAT IS THE MATTER? YOU...
I I DON'T KNOW. N-NOTHING LIKE THIS, IT JUST, NEVER HAPPENED BEFORE.
I--I GUESS, I MEAN, I HAD SO MUCH TO DRINK AT JOE'S...
STEVE, WHAT...WHAT IS THIS ABOUT? YOU ARE LEAVING?
I'M SORRY. I SHOULDN'T HAVE COME HERE.
I SHOULDN'T HAVE DONE THIS.
I'M SORRY.
JOE'S
FOOD
HOTEL

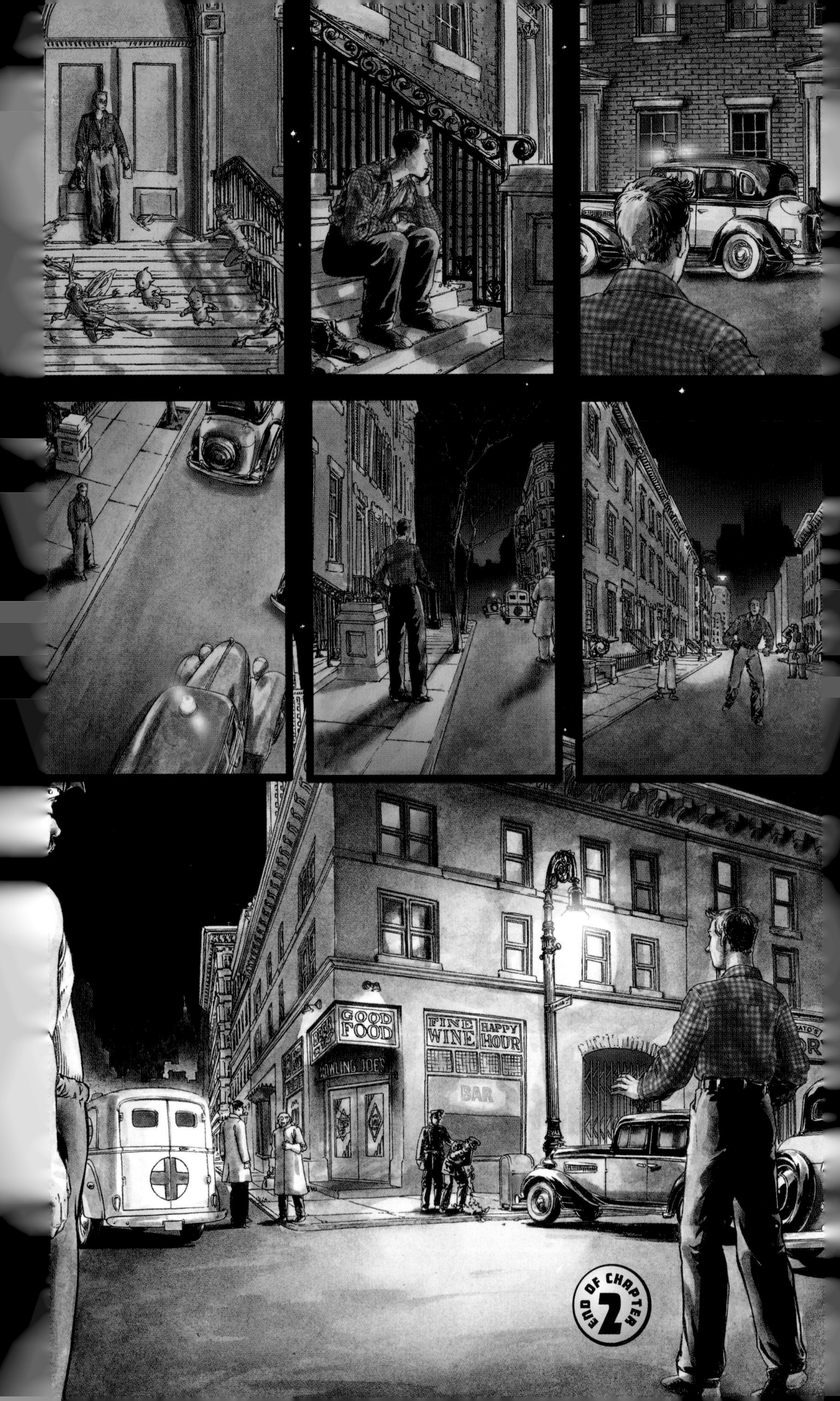
GOOD FOOD
FINE WINE
HAPPY HOUR
HOWLING JOE'S
BAR
END OF CHAPTER 2

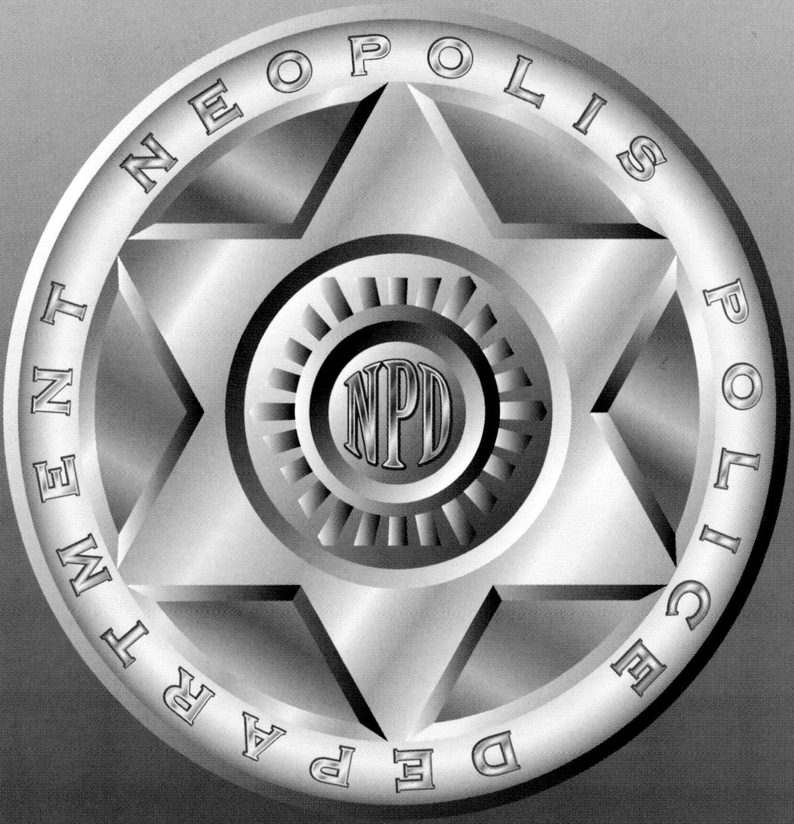
NEOPOLIS POLICE DEPARTMENT
NPD

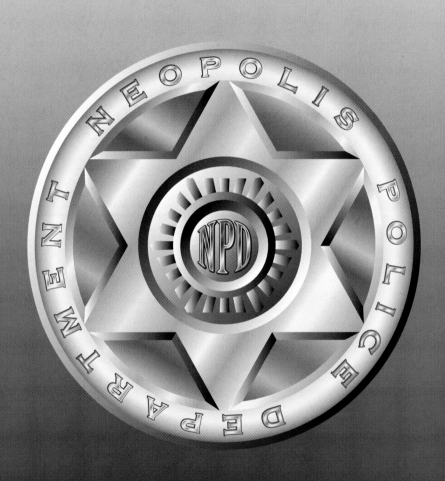

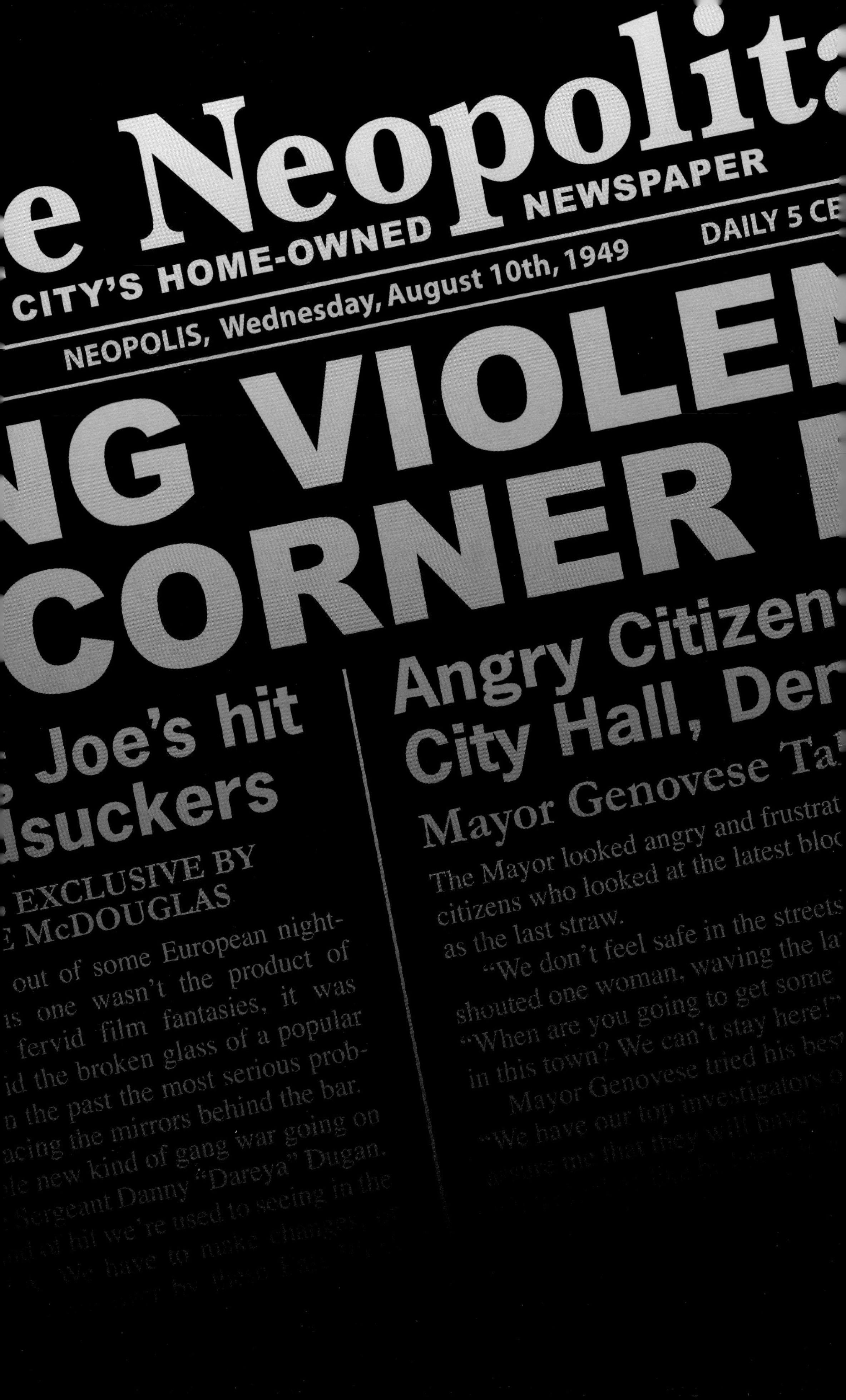

e Neopolita

CITY'S HOME-OWNED NEWSPAPER

NEOPOLIS, Wednesday, August 10th, 1949

DAILY 5 CE

NG VIOLE
CORNER

Joe's hit
suckers

EXCLUSIVE BY
McDOUGLAS

out of some European night-
s one wasn't the product of
fervid film fantasies, it was
d the broken glass of a popular
n the past the most serious prob-
acing the mirrors behind the bar.
e new kind of gang war going on
Sergeant Danny "Dareya" Dugan.
d of hit we're used to seeing in the
We have to make changes

Angry Citizen
City Hall, Den

Mayor Genovese Ta

The Mayor looked angry and frustrat
citizens who looked at the latest bloc
as the last straw.

"We don't feel safe in the streets
shouted one woman, waving the la
"When are you going to get some
in this town? We can't stay here!"

Mayor Genovese tried his best
"We have our top investigators
assure me that they will have

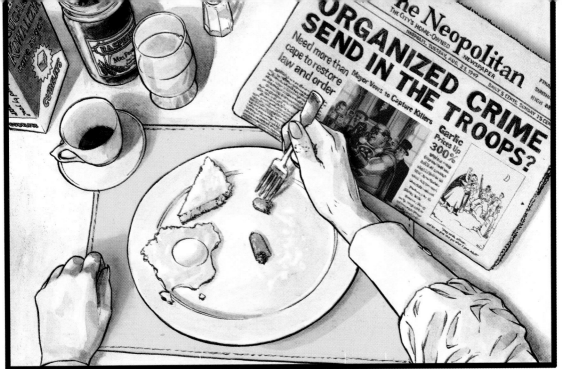

The Neopolitan
THE CITY'S HOME-OWNED NEWSPAPER
MINNEAPOLIS, TUESDAY, AUG. 23, 1943
DAILY 5 CENTS, SUNDAY 15 CENTS

ORGANIZED CRIME
SEND IN THE TROOPS?
Need more than cape to restore law and order
Mayor Vows to Capture Killers

Garlic Prices Up 300%

HM.

I HOPE THEY DO SOMETHING **SOON**, ABOUT THESE **BLOODSUCKER** GANGS.

I'M AFRAID TO GO **OUT** NIGHTS.

WELL, THE POLICE ARE DOING THEIR BEST.

OKAY, THAT'S MY RIDE TO WORK OUTSIDE.

I'LL SEE YOU TONIGHT, MRS. DOES-GOOD.

SURE THING, HON. HAVE A GOOD DAY.

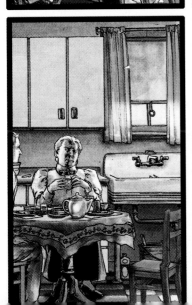

UM...WELL, I'D BETTER GET OVER TO THE **BASE.** THANKS FOR BREAKFAST, MRS. DOESGOOD.

YOU'RE WELCOME. TELL **SLOPPY** TO CALL ME.

TAKE CARE, NOW.

:HAHHH:

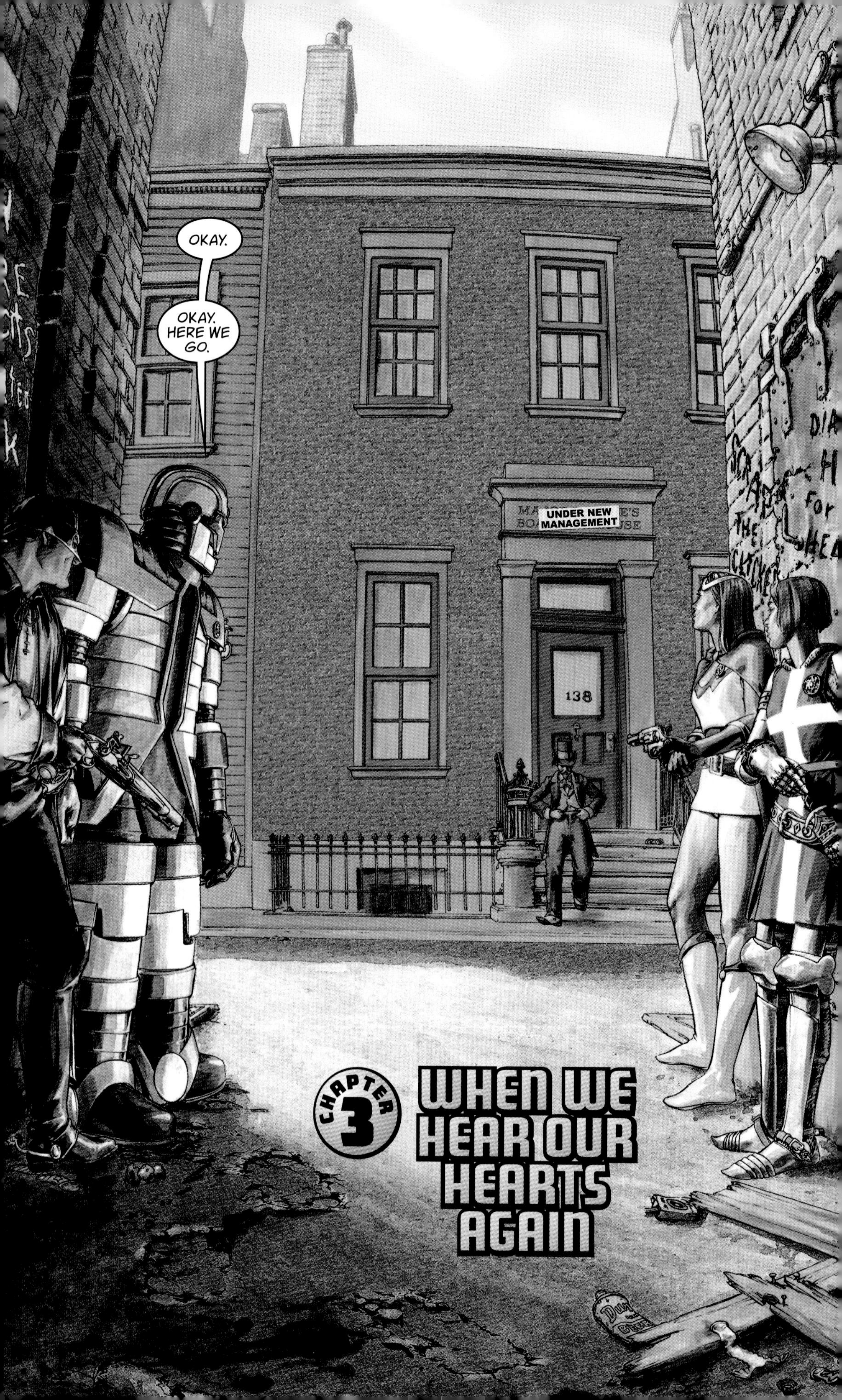
OKAY.
OKAY. HERE WE GO.
UNDER NEW MANAGEMENT
138
CHAPTER 3
WHEN WE HEAR OUR HEARTS AGAIN

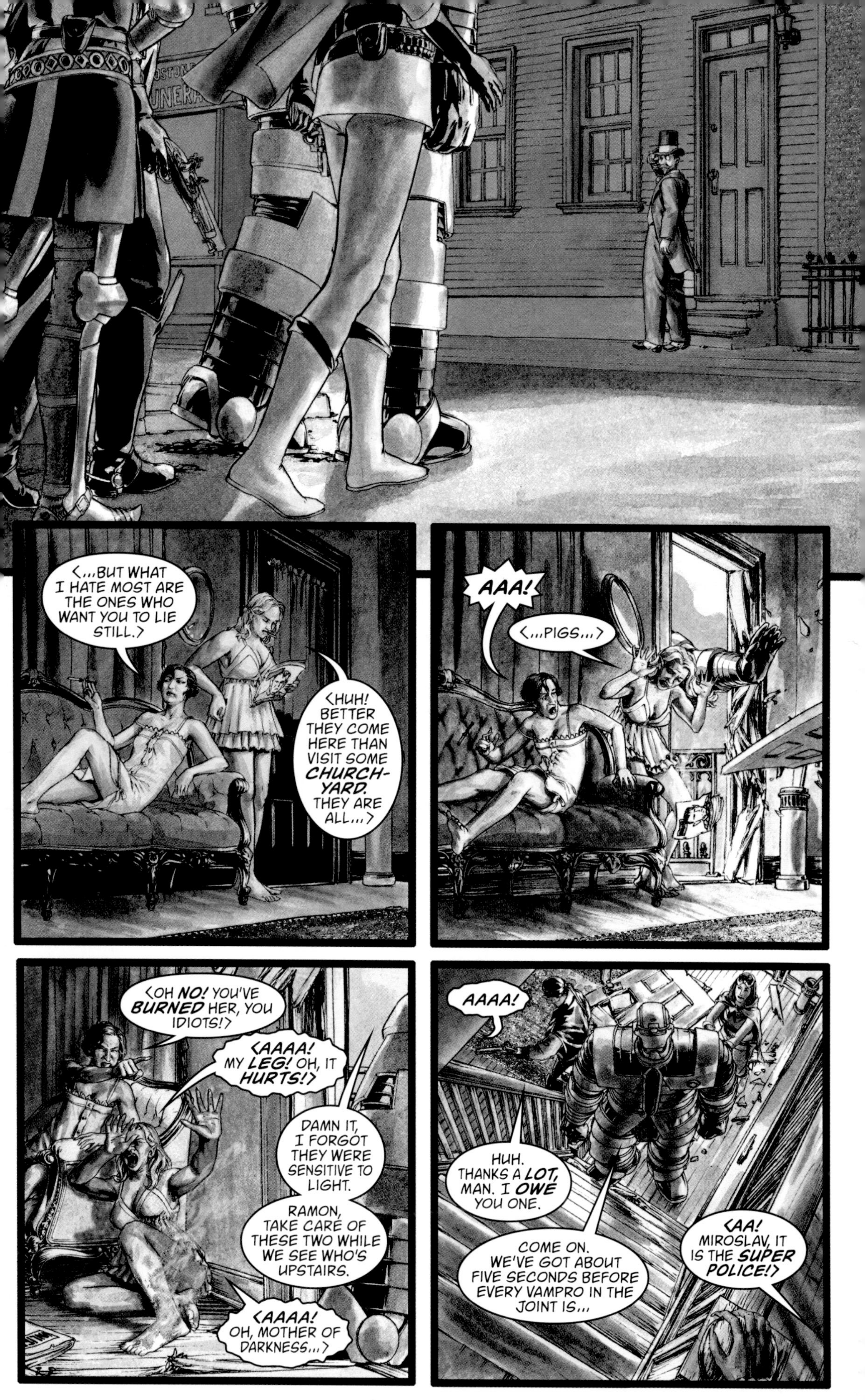

<...BUT WHAT I HATE MOST ARE THE ONES WHO WANT YOU TO LIE STILL.>
<HUH! BETTER THEY COME HERE THAN VISIT SOME **CHURCH-YARD.** THEY ARE ALL...>
AAA!
<...PIGS...>
<OH **NO!** YOU'VE **BURNED** HER, YOU IDIOTS!>
<AAAA! MY LEG! OH, IT HURTS!>
DAMN IT, I FORGOT THEY WERE SENSITIVE TO LIGHT.
RAMON, TAKE CARE OF THESE TWO WHILE WE SEE WHO'S UPSTAIRS.
<AAAA! OH, MOTHER OF DARKNESS...>
AAAA!
HUH. THANKS A **LOT,** MAN. I **OWE** YOU ONE.
COME ON. WE'VE GOT ABOUT FIVE SECONDS BEFORE EVERY VAMPRO IN THE JOINT IS...
<AA! MIROSLAV, IT IS THE **SUPER POLICE!>**

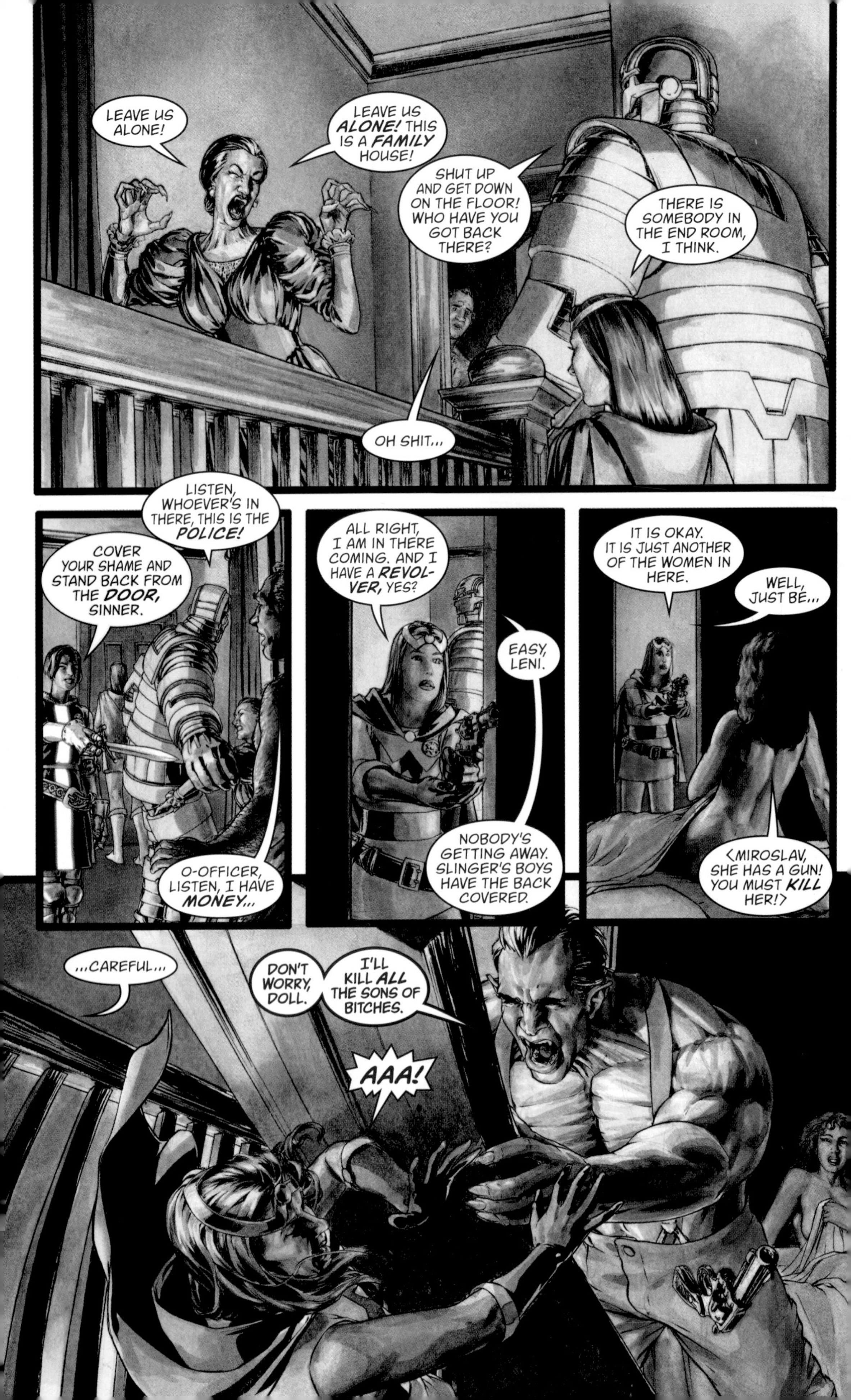
LEAVE US ALONE!
LEAVE US ALONE! THIS IS A FAMILY HOUSE!
SHUT UP AND GET DOWN ON THE FLOOR! WHO HAVE YOU GOT BACK THERE?
THERE IS SOMEBODY IN THE END ROOM, I THINK.
OH SHIT...
LISTEN, WHOEVER'S IN THERE, THIS IS THE POLICE!
COVER YOUR SHAME AND STAND BACK FROM THE DOOR, SINNER.
O-OFFICER, LISTEN, I HAVE MONEY...
ALL RIGHT, I AM IN THERE COMING. AND I HAVE A REVOLVER, YES?
EASY, LENI.
NOBODY'S GETTING AWAY. SLINGER'S BOYS HAVE THE BACK COVERED.
IT IS OKAY. IT IS JUST ANOTHER OF THE WOMEN IN HERE.
WELL, JUST BE...
<MIROSLAV, SHE HAS A GUN! YOU MUST KILL HER!>
...CAREFUL...
DON'T WORRY, DOLL.
I'LL KILL ALL THE SONS OF BITCHES.
AAA!

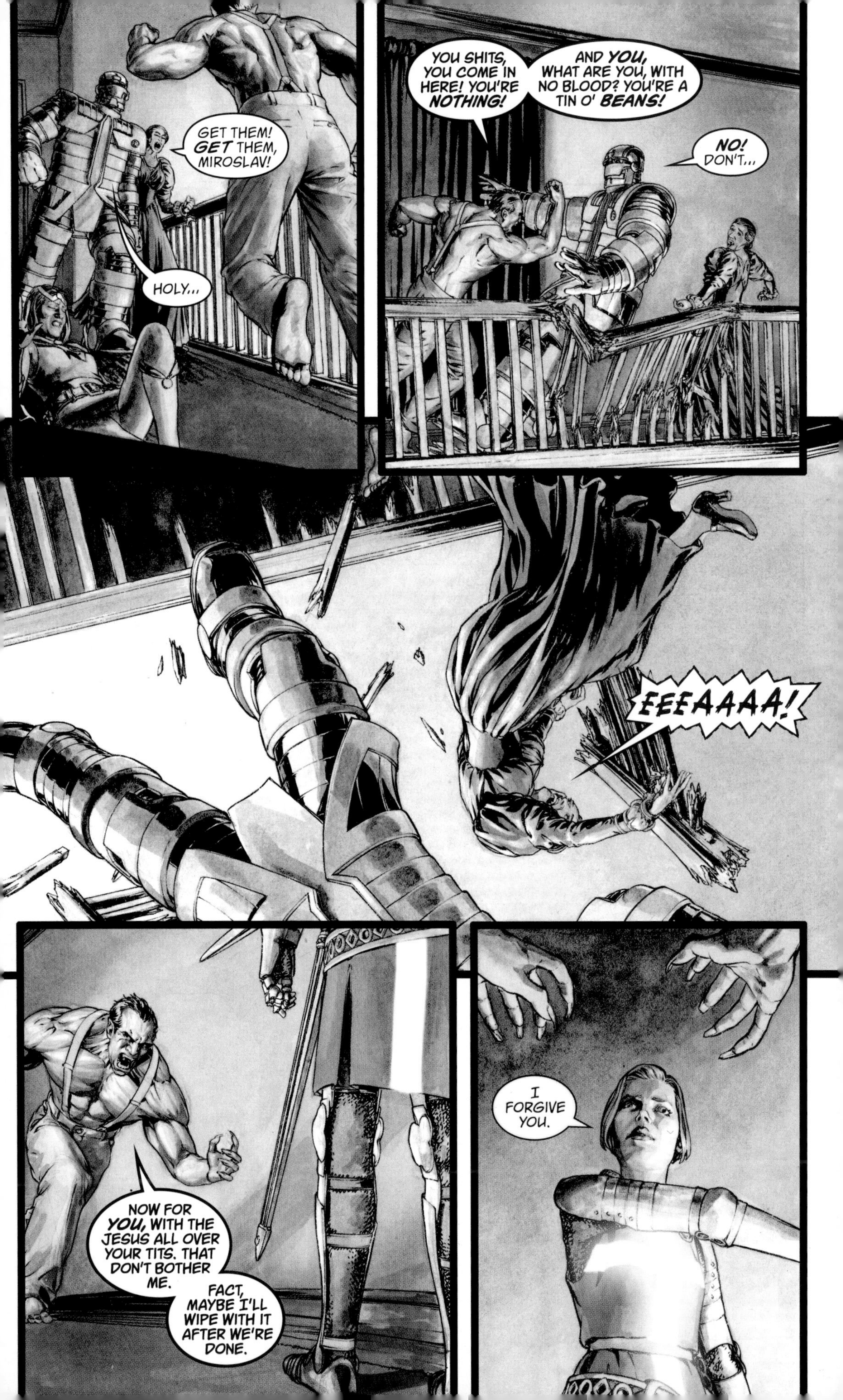
GET THEM! GET THEM, MIROSLAV!
HOLY...
YOU SHITS, YOU COME IN HERE! YOU'RE NOTHING!
AND YOU, WHAT ARE YOU, WITH NO BLOOD? YOU'RE A TIN O' BEANS!
NO! DON'T...
EEEAAAA!
NOW FOR YOU, WITH THE JESUS ALL OVER YOUR TITS. THAT DON'T BOTHER ME.
FACT, MAYBE I'LL WIPE WITH IT AFTER WE'RE DONE.
I FORGIVE YOU.

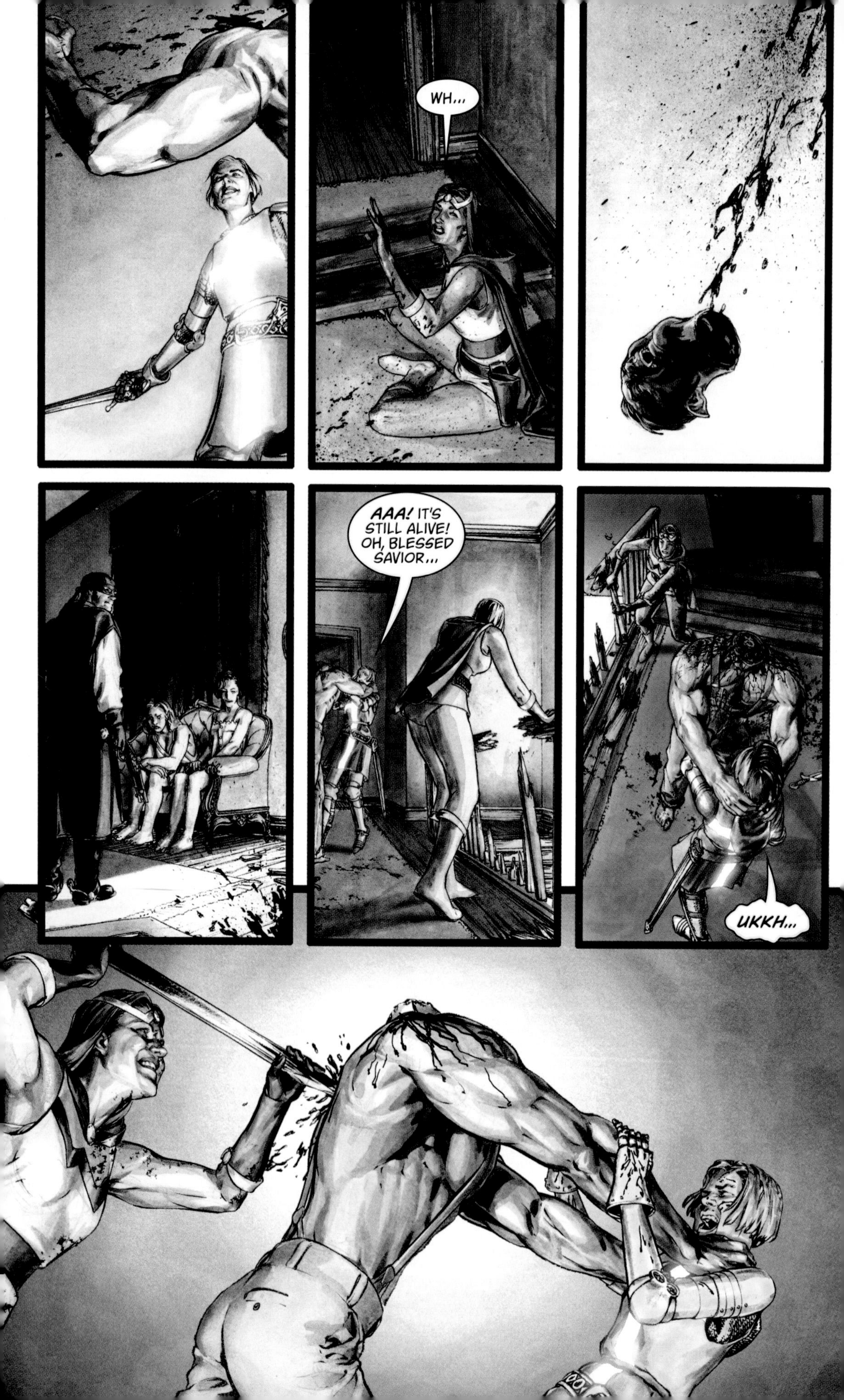
WH...
AAA! IT'S STILL ALIVE! OH, BLESSED SAVIOR...
UKKH...

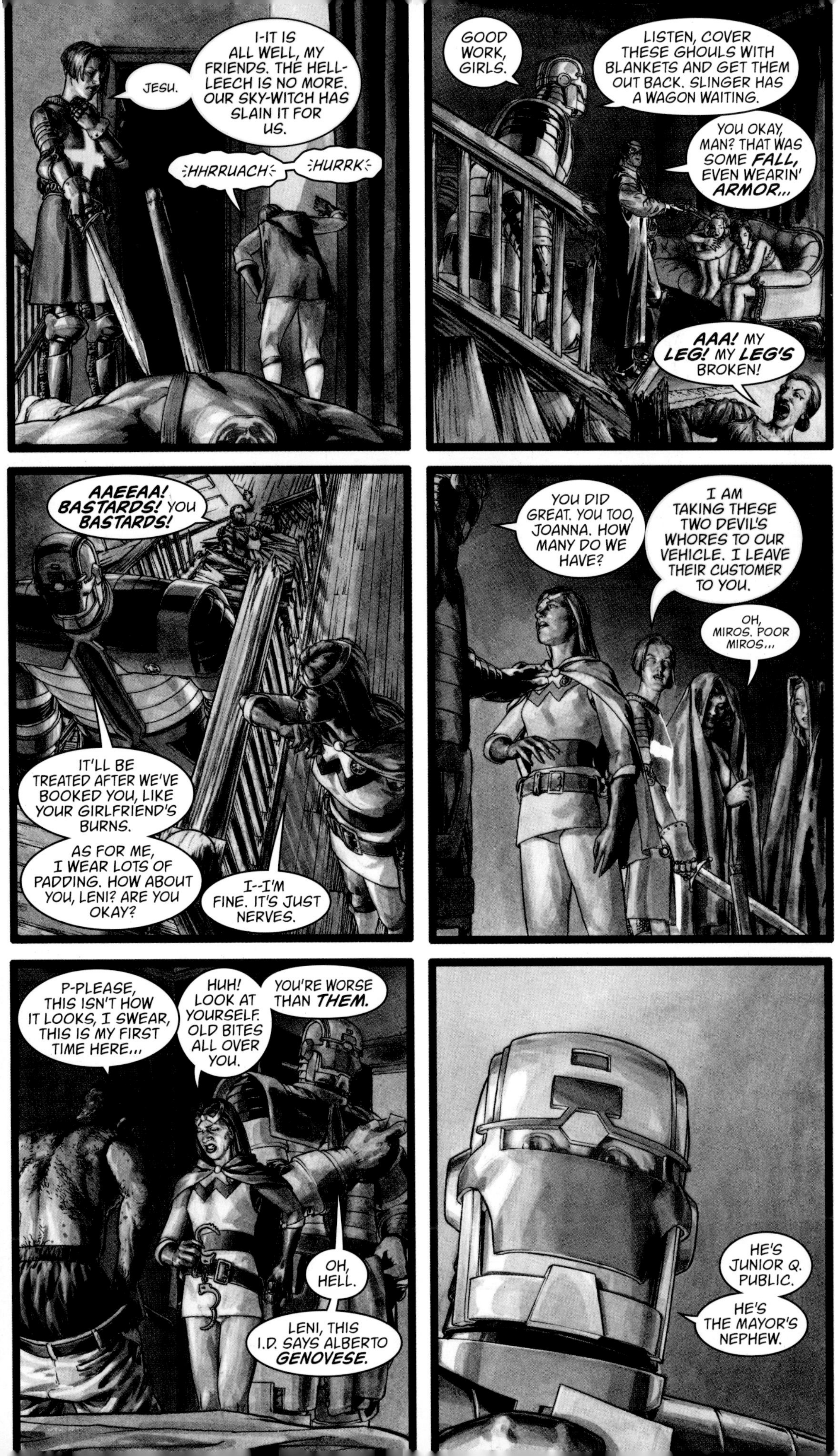
JESU.
I-IT IS ALL WELL, MY FRIENDS. THE HELL-LEECH IS NO MORE. OUR SKY-WITCH HAS SLAIN IT FOR US.
HHRRUACH
HURRK
GOOD WORK, GIRLS.
LISTEN, COVER THESE GHOULS WITH BLANKETS AND GET THEM OUT BACK. SLINGER HAS A WAGON WAITING.
YOU OKAY, MAN? THAT WAS SOME FALL, EVEN WEARIN' ARMOR...
AAA! MY LEG! MY LEG'S BROKEN!
AAEEAA! BASTARDS! YOU BASTARDS!
IT'LL BE TREATED AFTER WE'VE BOOKED YOU, LIKE YOUR GIRLFRIEND'S BURNS.
AS FOR ME, I WEAR LOTS OF PADDING. HOW ABOUT YOU, LENI? ARE YOU OKAY?
I--I'M FINE. IT'S JUST NERVES.
YOU DID GREAT. YOU TOO, JOANNA. HOW MANY DO WE HAVE?
I AM TAKING THESE TWO DEVIL'S WHORES TO OUR VEHICLE. I LEAVE THEIR CUSTOMER TO YOU.
OH, MIROS. POOR MIROS...
P-PLEASE, THIS ISN'T HOW IT LOOKS, I SWEAR, THIS IS MY FIRST TIME HERE...
HUH! LOOK AT YOURSELF. OLD BITES ALL OVER YOU.
YOU'RE WORSE THAN THEM.
OH, HELL.
LENI, THIS I.D. SAYS ALBERTO GENOVESE.
HE'S JUNIOR Q. PUBLIC.
HE'S THE MAYOR'S NEPHEW.

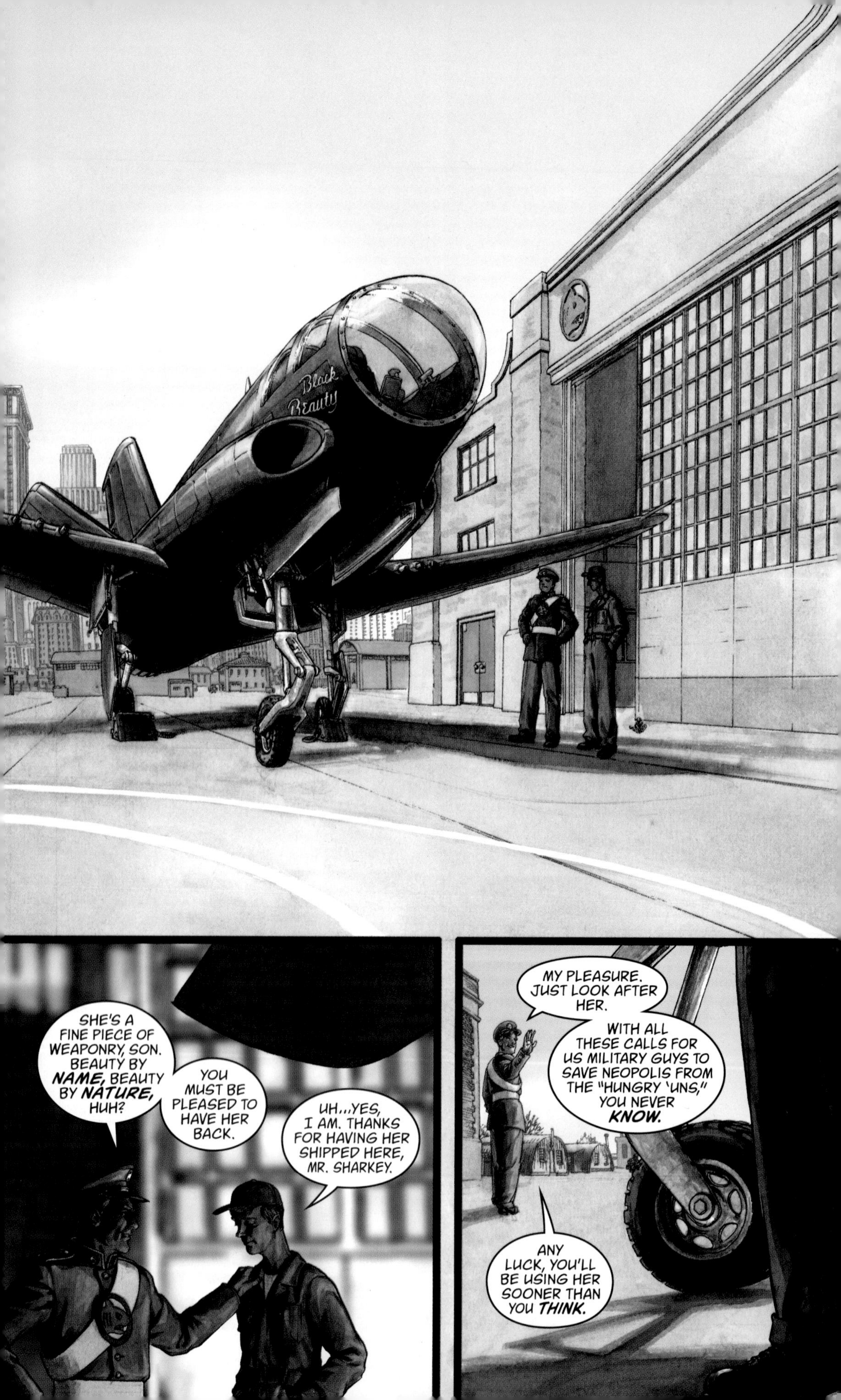
Black Beauty
SHE'S A FINE PIECE OF WEAPONRY, SON. BEAUTY BY NAME, BEAUTY BY NATURE, HUH?
YOU MUST BE PLEASED TO HAVE HER BACK.
UH...YES, I AM. THANKS FOR HAVING HER SHIPPED HERE, MR. SHARKEY.
MY PLEASURE. JUST LOOK AFTER HER.
WITH ALL THESE CALLS FOR US MILITARY GUYS TO SAVE NEOPOLIS FROM THE "HUNGRY 'UNS," YOU NEVER KNOW.
ANY LUCK, YOU'LL BE USING HER SOONER THAN YOU THINK.

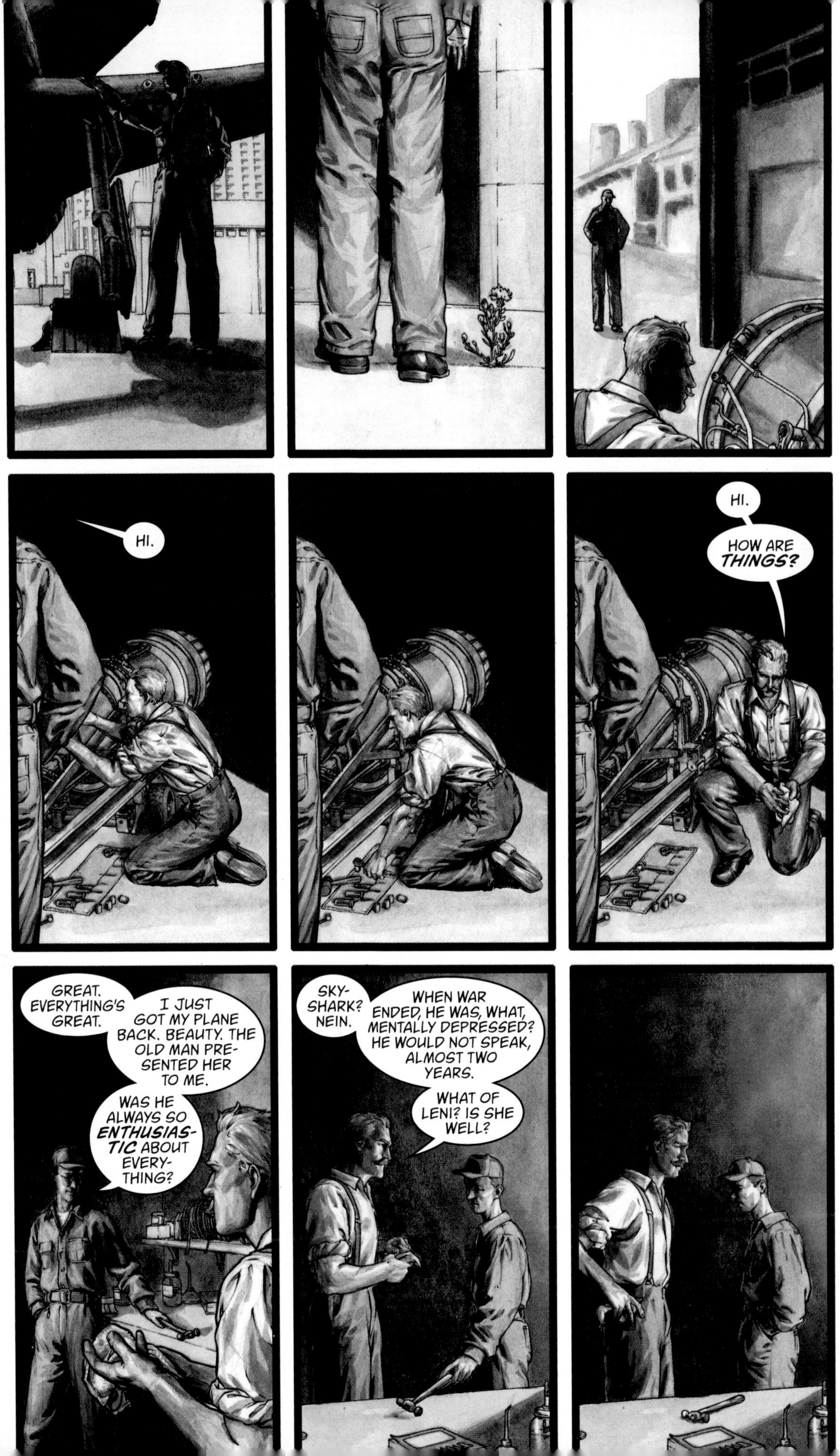
HI.
HI.
HOW ARE *THINGS?*
GREAT. EVERYTHING'S GREAT.
I JUST GOT MY PLANE BACK. BEAUTY. THE OLD MAN PRESENTED HER TO ME.
WAS HE ALWAYS SO *ENTHUSIASTIC* ABOUT EVERYTHING?
SKY-SHARK? NEIN.
WHEN WAR ENDED, HE WAS, WHAT, MENTALLY DEPRESSED? HE WOULD NOT SPEAK, ALMOST TWO YEARS.
WHAT OF LENI? IS SHE WELL?

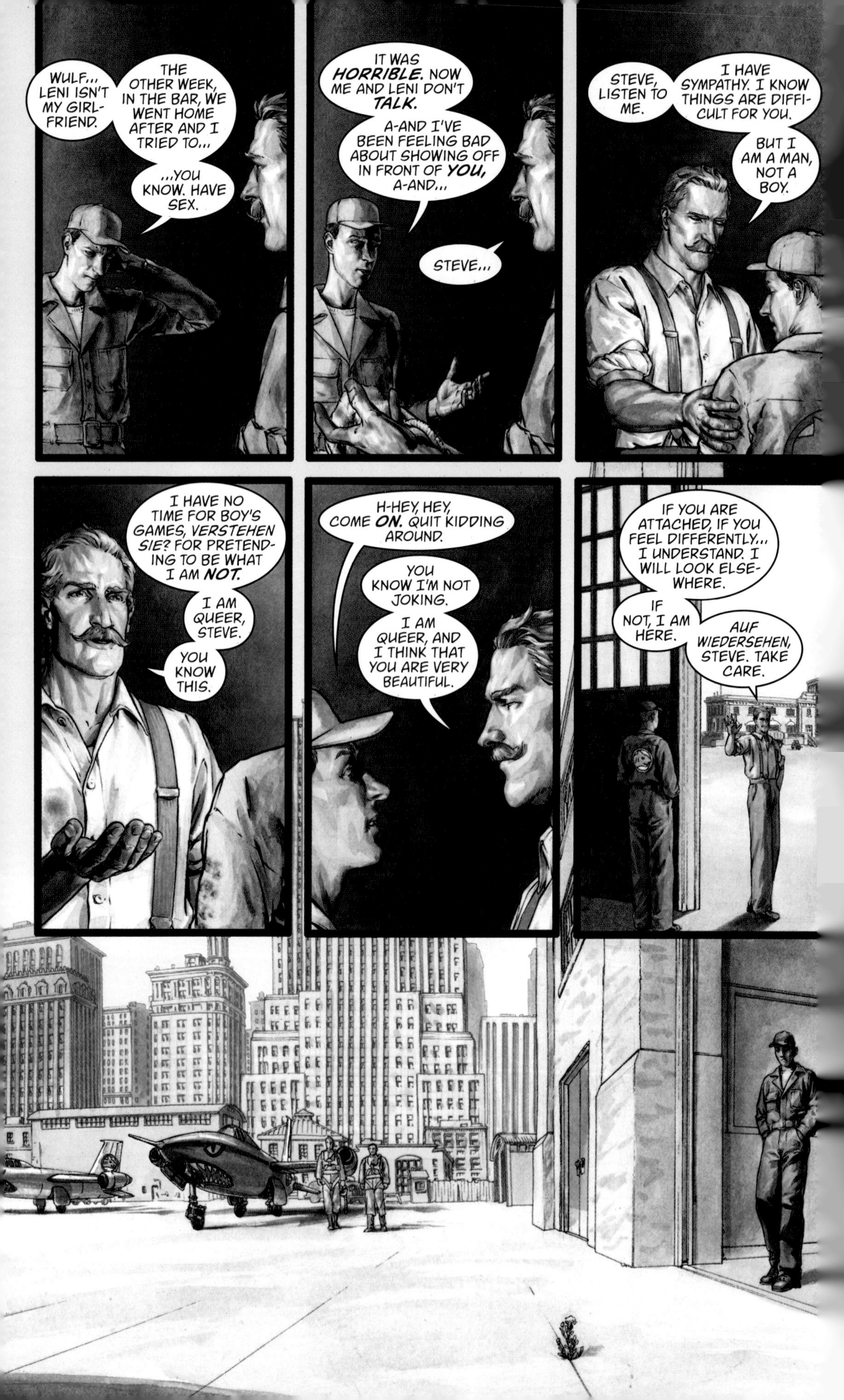
WULF... LENI ISN'T MY GIRL-FRIEND.
THE OTHER WEEK, IN THE BAR, WE WENT HOME AFTER AND I TRIED TO...
...YOU KNOW. HAVE SEX.
IT WAS **HORRIBLE.** NOW ME AND LENI DON'T **TALK.**
A-AND I'VE BEEN FEELING BAD ABOUT SHOWING OFF IN FRONT OF **YOU,** A-AND...
STEVE...
STEVE, LISTEN TO ME.
I HAVE SYMPATHY. I KNOW THINGS ARE DIFFI-CULT FOR YOU.
BUT I AM A MAN, NOT A BOY.
I HAVE NO TIME FOR BOY'S GAMES, *VERSTEHEN SIE?* FOR PRETEND-ING TO BE WHAT I AM **NOT.**
I AM QUEER, STEVE.
YOU KNOW THIS.
H-HEY, HEY, COME **ON.** QUIT KIDDING AROUND.
YOU KNOW I'M NOT JOKING.
I AM QUEER, AND I THINK THAT YOU ARE VERY BEAUTIFUL.
IF YOU ARE ATTACHED, IF YOU FEEL DIFFERENTLY... I UNDERSTAND. I WILL LOOK ELSE-WHERE.
IF NOT, I AM HERE.
AUF WIEDERSEHEN, STEVE. TAKE CARE.

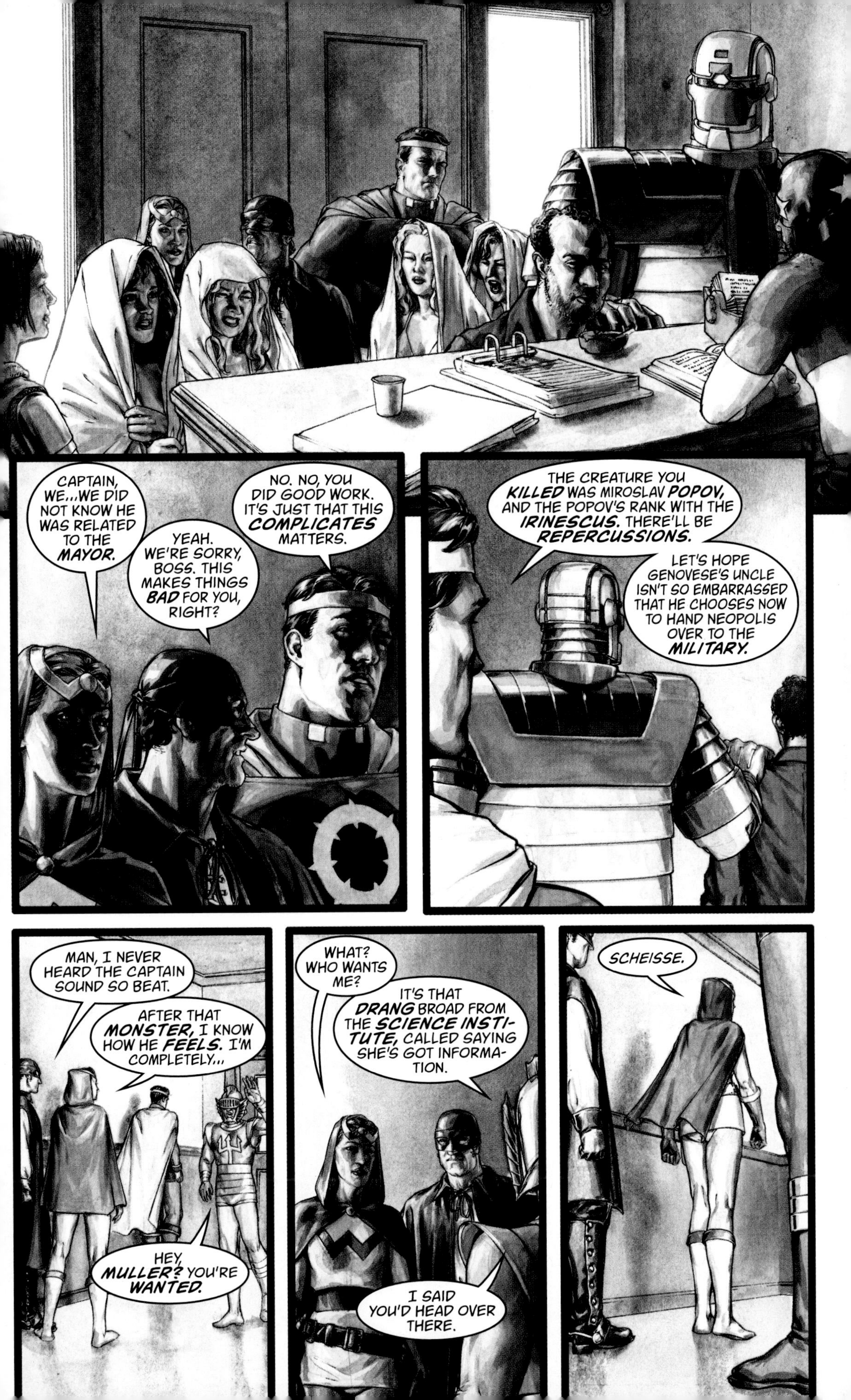
CAPTAIN, WE...WE DID NOT KNOW HE WAS RELATED TO THE MAYOR.
YEAH. WE'RE SORRY, BOSS. THIS MAKES THINGS BAD FOR YOU, RIGHT?
NO. NO, YOU DID GOOD WORK. IT'S JUST THAT THIS COMPLICATES MATTERS.
THE CREATURE YOU KILLED WAS MIROSLAV POPOV, AND THE POPOV'S RANK WITH THE IRINESCUS. THERE'LL BE REPERCUSSIONS.
LET'S HOPE GENOVESE'S UNCLE ISN'T SO EMBARRASSED THAT HE CHOOSES NOW TO HAND NEOPOLIS OVER TO THE MILITARY.
MAN, I NEVER HEARD THE CAPTAIN SOUND SO BEAT.
AFTER THAT MONSTER, I KNOW HOW HE FEELS. I'M COMPLETELY...
HEY, MULLER? YOU'RE WANTED.
WHAT? WHO WANTS ME?
IT'S THAT DRANG BROAD FROM THE SCIENCE INSTITUTE, CALLED SAYING SHE'S GOT INFORMATION.
I SAID YOU'D HEAD OVER THERE.
SCHEISSE.

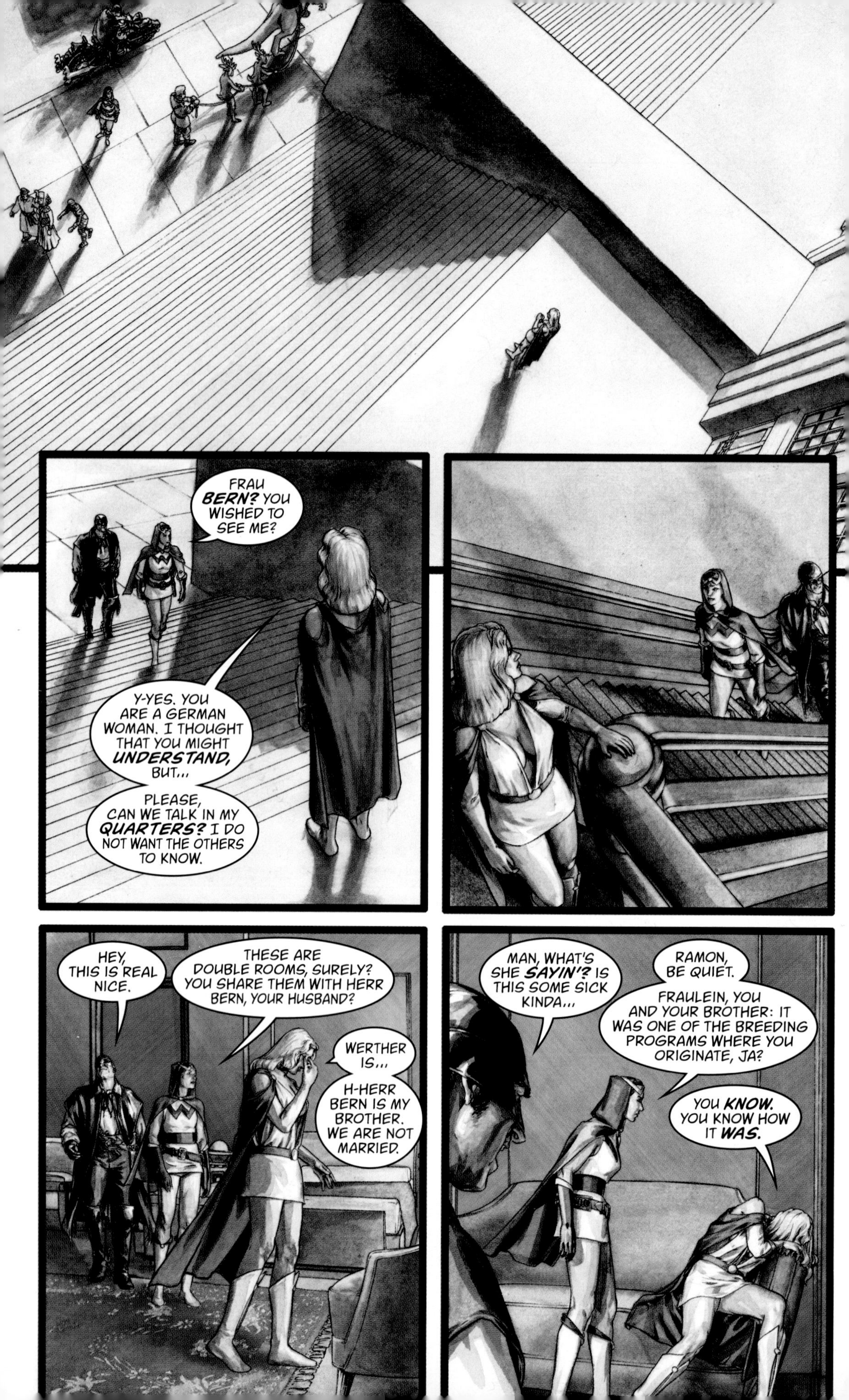
FRAU BERN? YOU WISHED TO SEE ME?
Y-YES. YOU ARE A GERMAN WOMAN. I THOUGHT THAT YOU MIGHT UNDERSTAND, BUT...
PLEASE, CAN WE TALK IN MY QUARTERS? I DO NOT WANT THE OTHERS TO KNOW.
HEY, THIS IS REAL NICE.
THESE ARE DOUBLE ROOMS, SURELY? YOU SHARE THEM WITH HERR BERN, YOUR HUSBAND?
WERTHER IS...
H-HERR BERN IS MY BROTHER. WE ARE NOT MARRIED.
MAN, WHAT'S SHE SAYIN'? IS THIS SOME SICK KINDA...
RAMON, BE QUIET.
FRAULEIN, YOU AND YOUR BROTHER: IT WAS ONE OF THE BREEDING PROGRAMS WHERE YOU ORIGINATE, JA?
YOU KNOW. YOU KNOW HOW IT WAS.

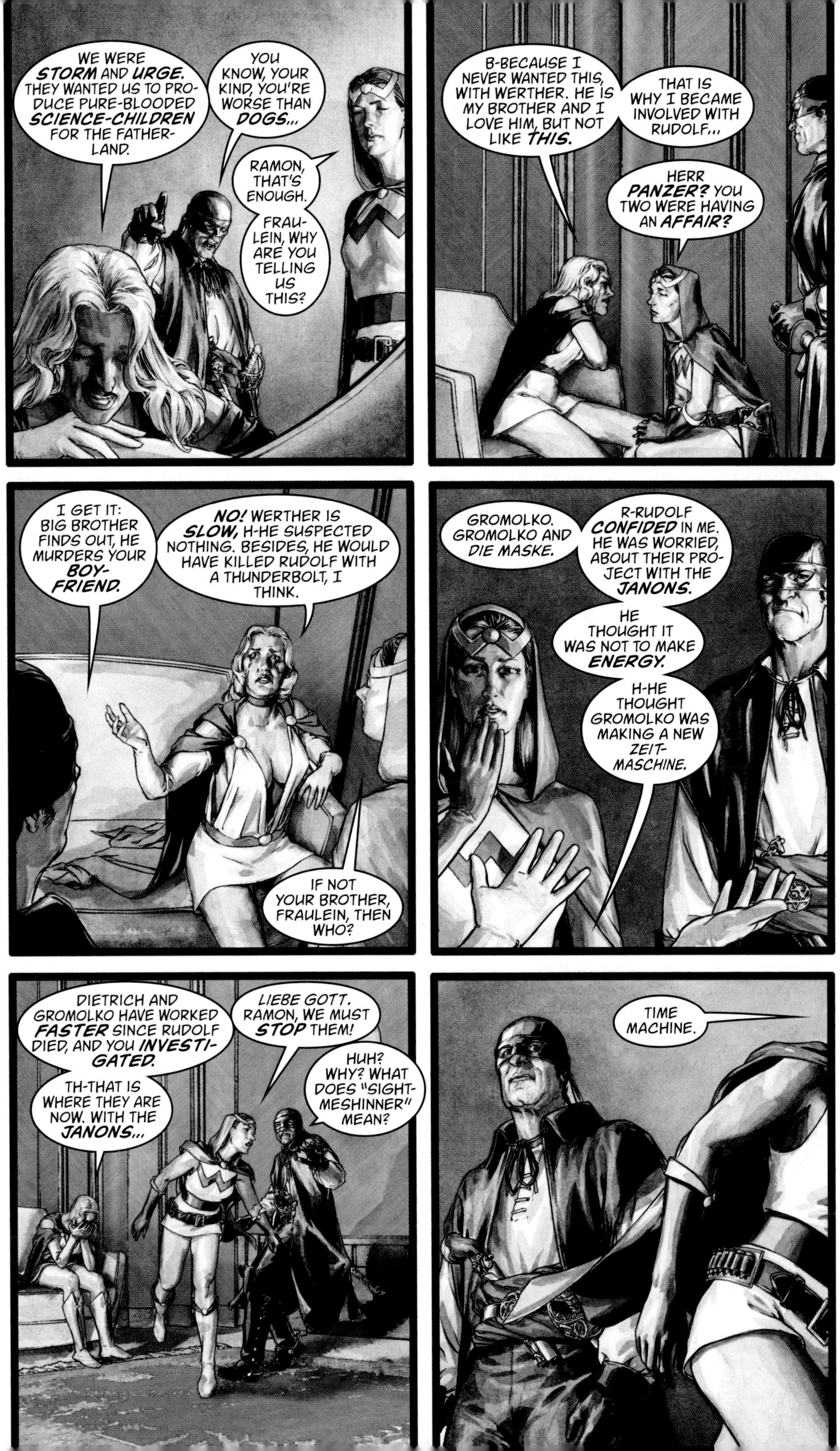

WE WERE STORM AND URGE. THEY WANTED US TO PRODUCE PURE-BLOODED SCIENCE-CHILDREN FOR THE FATHERLAND.
YOU KNOW, YOUR KIND, YOU'RE WORSE THAN DOGS...
RAMON, THAT'S ENOUGH.
FRAULEIN, WHY ARE YOU TELLING US THIS?
B-BECAUSE I NEVER WANTED THIS, WITH WERTHER. HE IS MY BROTHER AND I LOVE HIM, BUT NOT LIKE THIS.
THAT IS WHY I BECAME INVOLVED WITH RUDOLF...
HERR PANZER? YOU TWO WERE HAVING AN AFFAIR?
I GET IT: BIG BROTHER FINDS OUT, HE MURDERS YOUR BOY-FRIEND.
NO! WERTHER IS SLOW, H-HE SUSPECTED NOTHING. BESIDES, HE WOULD HAVE KILLED RUDOLF WITH A THUNDERBOLT, I THINK.
IF NOT YOUR BROTHER, FRAULEIN, THEN WHO?
GROMOLKO. GROMOLKO AND DIE MASKE.
R-RUDOLF CONFIDED IN ME. HE WAS WORRIED, ABOUT THEIR PROJECT WITH THE JANONS.
HE THOUGHT IT WAS NOT TO MAKE ENERGY.
H-HE THOUGHT GROMOLKO WAS MAKING A NEW ZEIT-MASCHINE.
DIETRICH AND GROMOLKO HAVE WORKED FASTER SINCE RUDOLF DIED, AND YOU INVESTIGATED.
TH-THAT IS WHERE THEY ARE NOW. WITH THE JANONS...
LIEBE GOTT. RAMON, WE MUST STOP THEM!
HUH? WHY? WHAT DOES "SIGHT-MESHINNER" MEAN?
TIME MACHINE.

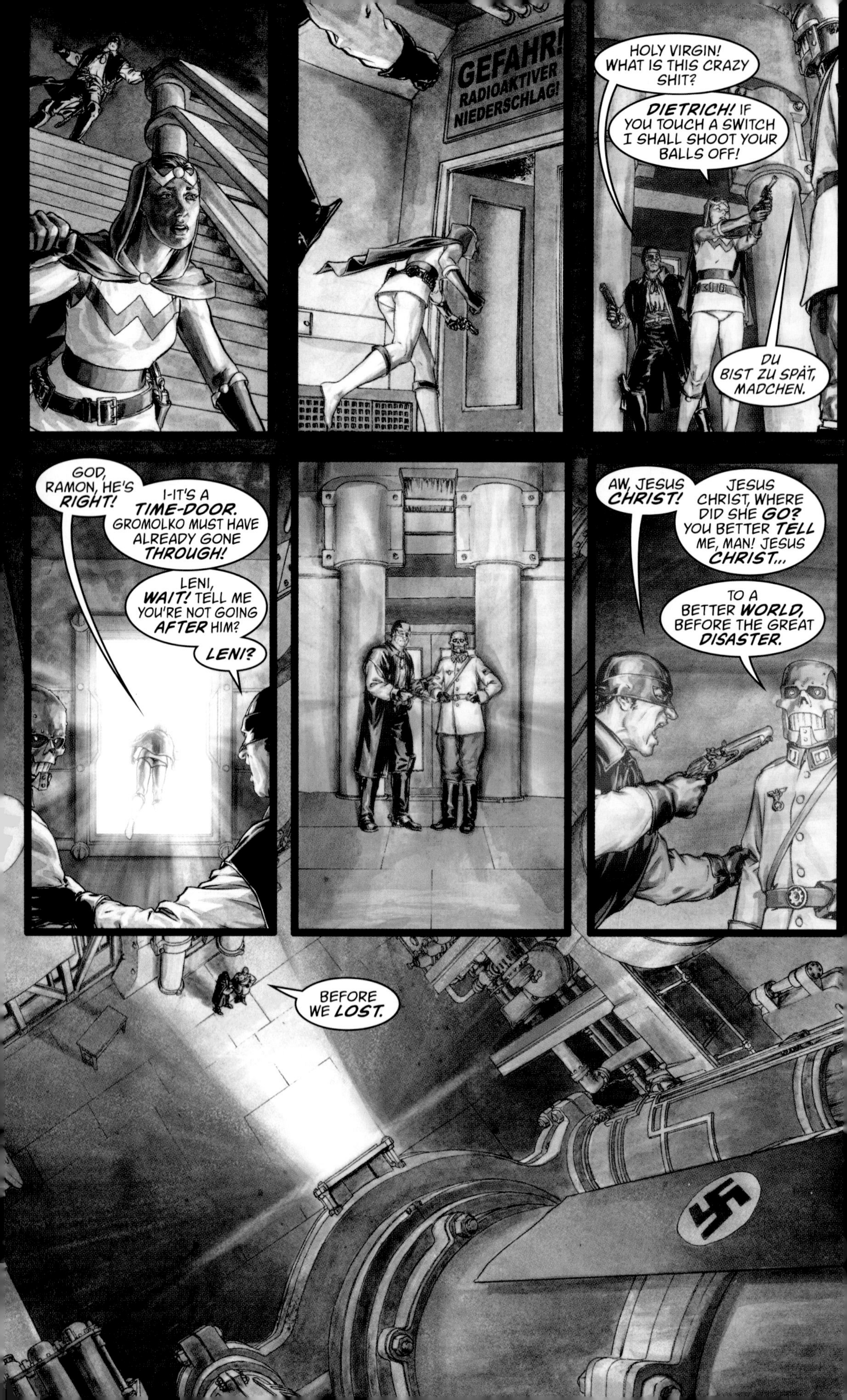
GEFAHR!
RADIOAKTIVER
NIEDERSCHLAG!
HOLY VIRGIN! WHAT IS THIS CRAZY SHIT?
DIETRICH! IF YOU TOUCH A SWITCH I SHALL SHOOT YOUR BALLS OFF!
DU BIST ZU SPÄT, MADCHEN.
GOD, RAMON, HE'S RIGHT!
I-IT'S A TIME-DOOR. GROMOLKO MUST HAVE ALREADY GONE THROUGH!
LENI, WAIT! TELL ME YOU'RE NOT GOING AFTER HIM?
LENI?
AW, JESUS CHRIST!
JESUS CHRIST, WHERE DID SHE GO? YOU BETTER TELL ME, MAN! JESUS CHRIST...
TO A BETTER WORLD, BEFORE THE GREAT DISASTER.
BEFORE WE LOST.

WHAT? WHAT ARE YOU SAYIN'?

I AM SAY-ING, *DU BASTARDE SPANIER*, THAT GUNTER IS IN BERLIN, IN 1943...

...TELLING *DER FUHRER* 1949'S *SECRETS*.

SECRETS? YOU MEAN LIKE THE A-BOMB?

JA. DIE *ATOMER BOMBE*. THEN THE *FUHRER* CAN MAKE HISTORY *RIGHT* AGAIN.

HE CAN CHANGE THE *FUTURE*.

YOU'RE NUTS. WE *CAUGHT* YOU. THAT AIN'T GONNA *HAPPEN*, MAN.

IT ALREADY *HAS*.

LOOK AT THE *ZEIT-EINFAHRT, MEIN FREUND*. SEE FOR YOURSELF.

politan
EWSPAPER

widely scattered light possible rain to-nite page 9 for more

NEOPOLIS, SUNDAY, AUG. 14, 1949

NAZIS RUN USA

Atque ea diversa penitus dum parte geruntur, trim de caelo misit Saturnia iuno audacem ad turnum. Luco turnum forte parentis pilumni turnus sacrata valle sedebat. Ad quem sic osco thaumantias ore turne, quod omitem

AW, GOD. THAT'S TOMORROW'S *PAPER!*

Y-YOU SAID THIS WAS A DOOR TO THE *PAST*...

THE *JANONS* GO *BOTH* WAYS IN TIME, *VERSTEHEN SIE?*

BESIDES, THIS WAS OUR FIRST TEST. WE COULD NOT PREDICT THE EFFECTS.

BUT NOW, I THINK, THE PREDICTION, IT IS VERY *CLEAR, NICHT WAHR?*

GUNTER HAS ALREADY *SUCCEEDED*, AND YOUR LITTLE TURNCOAT *PARTNER* HAS JUST AS CLEARLY *FAILED*.

SHE PROBABLY LIES DEAD.

IN BERLIN.

SIX YEARS AGO.

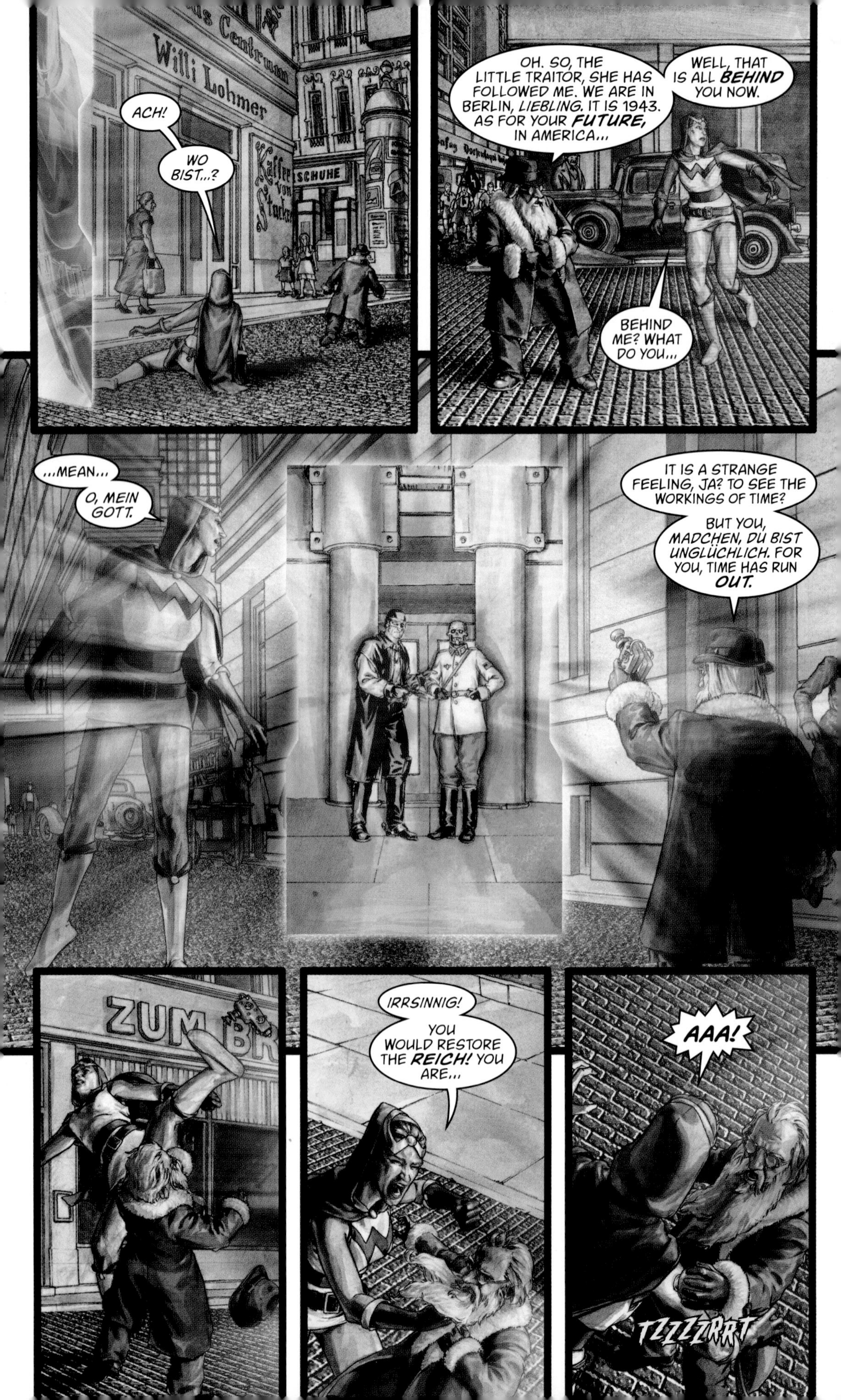
Willi Lohmer
ACH!
WO BIST...?
SCHUHE
OH. SO, THE LITTLE TRAITOR, SHE HAS FOLLOWED ME. WE ARE IN BERLIN, *LIEBLING.* IT IS 1943. AS FOR YOUR ***FUTURE,*** IN AMERICA...
WELL, THAT IS ALL ***BEHIND*** YOU NOW.
BEHIND ME? WHAT DO YOU...
...MEAN...
O, MEIN GOTT.
IT IS A STRANGE FEELING, JA? TO SEE THE WORKINGS OF TIME?
BUT YOU, MADCHEN, DU BIST UNGLÜCHLICH. FOR YOU, TIME HAS RUN ***OUT.***
ZUM BR
IRRSINNIG!
YOU WOULD RESTORE THE ***REICH!*** YOU ARE...
AAA!
TZZZZRRT

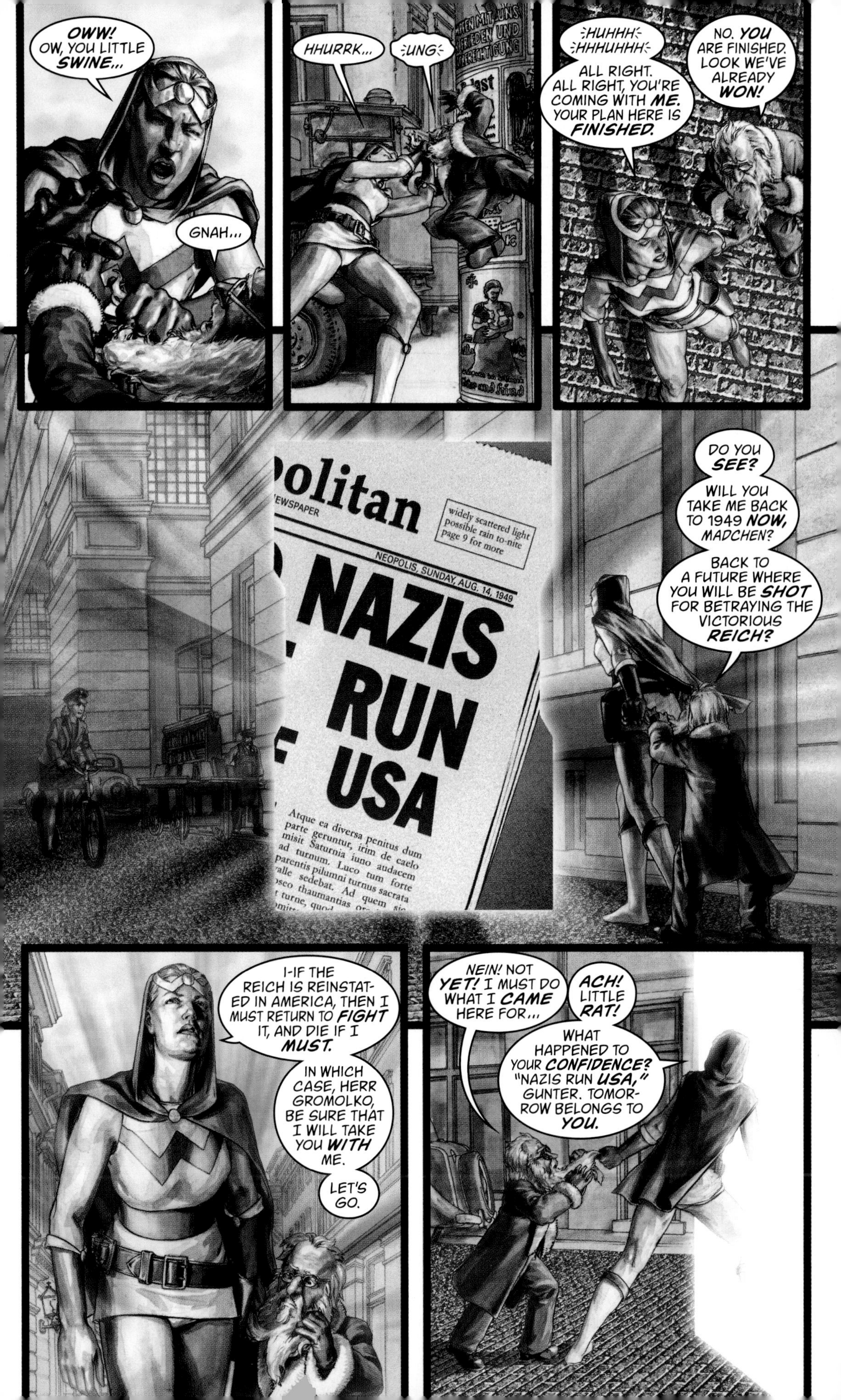
OWW! OW, YOU LITTLE SWINE...
GNAH...
HHURRK...
UNG
HUHHH HHHUHHH
ALL RIGHT. ALL RIGHT, YOU'RE COMING WITH ME. YOUR PLAN HERE IS FINISHED.
NO. YOU ARE FINISHED. LOOK WE'VE ALREADY WON!
olitan
NEWSPAPER
widely scattered light possible rain to-nite page 9 for more
NEOPOLIS, SUNDAY, AUG. 14, 1949
NAZIS RUN USA
Atque ea diversa penitus dum parte geruntur, írim de caelo misit Saturnia íuno audacem ad turnum. Luco tum forte parentis pilumni turnus sacrata valle sedebat. Ad quem
DO YOU SEE?
WILL YOU TAKE ME BACK TO 1949 NOW, MADCHEN?
BACK TO A FUTURE WHERE YOU WILL BE SHOT FOR BETRAYING THE VICTORIOUS REICH?
I-IF THE REICH IS REINSTATED IN AMERICA, THEN I MUST RETURN TO FIGHT IT, AND DIE IF I MUST.
IN WHICH CASE, HERR GROMOLKO, BE SURE THAT I WILL TAKE YOU WITH ME.
LET'S GO.
NEIN! NOT YET! I MUST DO WHAT I CAME HERE FOR...
ACH! LITTLE RAT!
WHAT HAPPENED TO YOUR CONFIDENCE? "NAZIS RUN USA," GUNTER. TOMORROW BELONGS TO YOU.

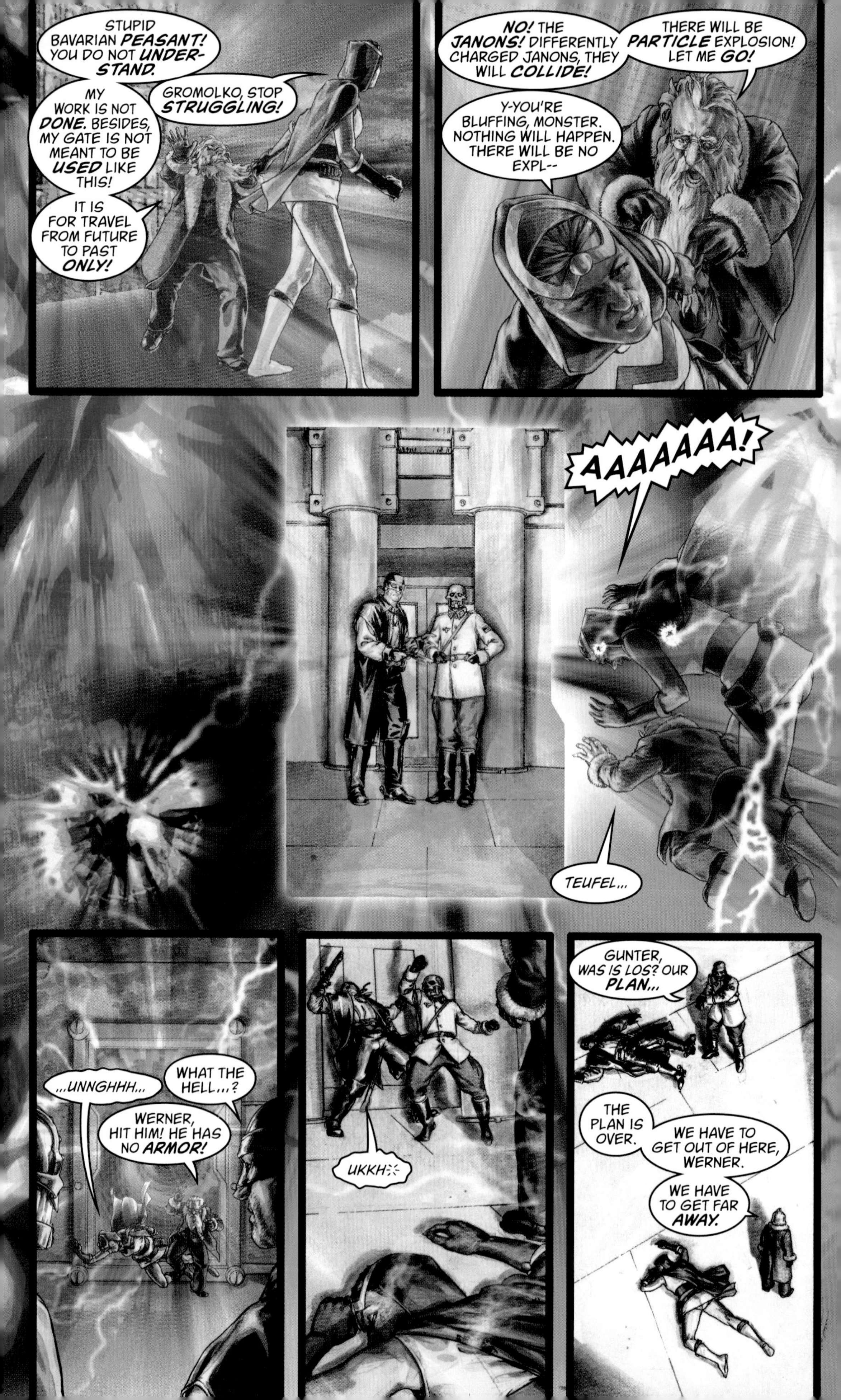
STUPID BAVARIAN PEASANT! YOU DO NOT UNDER-STAND.
GROMOLKO, STOP STRUGGLING!
MY WORK IS NOT DONE. BESIDES, MY GATE IS NOT MEANT TO BE USED LIKE THIS!
IT IS FOR TRAVEL FROM FUTURE TO PAST ONLY!
NO! THE JANONS! DIFFERENTLY CHARGED JANONS, THEY WILL COLLIDE!
THERE WILL BE PARTICLE EXPLOSION! LET ME GO!
Y-YOU'RE BLUFFING, MONSTER. NOTHING WILL HAPPEN. THERE WILL BE NO EXPL--
AAAAAAA!
TEUFEL...
...UNNGHHH...
WHAT THE HELL...?
WERNER, HIT HIM! HE HAS NO ARMOR!
UKKH
GUNTER, WAS IS LOS? OUR PLAN...
THE PLAN IS OVER.
WE HAVE TO GET OUT OF HERE, WERNER.
WE HAVE TO GET FAR AWAY.

Neopolitan
THE CITY'S ONLY HOME-OWNED NEWSPAPER

VOL. IV. NO. 86

widely scattered light
possible rain to-nite
Page 9 for more

NEOPOLIS, SUNDAY, AUG. 14, 1949

FORMED NAZIS
ON THE RUN
EMIES OF USA

Atque ea diversa penitus dum parte geruntur, irim de caelo misit Saturnia iuno audacem ad turnum. Luco tum forte parentis pilumni turnus sacrata valle sedebat. Ad quem sic roseo thaumantias ore loqui est turne, quod optanti...

UH...YOU WANTED TO SEE US, CAPTAIN?

YES, I DID.

RAMON, LENI, THAT WAS GOOD WORK YOU DID YESTERDAY.

CAPTAIN, THAT WAS ALL LENI, WAY SHE JUMPED IN THAT *TIME-HOLE...*

...ALL I DID WAS LET THEM GET *AWAY.*

THAT DOESN'T MATTER. WHAT'S IMPORTANT IS YOU STOPPED THEM. YOU'RE BOTH GETTING *RAISES.*

RAISES? BUT...

CAPTAIN, WE ONLY DID OUR *JOB...*

AND DID IT SPLENDIDLY.

AS FOR YOU, LENI, I HAVE A SPECIAL SURPRISE FOR YOU THROUGH HERE...

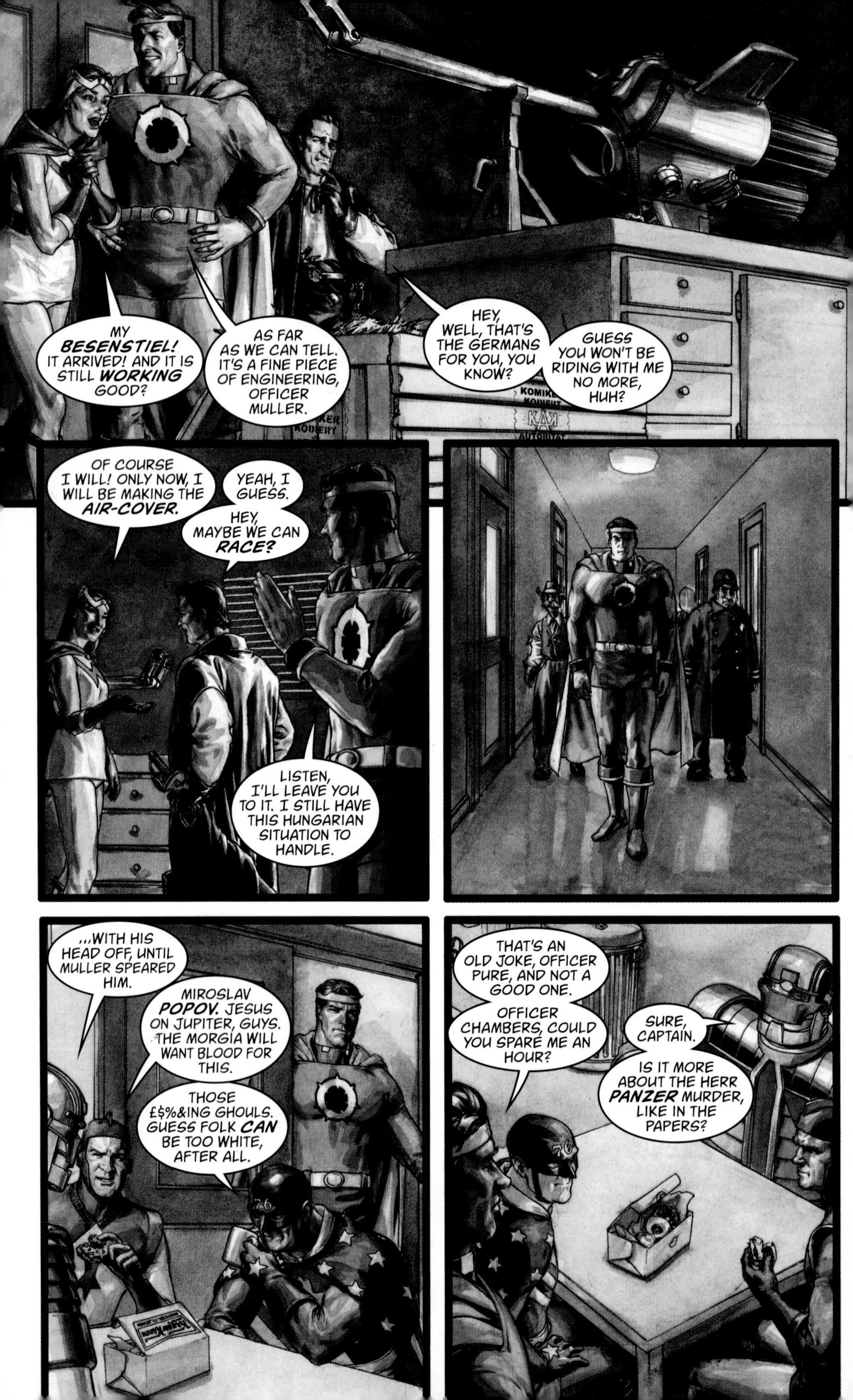
MY BESENSTIEL! IT ARRIVED! AND IT IS STILL WORKING GOOD?
AS FAR AS WE CAN TELL. IT'S A FINE PIECE OF ENGINEERING, OFFICER MULLER.
HEY, WELL, THAT'S THE GERMANS FOR YOU, YOU KNOW?
GUESS YOU WON'T BE RIDING WITH ME NO MORE, HUH?
OF COURSE I WILL! ONLY NOW, I WILL BE MAKING THE AIR-COVER.
YEAH, I GUESS.
HEY, MAYBE WE CAN RACE?
LISTEN, I'LL LEAVE YOU TO IT. I STILL HAVE THIS HUNGARIAN SITUATION TO HANDLE.
...WITH HIS HEAD OFF, UNTIL MULLER SPEARED HIM.
MIROSLAV POPOV. JESUS ON JUPITER, GUYS. THE MORGIA WILL WANT BLOOD FOR THIS.
THOSE £$%&ING GHOULS. GUESS FOLK CAN BE TOO WHITE, AFTER ALL.
THAT'S AN OLD JOKE, OFFICER PURE, AND NOT A GOOD ONE.
OFFICER CHAMBERS, COULD YOU SPARE ME AN HOUR?
SURE, CAPTAIN.
IS IT MORE ABOUT THE HERR PANZER MURDER, LIKE IN THE PAPERS?

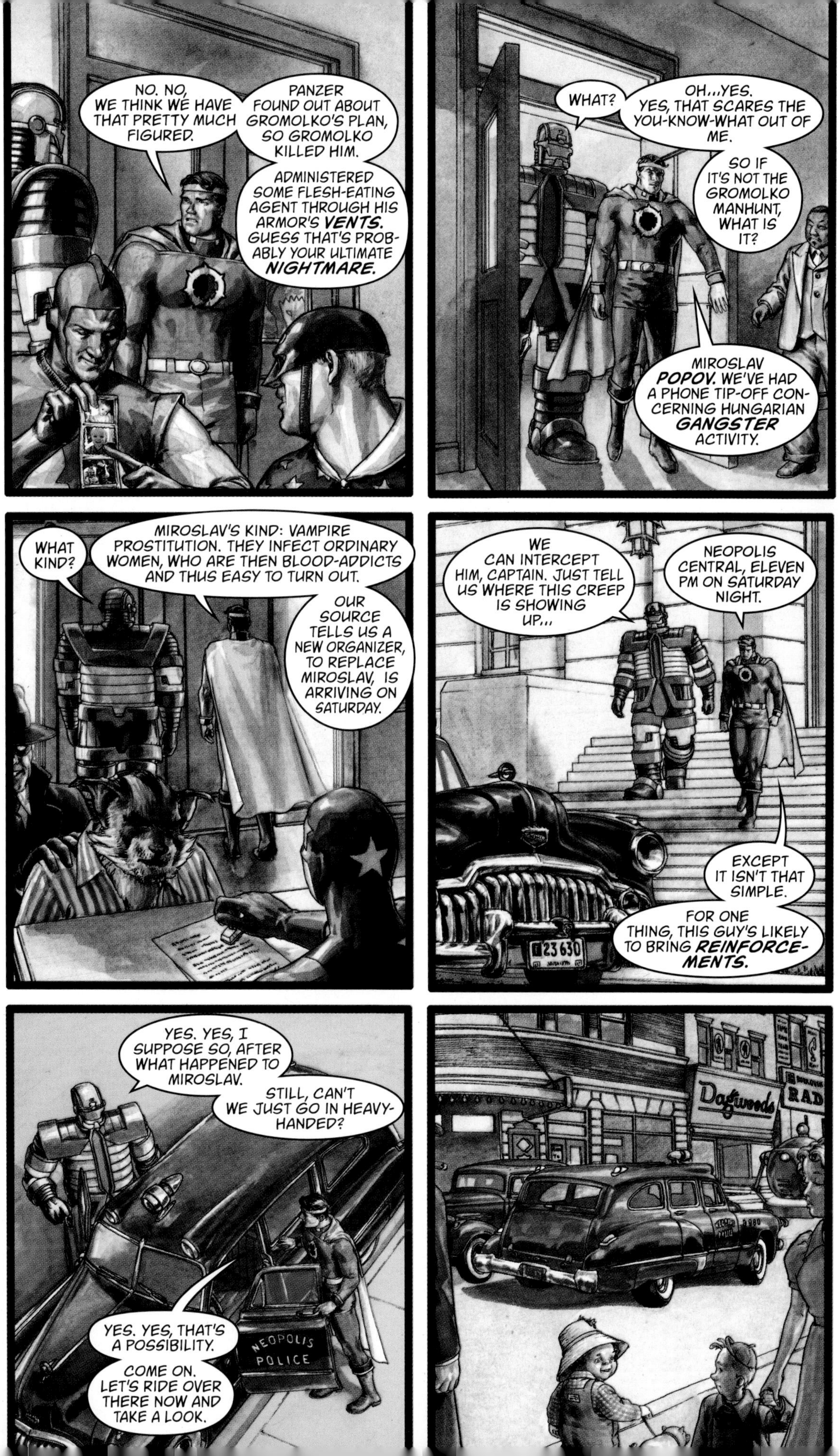
NO. NO, WE THINK WE HAVE THAT PRETTY MUCH FIGURED.
PANZER FOUND OUT ABOUT GROMOLKO'S PLAN, SO GROMOLKO KILLED HIM.
ADMINISTERED SOME FLESH-EATING AGENT THROUGH HIS ARMOR'S VENTS. GUESS THAT'S PROBABLY YOUR ULTIMATE NIGHTMARE.
WHAT?
OH...YES. YES, THAT SCARES THE YOU-KNOW-WHAT OUT OF ME.
SO IF IT'S NOT THE GROMOLKO MANHUNT, WHAT IS IT?
MIROSLAV POPOV. WE'VE HAD A PHONE TIP-OFF CONCERNING HUNGARIAN GANGSTER ACTIVITY.
WHAT KIND?
MIROSLAV'S KIND: VAMPIRE PROSTITUTION. THEY INFECT ORDINARY WOMEN, WHO ARE THEN BLOOD-ADDICTS AND THUS EASY TO TURN OUT.
OUR SOURCE TELLS US A NEW ORGANIZER, TO REPLACE MIROSLAV, IS ARRIVING ON SATURDAY.
WE CAN INTERCEPT HIM, CAPTAIN. JUST TELL US WHERE THIS CREEP IS SHOWING UP...
NEOPOLIS CENTRAL, ELEVEN PM ON SATURDAY NIGHT.
EXCEPT IT ISN'T THAT SIMPLE.
FOR ONE THING, THIS GUY'S LIKELY TO BRING REINFORCEMENTS.
23 630
YES. YES, I SUPPOSE SO, AFTER WHAT HAPPENED TO MIROSLAV.
STILL, CAN'T WE JUST GO IN HEAVY-HANDED?
YES. YES, THAT'S A POSSIBILITY.
COME ON. LET'S RIDE OVER THERE NOW AND TAKE A LOOK.
NEOPOLIS POLICE
Dagwoods
RAD

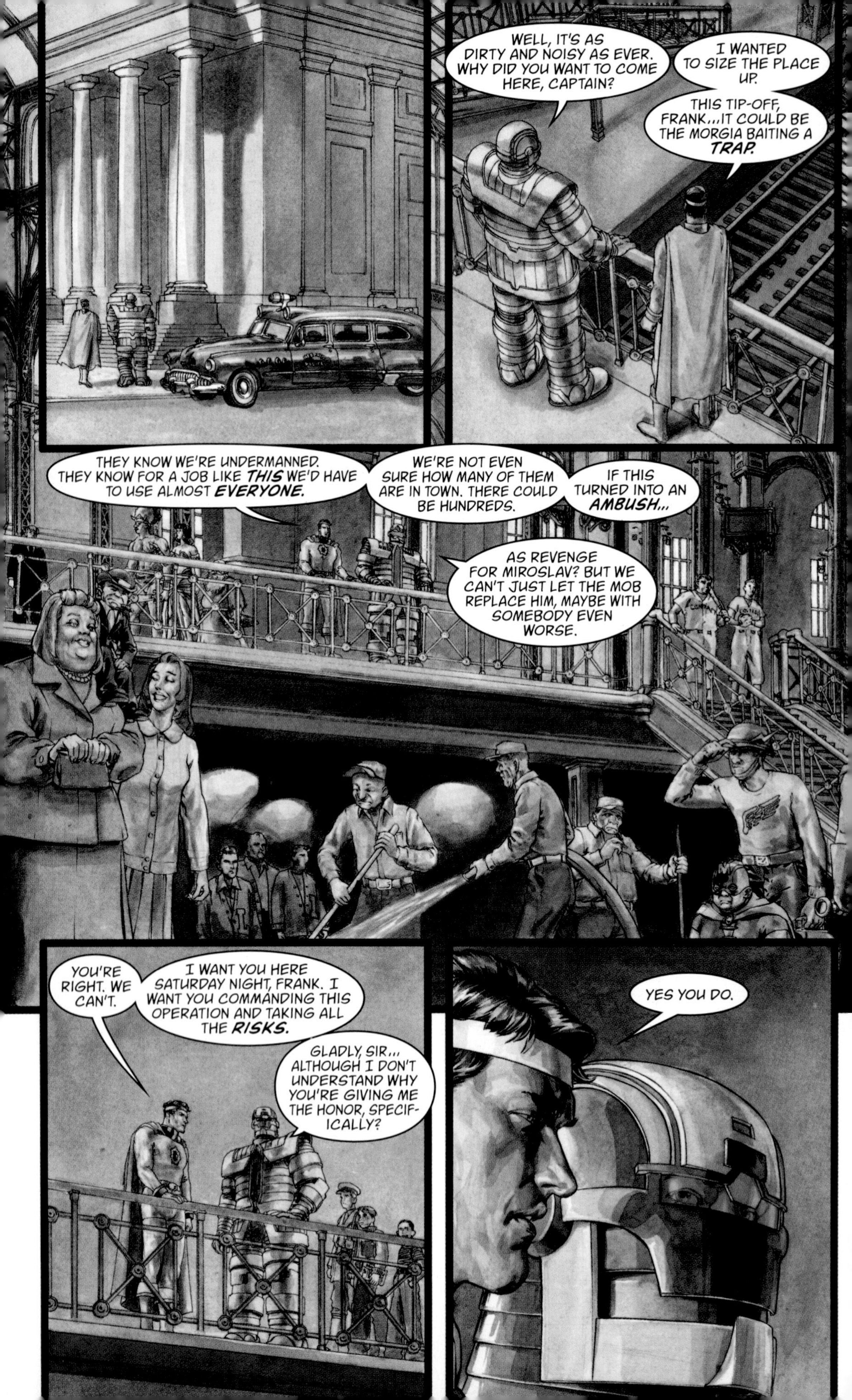

WELL, IT'S AS DIRTY AND NOISY AS EVER. WHY DID YOU WANT TO COME HERE, CAPTAIN?
I WANTED TO SIZE THE PLACE UP.
THIS TIP-OFF, FRANK...IT COULD BE THE MORGIA BAITING A TRAP.
THEY KNOW WE'RE UNDERMANNED. THEY KNOW FOR A JOB LIKE THIS WE'D HAVE TO USE ALMOST EVERYONE.
WE'RE NOT EVEN SURE HOW MANY OF THEM ARE IN TOWN. THERE COULD BE HUNDREDS.
IF THIS TURNED INTO AN AMBUSH...
AS REVENGE FOR MIROSLAV? BUT WE CAN'T JUST LET THE MOB REPLACE HIM, MAYBE WITH SOMEBODY EVEN WORSE.
YOU'RE RIGHT. WE CAN'T.
I WANT YOU HERE SATURDAY NIGHT, FRANK. I WANT YOU COMMANDING THIS OPERATION AND TAKING ALL THE RISKS.
GLADLY, SIR... ALTHOUGH I DON'T UNDERSTAND WHY YOU'RE GIVING ME THE HONOR, SPECIFICALLY?
YES YOU DO.

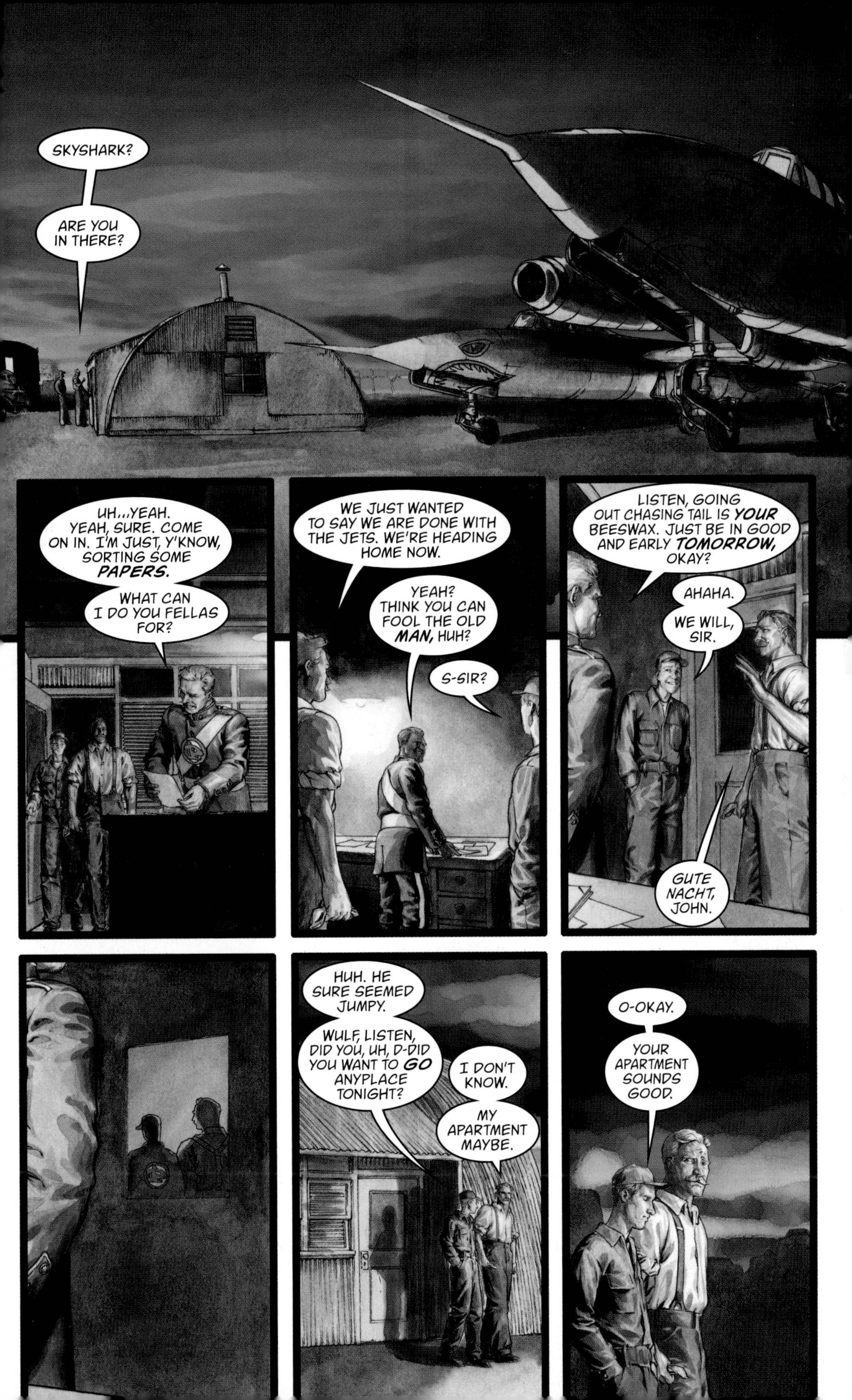
SKYSHARK?
ARE YOU IN THERE?
UH...YEAH. YEAH, SURE. COME ON IN. I'M JUST, Y'KNOW, SORTING SOME PAPERS.
WHAT CAN I DO YOU FELLAS FOR?
WE JUST WANTED TO SAY WE ARE DONE WITH THE JETS. WE'RE HEADING HOME NOW.
YEAH? THINK YOU CAN FOOL THE OLD MAN, HUH?
S-SIR?
LISTEN, GOING OUT CHASING TAIL IS YOUR BEESWAX. JUST BE IN GOOD AND EARLY TOMORROW, OKAY?
AHAHA.
WE WILL, SIR.
GUTE NACHT, JOHN.
HUH. HE SURE SEEMED JUMPY.
WULF, LISTEN, DID YOU, UH, D-DID YOU WANT TO GO ANYPLACE TONIGHT?
I DON'T KNOW.
MY APARTMENT MAYBE.
O-OKAY.
YOUR APARTMENT SOUNDS GOOD.

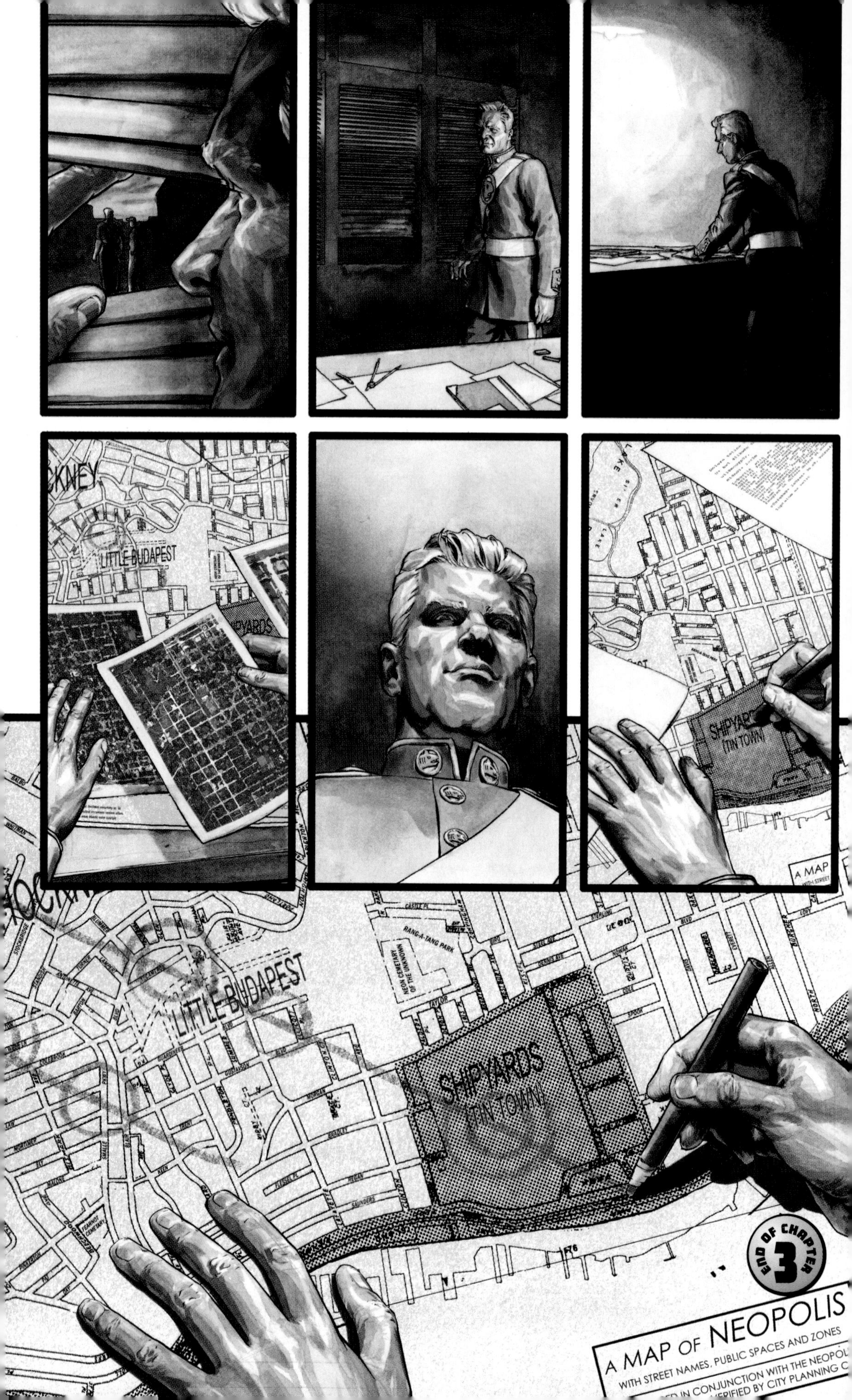

CKNEY
LITTLE BUDAPEST
SHIPYARDS
SHIPYARDS
(TIN TOWN)
A MAP
RANG-A-TANG PARK
NEON CEMETERY OF THE UNKNOWN
LITTLE BUDAPEST
SHIPYARDS
(TIN TOWN)
END OF CHAPTER
3
A MAP OF NEOPOLIS
WITH STREET NAMES, PUBLIC SPACES AND ZONES

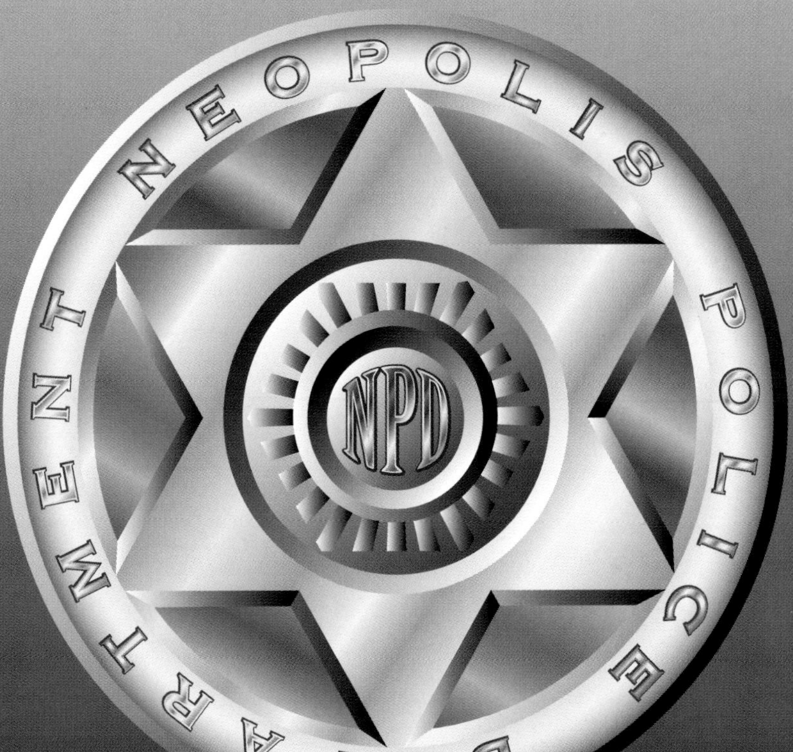
NEOPOLIS POLICE DEPARTMENT
NPD

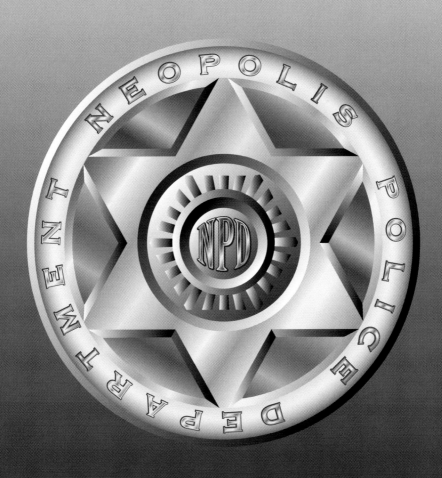

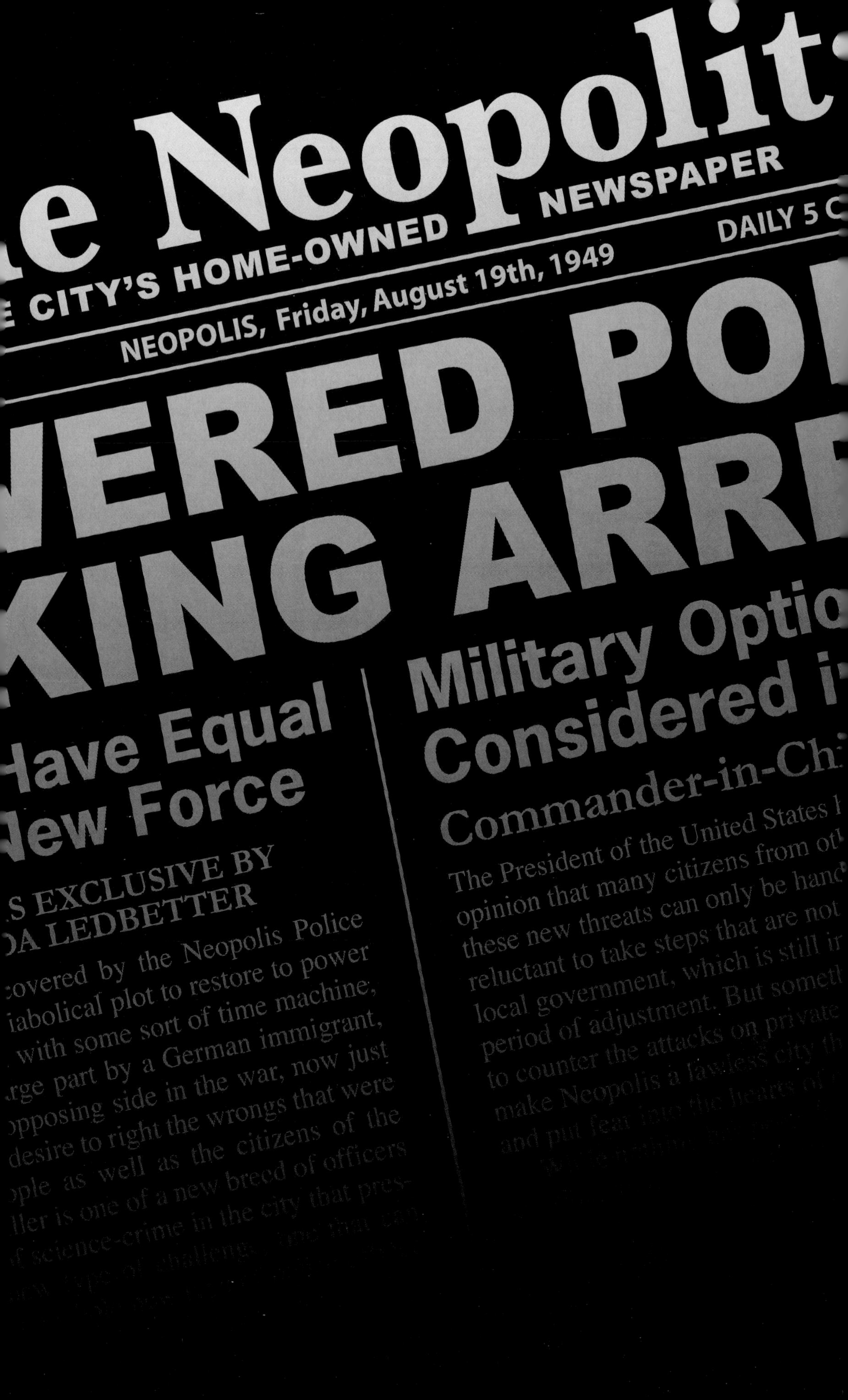

e Neopolit

E CITY'S HOME-OWNED NEWSPAPER

NEOPOLIS, Friday, August 19th, 1949 DAILY 5 C

VERED PO
XING ARR

Have Equal
New Force

S EXCLUSIVE BY
DA LEDBETTER

covered by the Neopolis Police
iabolical plot to restore to power
with some sort of time machine,
rge part by a German immigrant,
pposing side in the war, now just
desire to right the wrongs that were
ple as well as the citizens of the
ller is one of a new breed of officers
f science-crime in the city that pres-

Military Optio
Considered i

Commander-in-Ch

The President of the United States h
opinion that many citizens from ot
these new threats can only be hand
reluctant to take steps that are not
local government, which is still in
period of adjustment. But someth
to counter the attacks on private
make Neopolis a lawless city th
and put fear into the hearts of

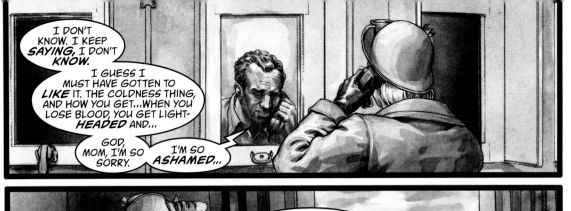

I DON'T KNOW. I KEEP SAYING, I DON'T KNOW.
I GUESS I MUST HAVE GOTTEN TO LIKE IT. THE COLDNESS THING, AND HOW YOU GET...WHEN YOU LOSE BLOOD, YOU GET LIGHT-HEADED AND...
GOD, MOM, I'M SO SORRY.
I'M SO ASHAMED...
NO.
NO. I'M BACK IN MARDALE NOW. JOHNNY, HE WAS WEEPING. YEAH. WEEPING.
YOU GOT HIM INTO THIS STUPID LIFE, JOHNNY. YOU AND YOUR STUPID CITY.
YEAH? WELL, WAY I HEAR IT, IT'S CRAWLIN' WITH DRACULAS...
The Neopolitan
HEMO HOODS IN HOSPITAL HORROR
BLOOD-BANK BLOODBATH
DOODLEHEAD NEXT TOP COP
The Neopolitan
REFORMED NAZIS
NO, CAPTAIN, YOU LISTEN.
DO YOU KNOW THE SHIT MY SISTER-IN-LAW PUT ME THROUGH SINCE YOU ARRESTED JUNIOR Q.?
NOW THERE'S £$%&IN' VAMPIRES EVERYWHERE. HOW COULD JIM GRANITE OR THE MILITARY DO A WORSE JOB THAN YOUR GUYS?
...ANY MISTAKES, FRANK. I WANT YOU TO TAKE OFFICERS DARK, MULLER AND MORALES. CHECK THE STATION TOP TO BOTTOM.
IF TONIGHT'S ARREST GOES WRONG, NEOPOLIS COULD BE LOOKING AT MARTIAL LAW WITHIN FORTY-EIGHT HOURS.
35
34
33
...OVER THE INTERIOR WITH A FINE-TOOTH COMB, AND THERE'S NO BOOBY-TRAPS. WE'RE HEADING OUT TO THE FRONT OF THE STATION NOW.
HOW ABOUT YOU, LENI? HOW'S IT LOOK FROM UP TOP?

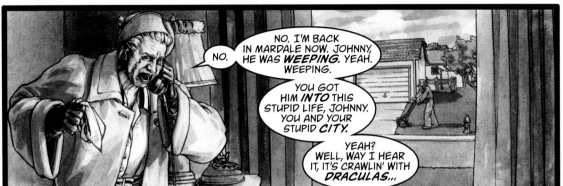

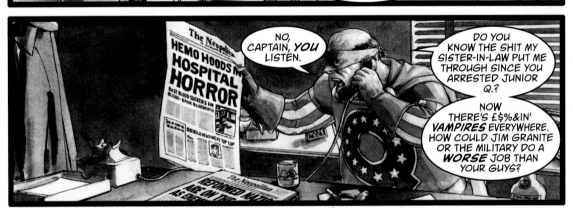

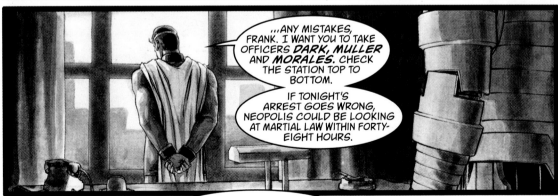

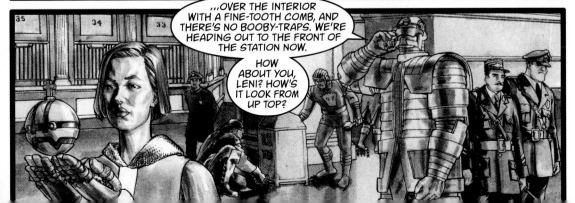

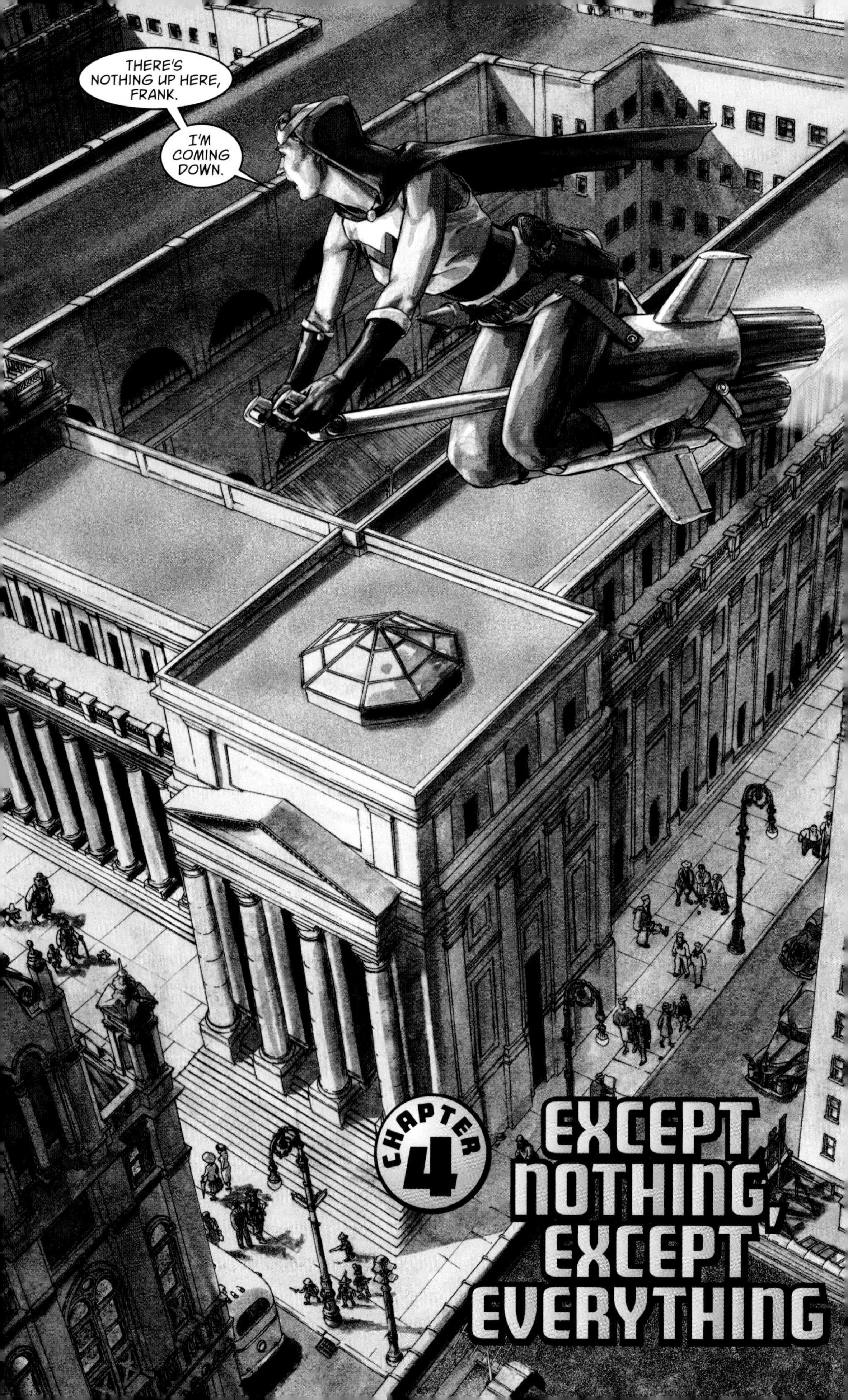
THERE'S NOTHING UP HERE, FRANK.
I'M COMING DOWN.
CHAPTER 4
EXCEPT NOTHING, EXCEPT EVERYTHING

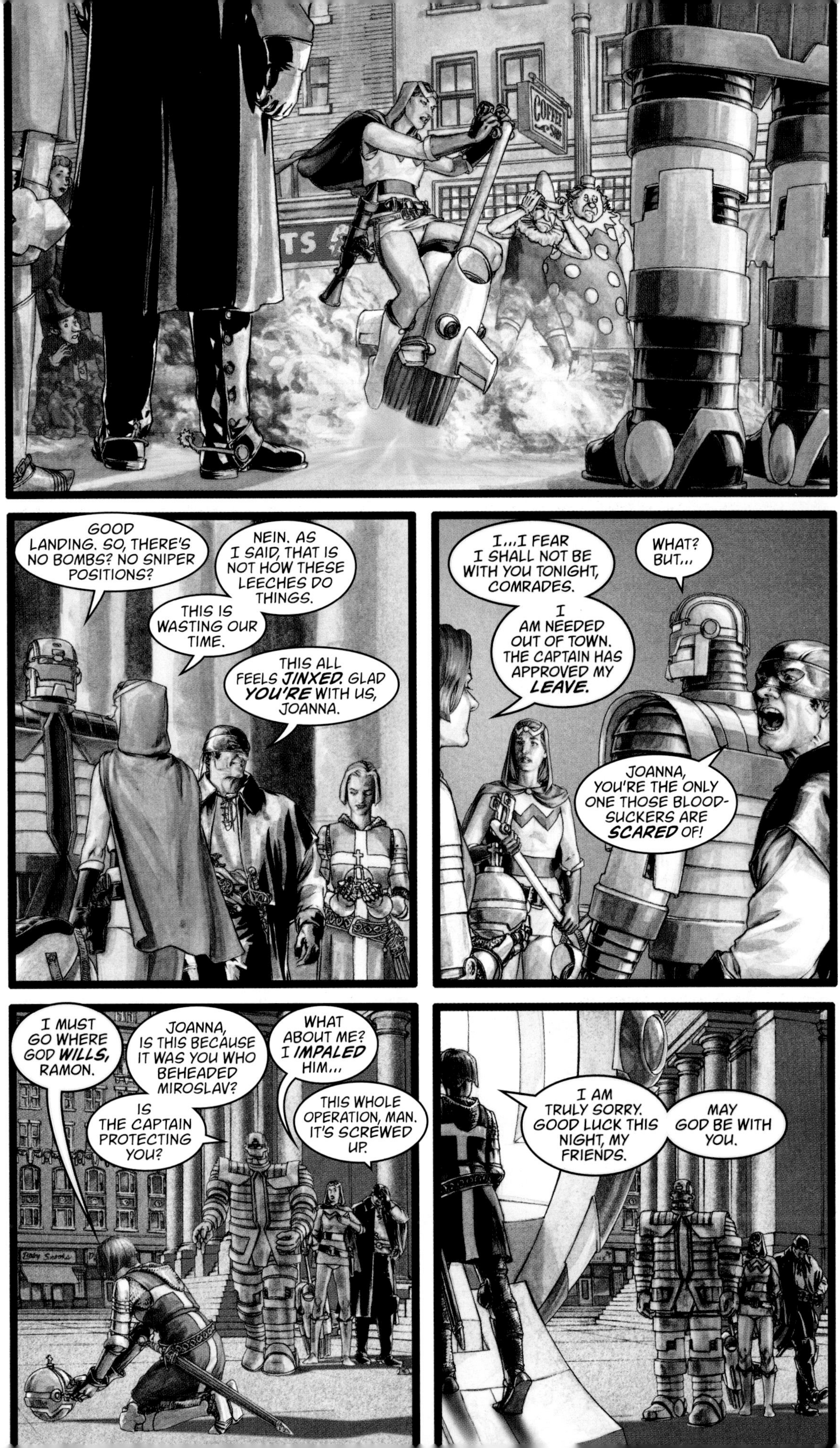
COFFEE SHOP
GOOD LANDING. SO, THERE'S NO BOMBS? NO SNIPER POSITIONS?
NEIN. AS I SAID, THAT IS NOT HOW THESE LEECHES DO THINGS.
THIS IS WASTING OUR TIME.
THIS ALL FEELS *JINXED.* GLAD *YOU'RE* WITH US, JOANNA.
I...I FEAR I SHALL NOT BE WITH YOU TONIGHT, COMRADES.
I AM NEEDED OUT OF TOWN. THE CAPTAIN HAS APPROVED MY *LEAVE.*
WHAT? BUT...
JOANNA, YOU'RE THE ONLY ONE THOSE BLOOD-SUCKERS ARE *SCARED* OF!
I MUST GO WHERE GOD *WILLS,* RAMON.
JOANNA, IS THIS BECAUSE IT WAS YOU WHO BEHEADED MIROSLAV?
IS THE CAPTAIN PROTECTING YOU?
WHAT ABOUT ME? I *IMPALED* HIM...
THIS WHOLE OPERATION, MAN. IT'S SCREWED UP.
I AM TRULY SORRY. GOOD LUCK THIS NIGHT, MY FRIENDS.
MAY GOD BE WITH YOU.

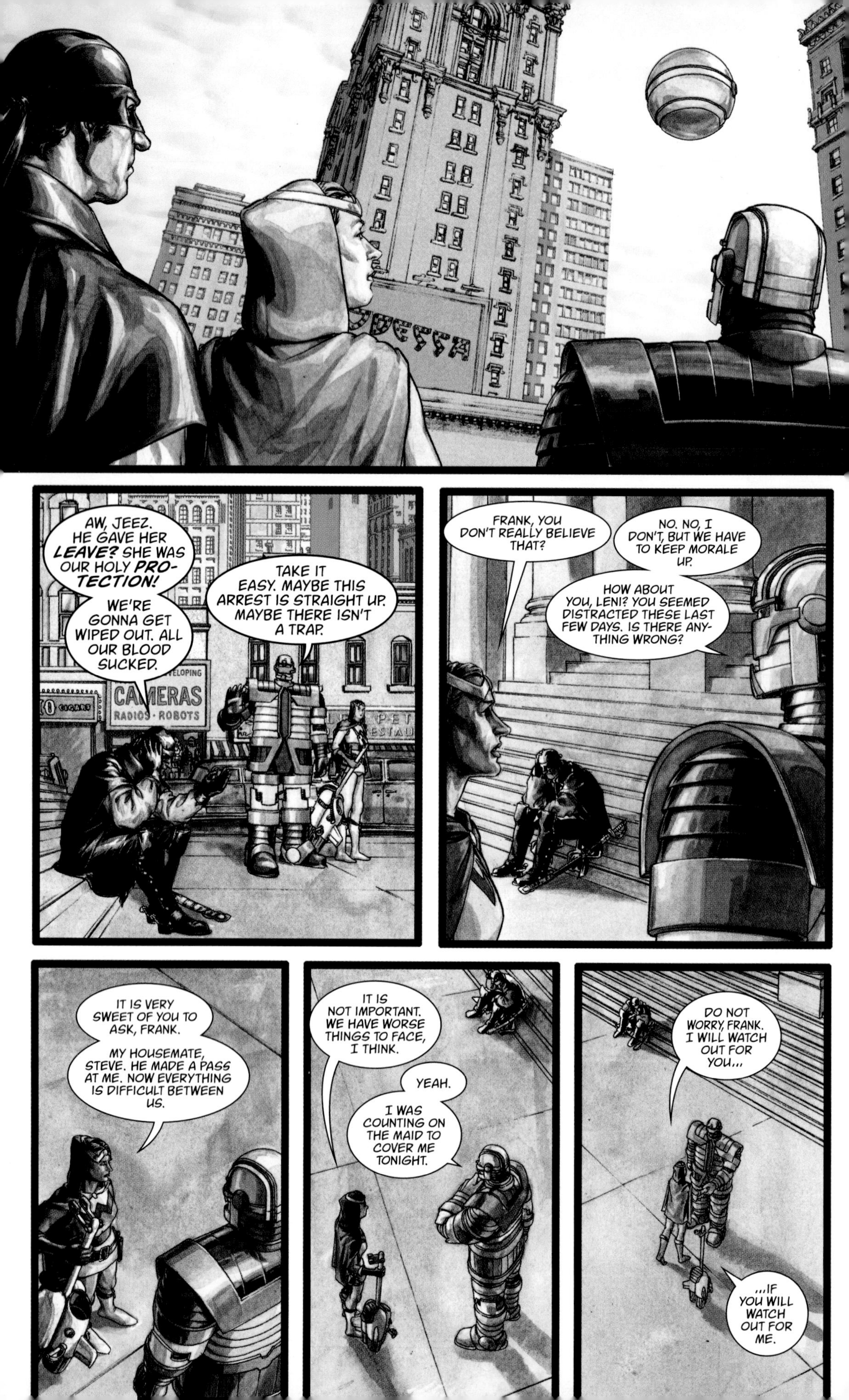

AW, JEEZ. HE GAVE HER ***LEAVE?*** SHE WAS OUR HOLY ***PRO-TECTION!***
WE'RE GONNA GET WIPED OUT. ALL OUR BLOOD SUCKED.
TAKE IT EASY. MAYBE THIS ARREST IS STRAIGHT UP. MAYBE THERE ISN'T A TRAP.
CAMERAS
RADIOS · ROBOTS
FRANK, YOU DON'T REALLY BELIEVE THAT?
NO. NO, I DON'T, BUT WE HAVE TO KEEP MORALE UP.
HOW ABOUT YOU, LENI? YOU SEEMED DISTRACTED THESE LAST FEW DAYS. IS THERE ANY-THING WRONG?
IT IS VERY SWEET OF YOU TO ASK, FRANK.
MY HOUSEMATE, STEVE. HE MADE A PASS AT ME. NOW EVERYTHING IS DIFFICULT BETWEEN US.
IT IS NOT IMPORTANT. WE HAVE WORSE THINGS TO FACE, I THINK.
YEAH.
I WAS COUNTING ON THE MAID TO COVER ME TONIGHT.
DO NOT WORRY, FRANK. I WILL WATCH OUT FOR YOU...
...IF YOU WILL WATCH OUT FOR ME.

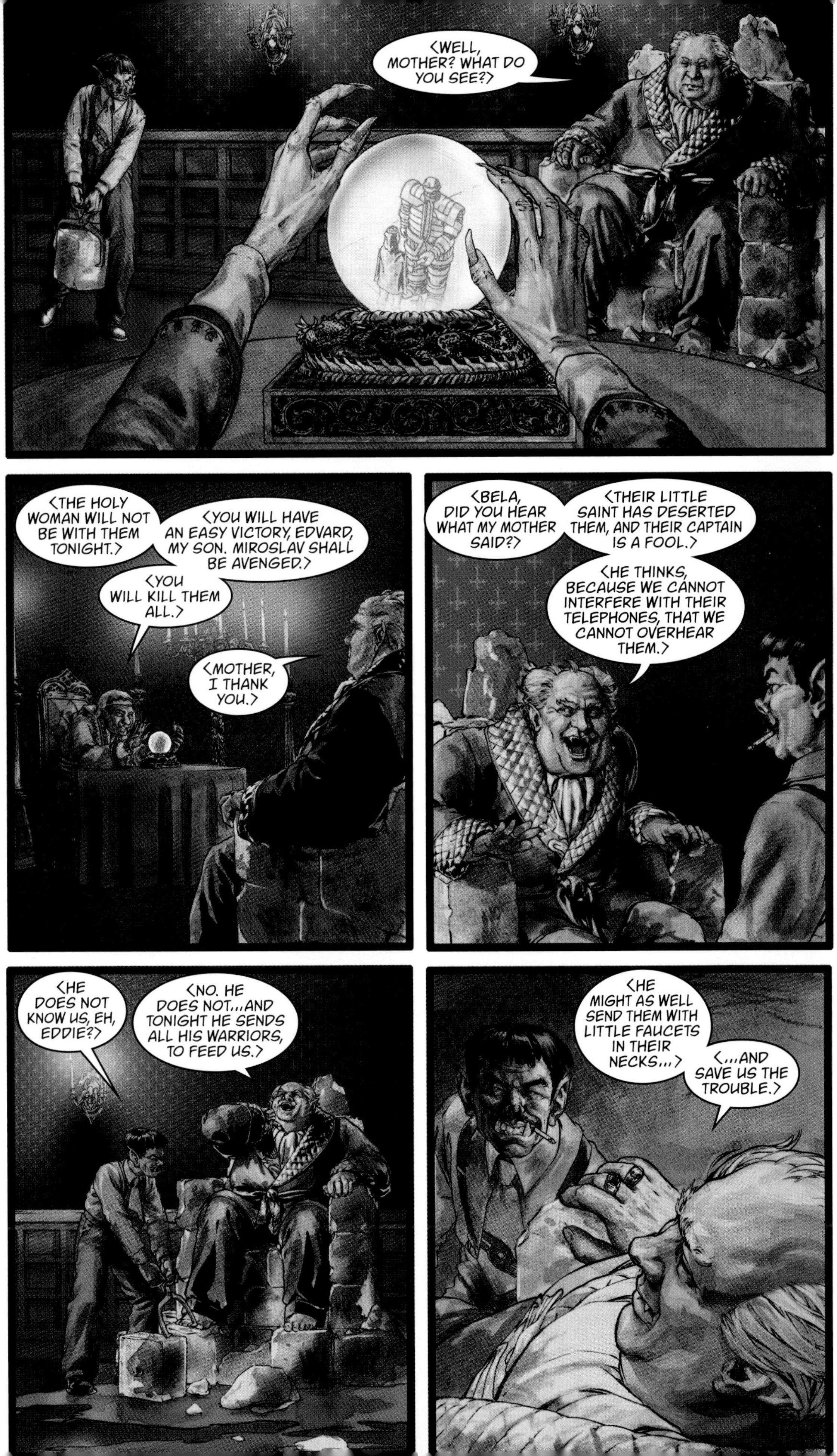

<WELL, MOTHER? WHAT DO YOU SEE?>
<THE HOLY WOMAN WILL NOT BE WITH THEM TONIGHT.>
<YOU WILL HAVE AN EASY VICTORY, EDVARD, MY SON. MIROSLAV SHALL BE AVENGED.>
<YOU WILL KILL THEM ALL.>
<MOTHER, I THANK YOU.>
<BELA, DID YOU HEAR WHAT MY MOTHER SAID?>
<THEIR LITTLE SAINT HAS DESERTED THEM, AND THEIR CAPTAIN IS A FOOL.>
<HE THINKS, BECAUSE WE CANNOT INTERFERE WITH THEIR TELEPHONES, THAT WE CANNOT OVERHEAR THEM.>
<HE DOES NOT KNOW US, EH, EDDIE?>
<NO. HE DOES NOT...AND TONIGHT HE SENDS ALL HIS WARRIORS, TO FEED US.>
<HE MIGHT AS WELL SEND THEM WITH LITTLE FAUCETS IN THEIR NECKS...>
<...AND SAVE US THE TROUBLE.>

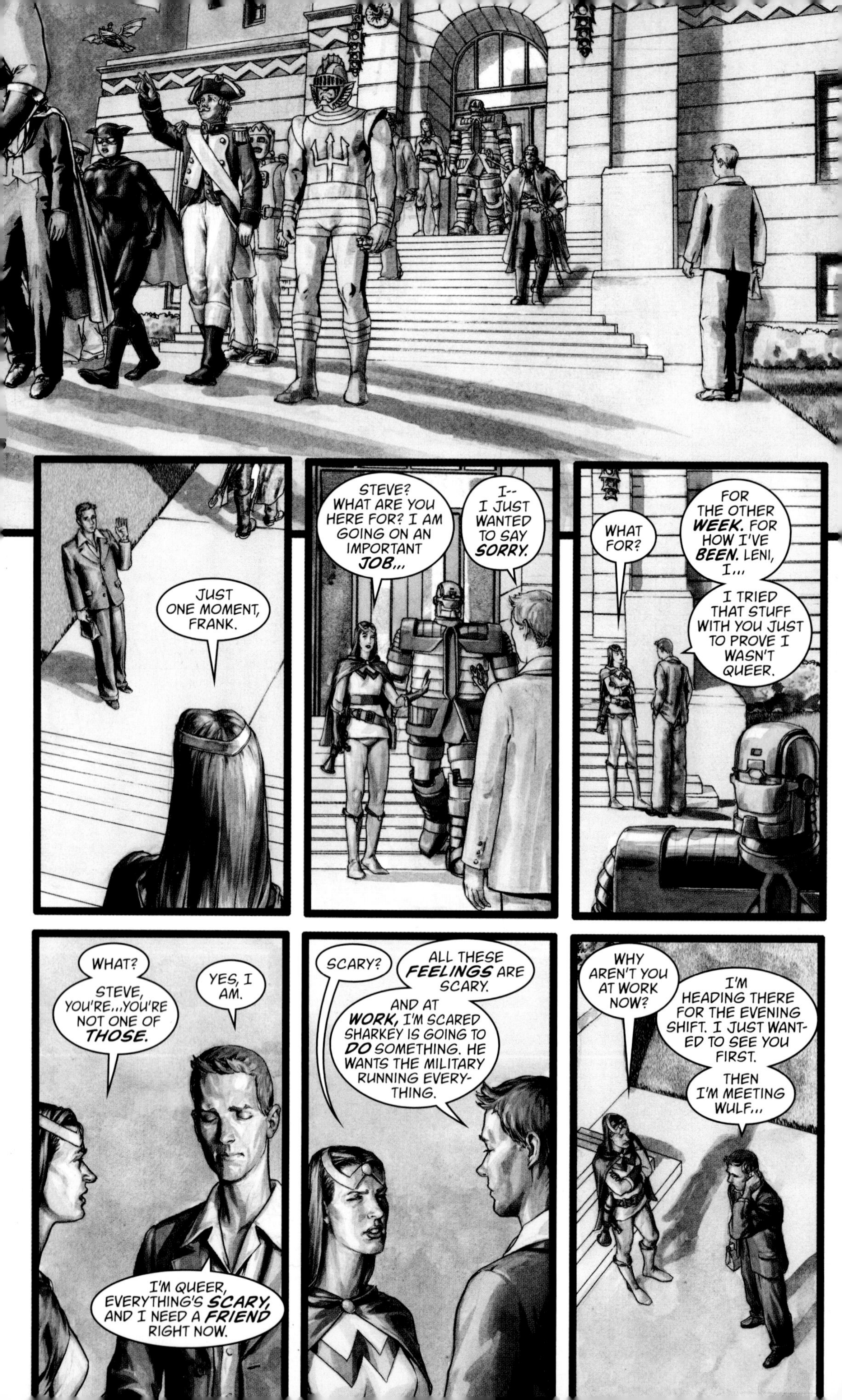
JUST ONE MOMENT, FRANK.
STEVE? WHAT ARE YOU HERE FOR? I AM GOING ON AN IMPORTANT JOB...
I-- I JUST WANTED TO SAY SORRY.
WHAT FOR?
FOR THE OTHER WEEK. FOR HOW I'VE BEEN. LENI, I...
I TRIED THAT STUFF WITH YOU JUST TO PROVE I WASN'T QUEER.
WHAT?
STEVE, YOU'RE...YOU'RE NOT ONE OF THOSE.
YES, I AM.
I'M QUEER, EVERYTHING'S SCARY, AND I NEED A FRIEND RIGHT NOW.
SCARY?
ALL THESE FEELINGS ARE SCARY.
AND AT WORK, I'M SCARED SHARKEY IS GOING TO DO SOMETHING. HE WANTS THE MILITARY RUNNING EVERY-THING.
WHY AREN'T YOU AT WORK NOW?
I'M HEADING THERE FOR THE EVENING SHIFT. I JUST WANT-ED TO SEE YOU FIRST.
THEN I'M MEETING WULF...

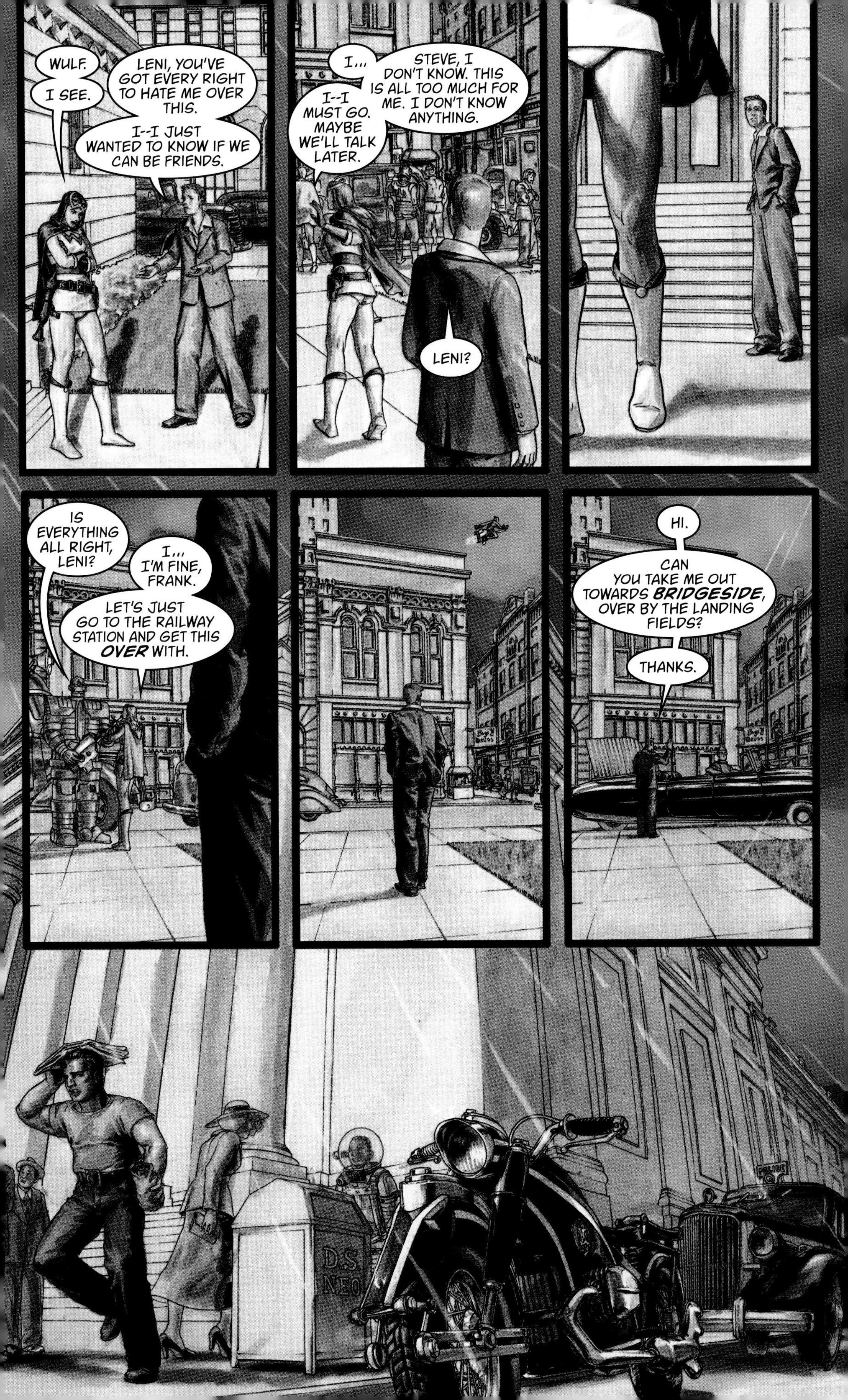
WULF.
I SEE.
LENI, YOU'VE GOT EVERY RIGHT TO HATE ME OVER THIS.
I--I JUST WANTED TO KNOW IF WE CAN BE FRIENDS.
I...
STEVE, I DON'T KNOW. THIS IS ALL TOO MUCH FOR ME. I DON'T KNOW ANYTHING.
I--I MUST GO. MAYBE WE'LL TALK LATER.
LENI?
IS EVERYTHING ALL RIGHT, LENI?
I... I'M FINE, FRANK.
LET'S JUST GO TO THE RAILWAY STATION AND GET THIS OVER WITH.
HI.
CAN YOU TAKE ME OUT TOWARDS BRIDGESIDE, OVER BY THE LANDING FIELDS?
THANKS.
D.S. NEO
POLICE

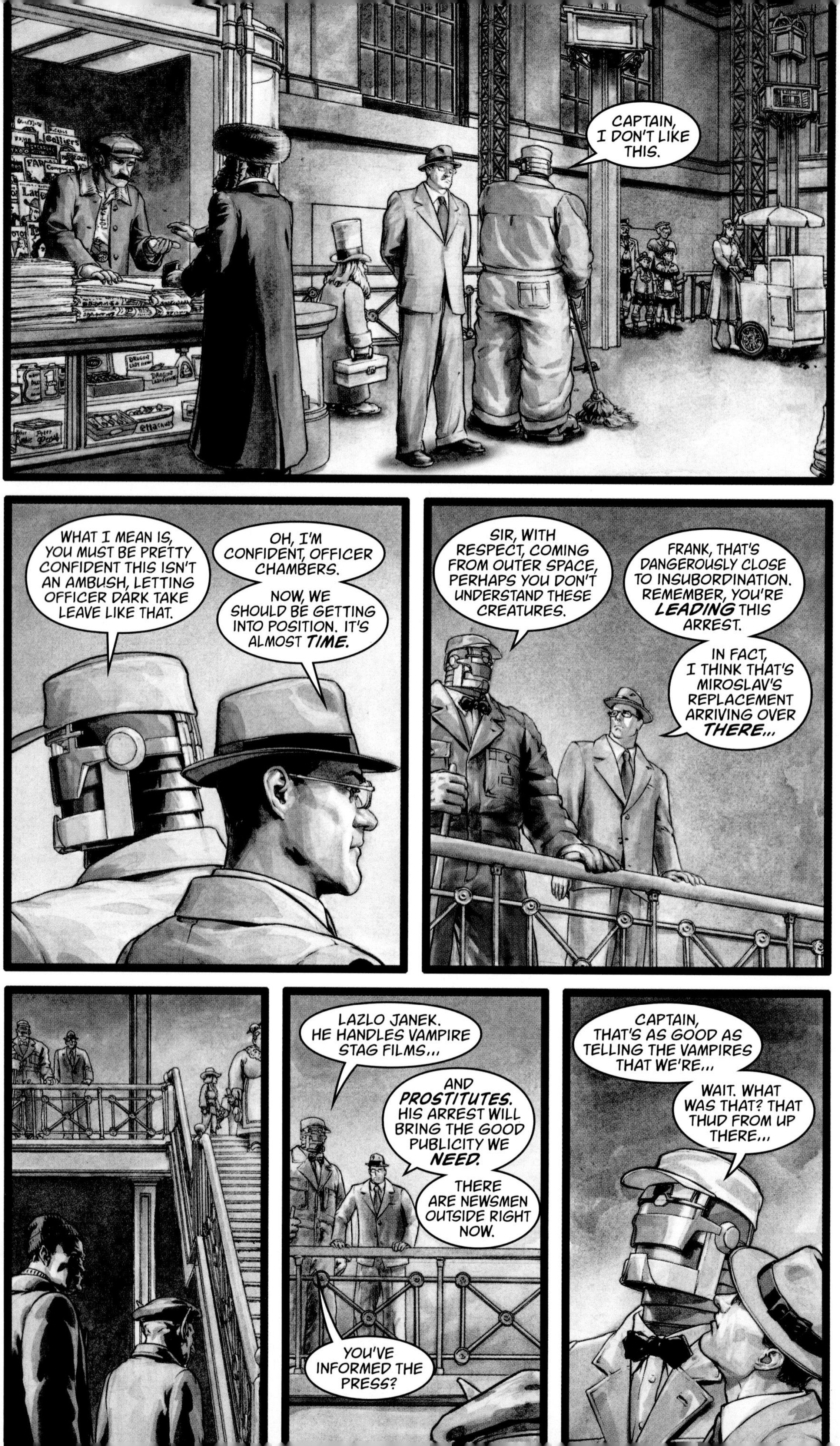

CAPTAIN, I DON'T LIKE THIS.
WHAT I MEAN IS, YOU MUST BE PRETTY CONFIDENT THIS ISN'T AN AMBUSH, LETTING OFFICER DARK TAKE LEAVE LIKE THAT.
OH, I'M CONFIDENT, OFFICER CHAMBERS.
NOW, WE SHOULD BE GETTING INTO POSITION. IT'S ALMOST *TIME*.
SIR, WITH RESPECT, COMING FROM OUTER SPACE, PERHAPS YOU DON'T UNDERSTAND THESE CREATURES.
FRANK, THAT'S DANGEROUSLY CLOSE TO INSUBORDINATION. REMEMBER, YOU'RE ***LEADING*** THIS ARREST.
IN FACT, I THINK THAT'S MIROSLAV'S REPLACEMENT ARRIVING OVER ***THERE...***
LAZLO JANEK. HE HANDLES VAMPIRE STAG FILMS...
AND ***PROSTITUTES.*** HIS ARREST WILL BRING THE GOOD PUBLICITY WE ***NEED.***
THERE ARE NEWSMEN OUTSIDE RIGHT NOW.
YOU'VE INFORMED THE PRESS?
CAPTAIN, THAT'S AS GOOD AS TELLING THE VAMPIRES THAT WE'RE...
WAIT. WHAT WAS THAT? THAT THUD FROM UP THERE...

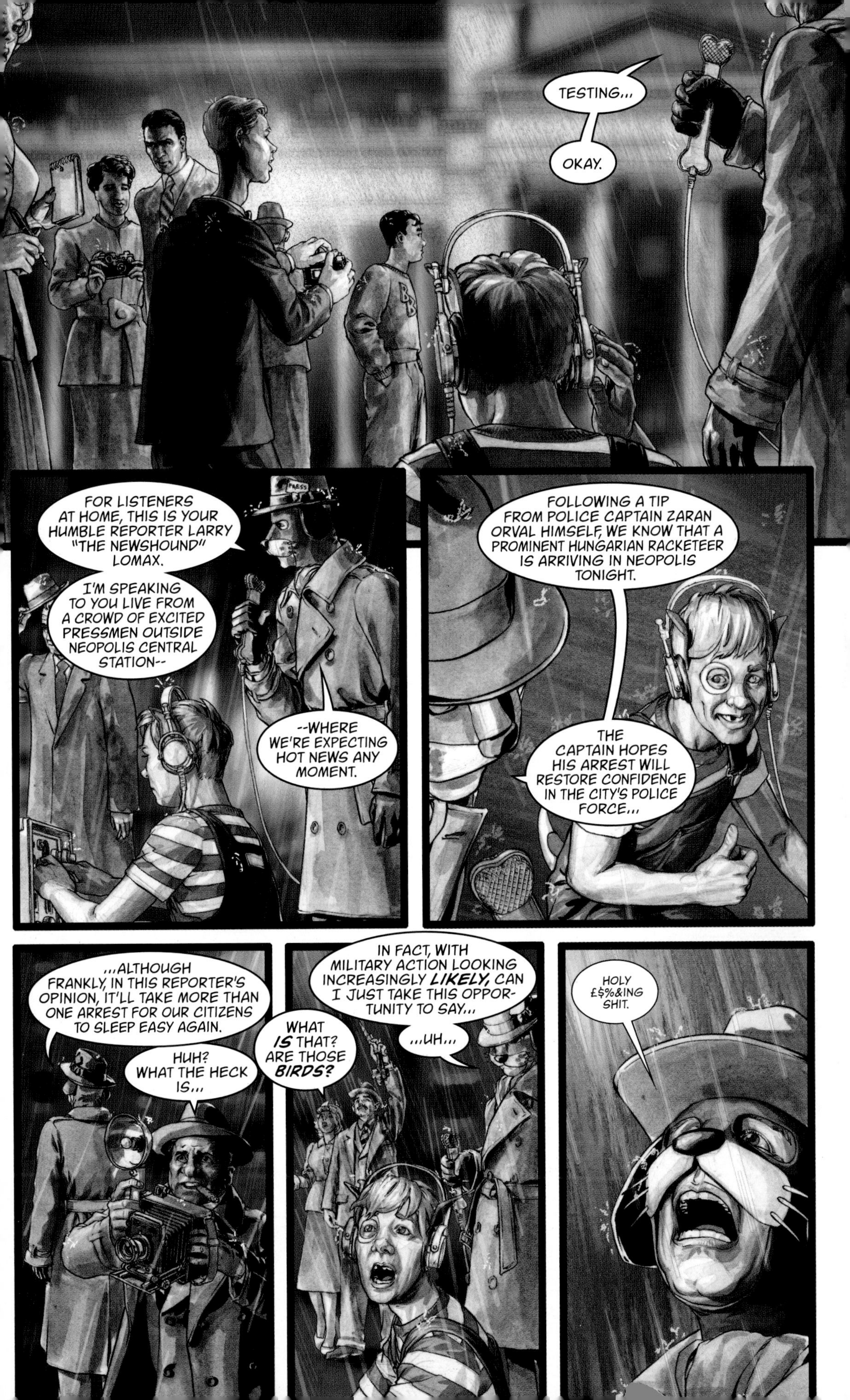
TESTING...
OKAY.
FOR LISTENERS AT HOME, THIS IS YOUR HUMBLE REPORTER LARRY "THE NEWSHOUND" LOMAX.
I'M SPEAKING TO YOU LIVE FROM A CROWD OF EXCITED PRESSMEN OUTSIDE NEOPOLIS CENTRAL STATION--
--WHERE WE'RE EXPECTING HOT NEWS ANY MOMENT.
FOLLOWING A TIP FROM POLICE CAPTAIN ZARAN ORVAL HIMSELF, WE KNOW THAT A PROMINENT HUNGARIAN RACKETEER IS ARRIVING IN NEOPOLIS TONIGHT.
THE CAPTAIN HOPES HIS ARREST WILL RESTORE CONFIDENCE IN THE CITY'S POLICE FORCE...
...ALTHOUGH FRANKLY, IN THIS REPORTER'S OPINION, IT'LL TAKE MORE THAN ONE ARREST FOR OUR CITIZENS TO SLEEP EASY AGAIN.
HUH? WHAT THE HECK IS...
IN FACT, WITH MILITARY ACTION LOOKING INCREASINGLY LIKELY, CAN I JUST TAKE THIS OPPOR-TUNITY TO SAY...
WHAT IS THAT? ARE THOSE BIRDS?
...UH...
HOLY £$%&ING SHIT.

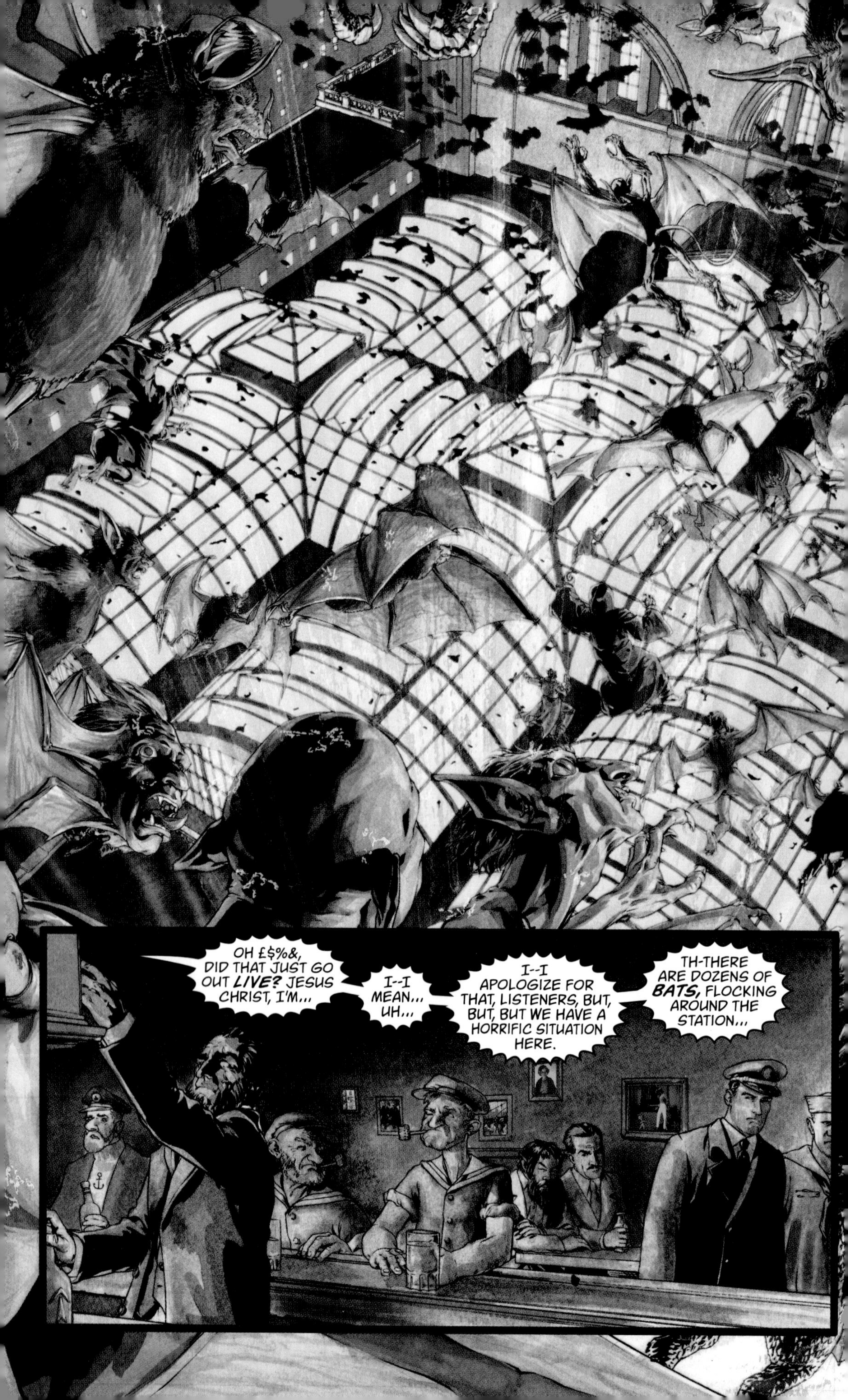
OH £$%&, DID THAT JUST GO OUT LIVE? JESUS CHRIST, I'M...
I--I MEAN... UH...
I--I APOLOGIZE FOR THAT, LISTENERS, BUT, BUT, BUT WE HAVE A HORRIFIC SITUATION HERE.
TH-THERE ARE DOZENS OF BATS, FLOCKING AROUND THE STATION...

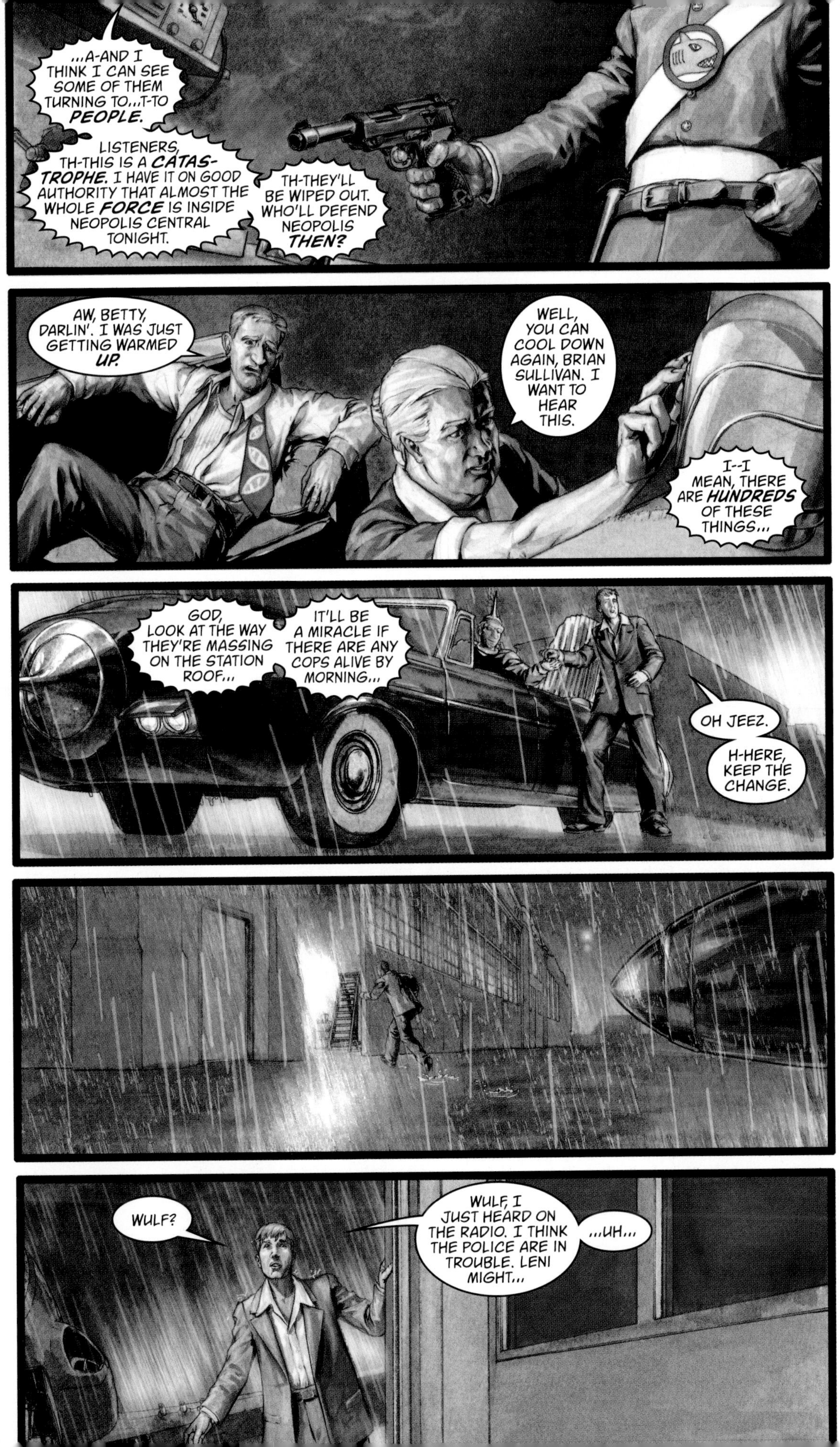
...A-AND I THINK I CAN SEE SOME OF THEM TURNING TO...T-TO **PEOPLE**.
LISTENERS, TH-THIS IS A **CATASTROPHE**. I HAVE IT ON GOOD AUTHORITY THAT ALMOST THE WHOLE **FORCE** IS INSIDE NEOPOLIS CENTRAL TONIGHT.
TH-THEY'LL BE WIPED OUT. WHO'LL DEFEND NEOPOLIS **THEN?**
AW, BETTY, DARLIN'. I WAS JUST GETTING WARMED **UP.**
WELL, YOU CAN COOL DOWN AGAIN, BRIAN SULLIVAN. I WANT TO HEAR THIS.
I--I MEAN, THERE ARE **HUNDREDS** OF THESE THINGS...
GOD, LOOK AT THE WAY THEY'RE MASSING ON THE STATION ROOF...
IT'LL BE A MIRACLE IF THERE ARE ANY COPS ALIVE BY MORNING...
OH JEEZ.
H-HERE, KEEP THE CHANGE.
WULF?
WULF, I JUST HEARD ON THE RADIO. I THINK THE POLICE ARE IN TROUBLE. LENI MIGHT...
...UH...

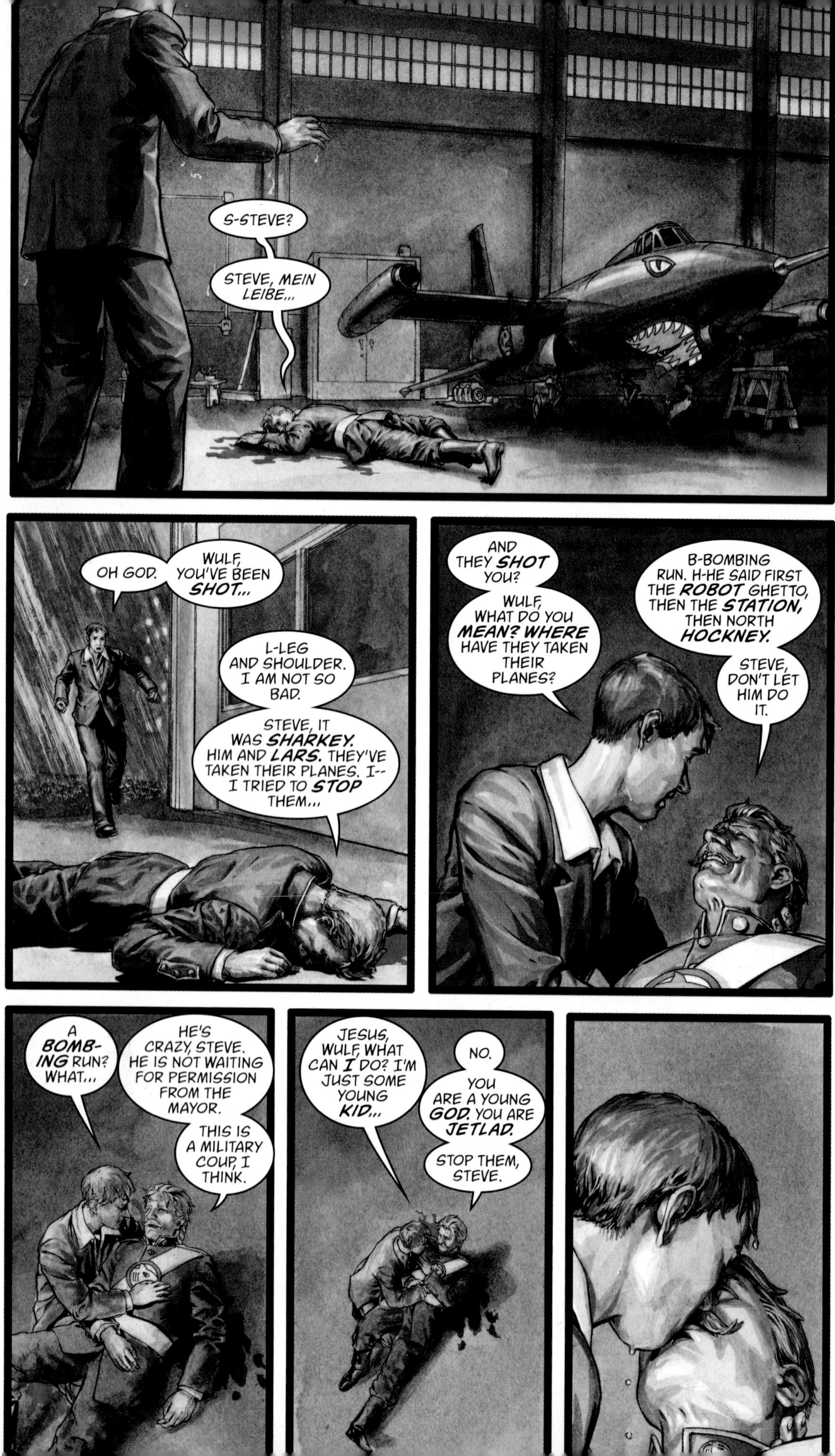
S-STEVE?
STEVE, MEIN LEIBE...
OH GOD.
WULF, YOU'VE BEEN SHOT...
L-LEG AND SHOULDER. I AM NOT SO BAD.
STEVE, IT WAS SHARKEY. HIM AND LARS. THEY'VE TAKEN THEIR PLANES. I-- I TRIED TO STOP THEM...
AND THEY SHOT YOU?
WULF, WHAT DO YOU MEAN? WHERE HAVE THEY TAKEN THEIR PLANES?
B-BOMBING RUN. H-HE SAID FIRST THE ROBOT GHETTO, THEN THE STATION, THEN NORTH HOCKNEY.
STEVE, DON'T LET HIM DO IT.
A BOMBING RUN? WHAT...
HE'S CRAZY, STEVE. HE IS NOT WAITING FOR PERMISSION FROM THE MAYOR.
THIS IS A MILITARY COUP, I THINK.
JESUS, WULF, WHAT CAN I DO? I'M JUST SOME YOUNG KID...
NO.
YOU ARE A YOUNG GOD. YOU ARE JETLAD.
STOP THEM, STEVE.

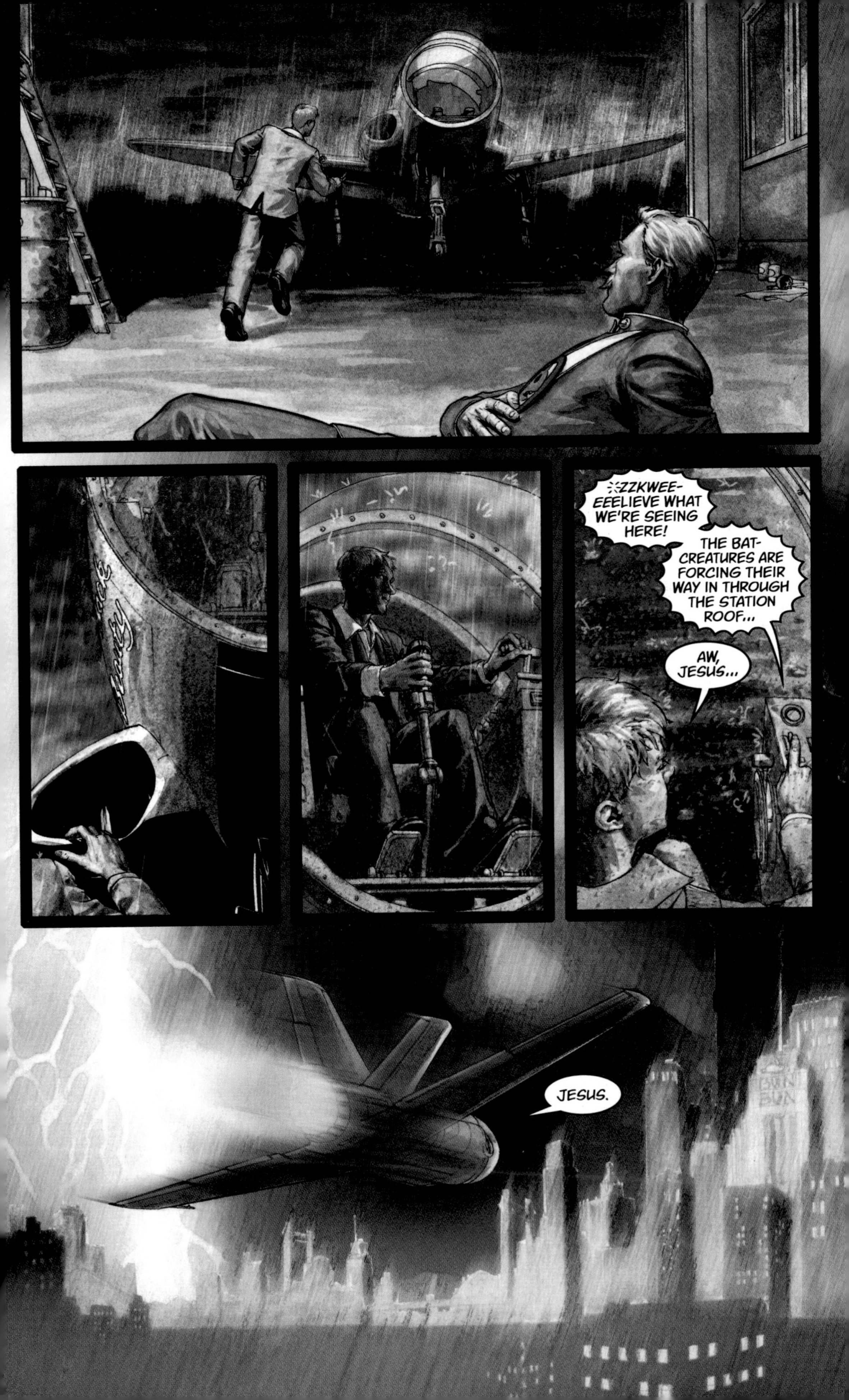
ZZKWEE-EEELIEVE WHAT WE'RE SEEING HERE!
THE BAT-CREATURES ARE FORCING THEIR WAY IN THROUGH THE STATION ROOF...
AW, JESUS...
JESUS.

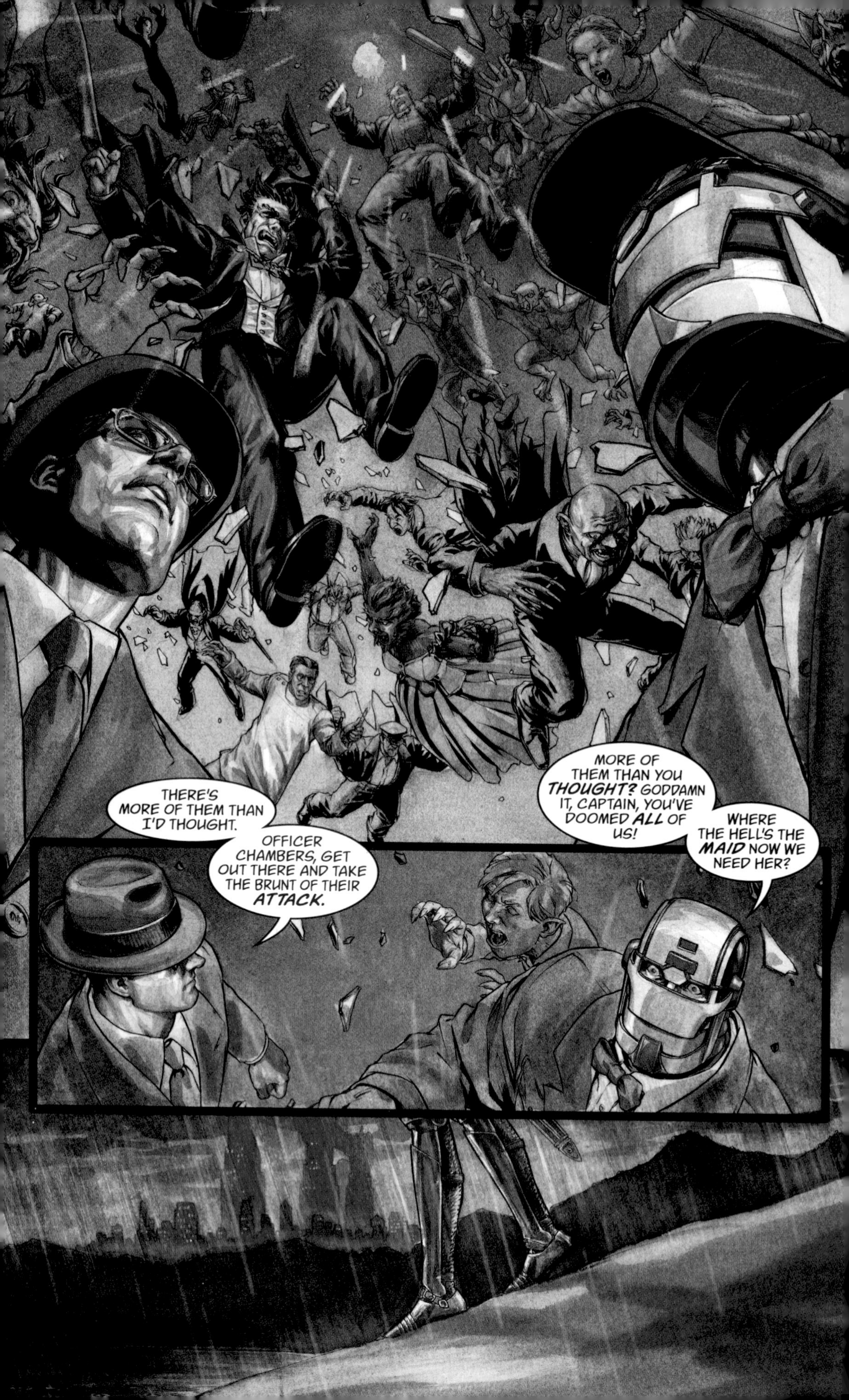
THERE'S MORE OF THEM THAN I'D THOUGHT.
OFFICER CHAMBERS, GET OUT THERE AND TAKE THE BRUNT OF THEIR *ATTACK.*
MORE OF THEM THAN YOU *THOUGHT?* GODDAMN IT, CAPTAIN, YOU'VE DOOMED *ALL* OF US!
WHERE THE HELL'S THE *MAID* NOW WE NEED HER?

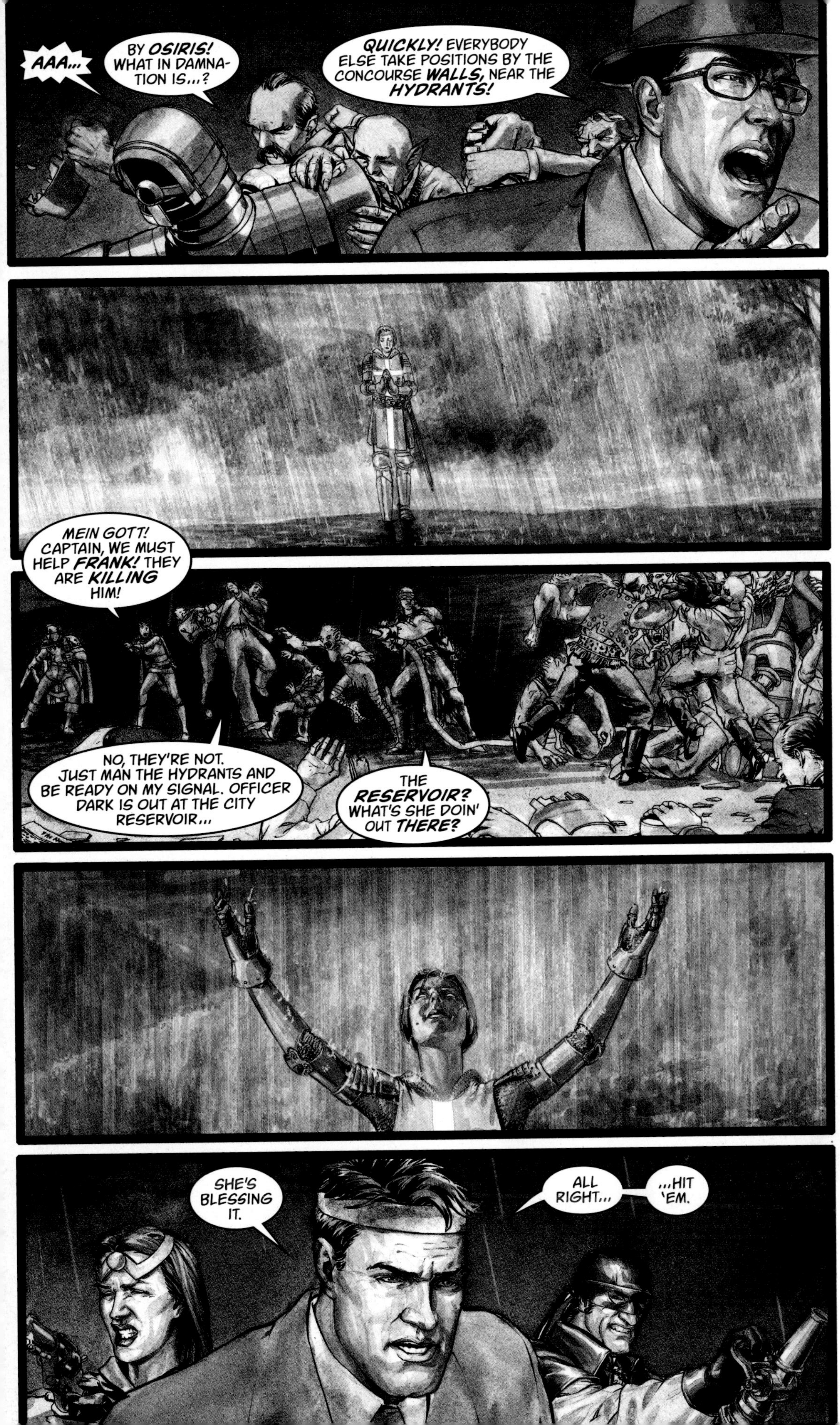
AAA...
BY OSIRIS! WHAT IN DAMNATION IS...?
QUICKLY! EVERYBODY ELSE TAKE POSITIONS BY THE CONCOURSE WALLS, NEAR THE HYDRANTS!
MEIN GOTT! CAPTAIN, WE MUST HELP FRANK! THEY ARE KILLING HIM!
NO, THEY'RE NOT. JUST MAN THE HYDRANTS AND BE READY ON MY SIGNAL. OFFICER DARK IS OUT AT THE CITY RESERVOIR...
THE RESERVOIR? WHAT'S SHE DOIN' OUT THERE?
SHE'S BLESSING IT.
ALL RIGHT...
...HIT 'EM.

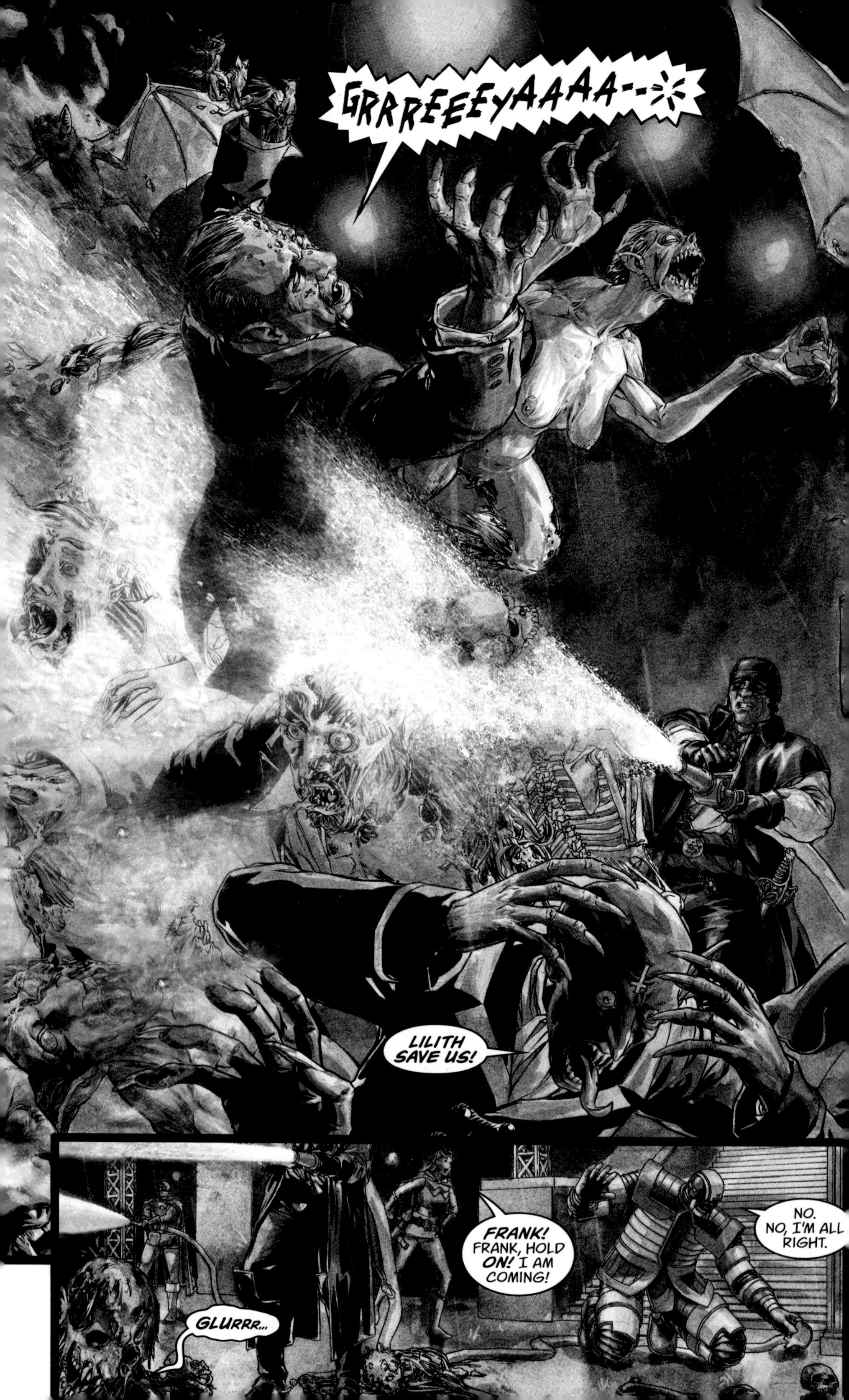
GRRREEEYAAAA--
LILITH SAVE US!
GLURRR...
FRANK! FRANK, HOLD ON! I AM COMING!
NO. NO, I'M ALL RIGHT.

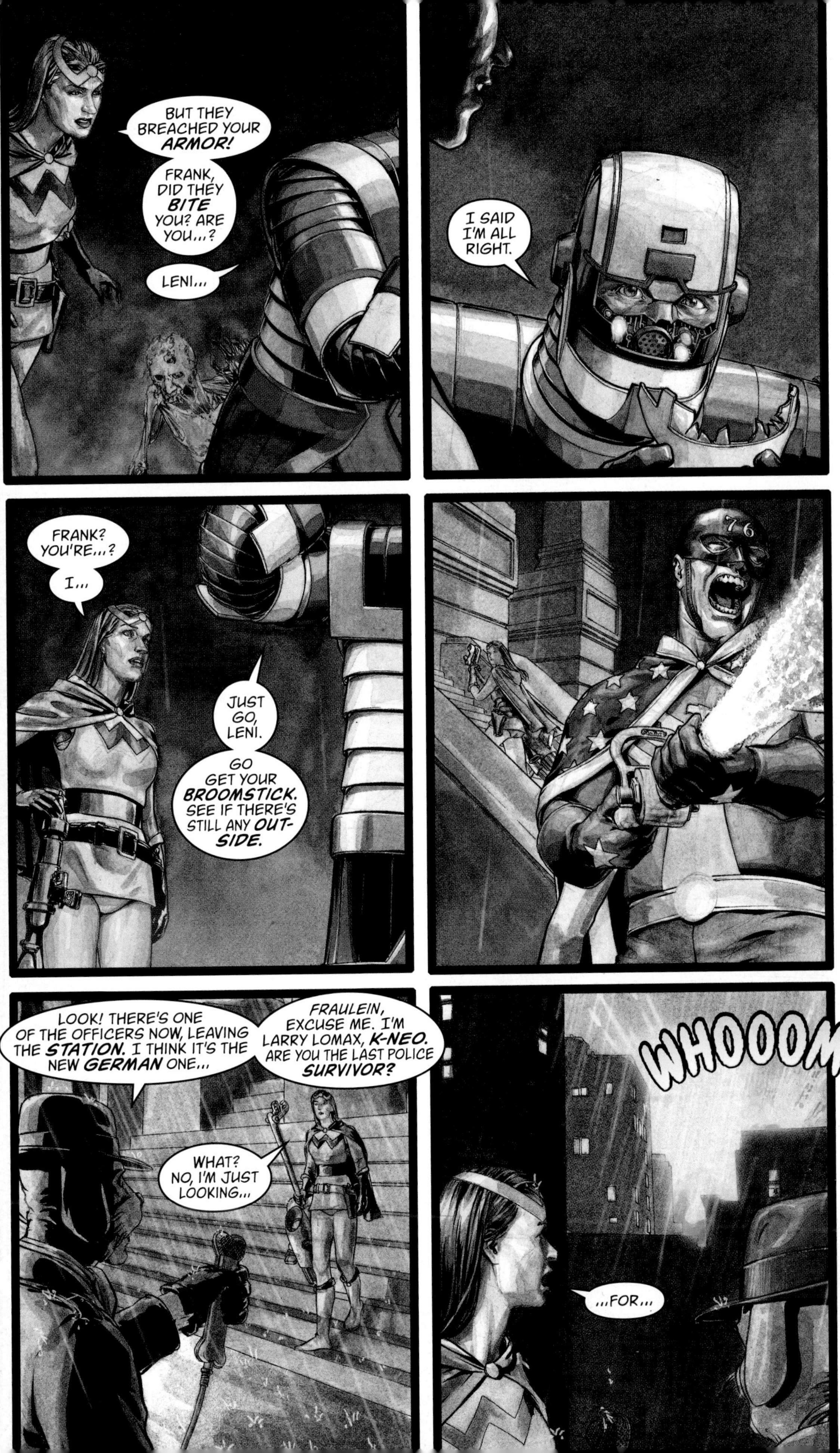

BUT THEY BREACHED YOUR ARMOR!
FRANK, DID THEY BITE YOU? ARE YOU...?
LENI...
I SAID I'M ALL RIGHT.
FRANK? YOU'RE...?
I...
JUST GO, LENI.
GO GET YOUR BROOMSTICK. SEE IF THERE'S STILL ANY OUT-SIDE.
76
LOOK! THERE'S ONE OF THE OFFICERS NOW, LEAVING THE STATION. I THINK IT'S THE NEW GERMAN ONE...
FRAULEIN, EXCUSE ME. I'M LARRY LOMAX, K-NEO. ARE YOU THE LAST POLICE SURVIVOR?
WHAT? NO, I'M JUST LOOKING...
WHOOOM
...FOR...

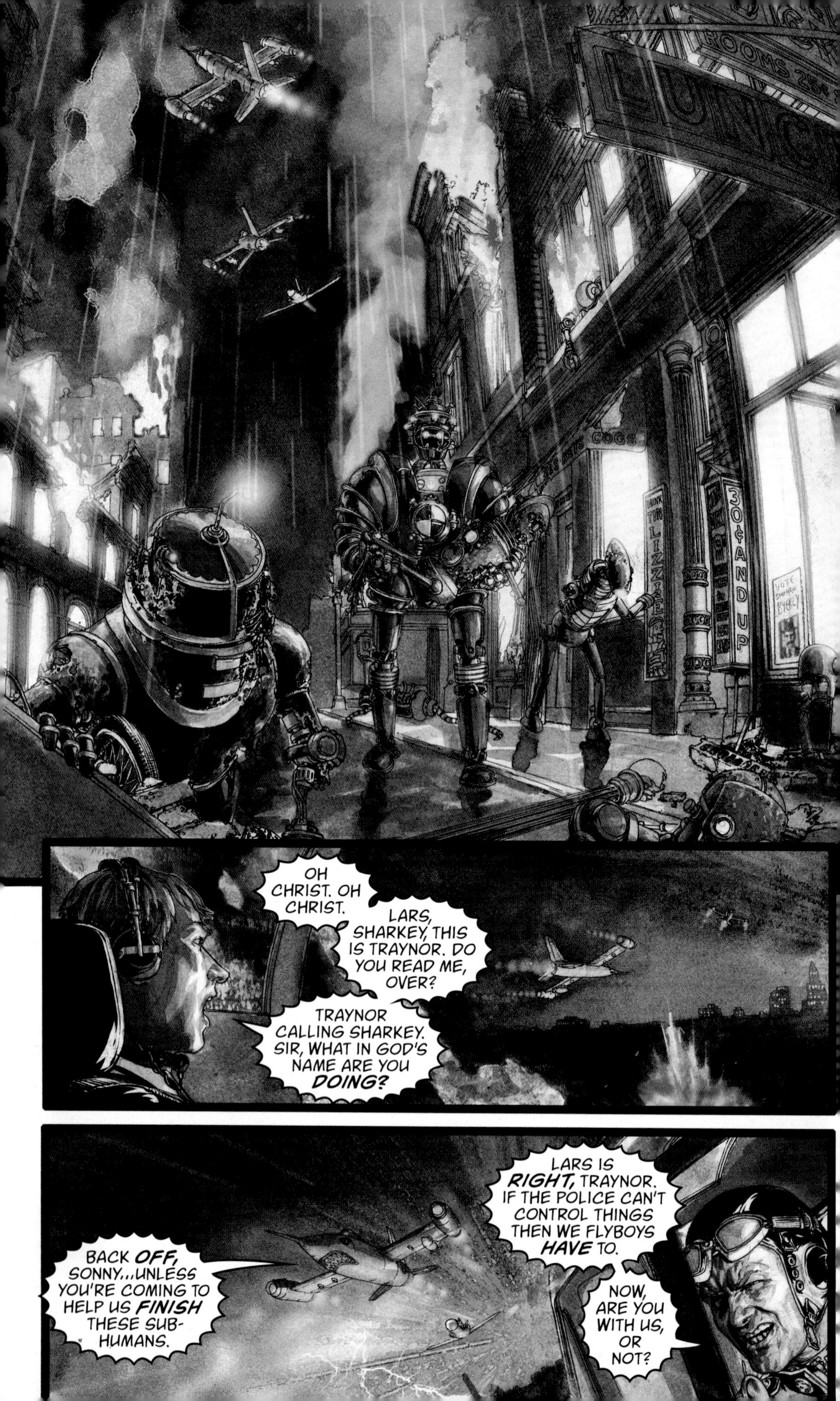

ROOMS 25¢
COGS
TIN LIZZIE
30¢ AND UP
VOTE
OH CHRIST. OH CHRIST.
LARS, SHARKEY, THIS IS TRAYNOR. DO YOU READ ME, OVER?
TRAYNOR CALLING SHARKEY. SIR, WHAT IN GOD'S NAME ARE YOU **DOING?**
LARS IS **RIGHT,** TRAYNOR. IF THE POLICE CAN'T CONTROL THINGS THEN WE FLYBOYS **HAVE** TO.
BACK **OFF,** SONNY...UNLESS YOU'RE COMING TO HELP US **FINISH** THESE SUB-HUMANS.
NOW, ARE YOU WITH US, OR NOT?

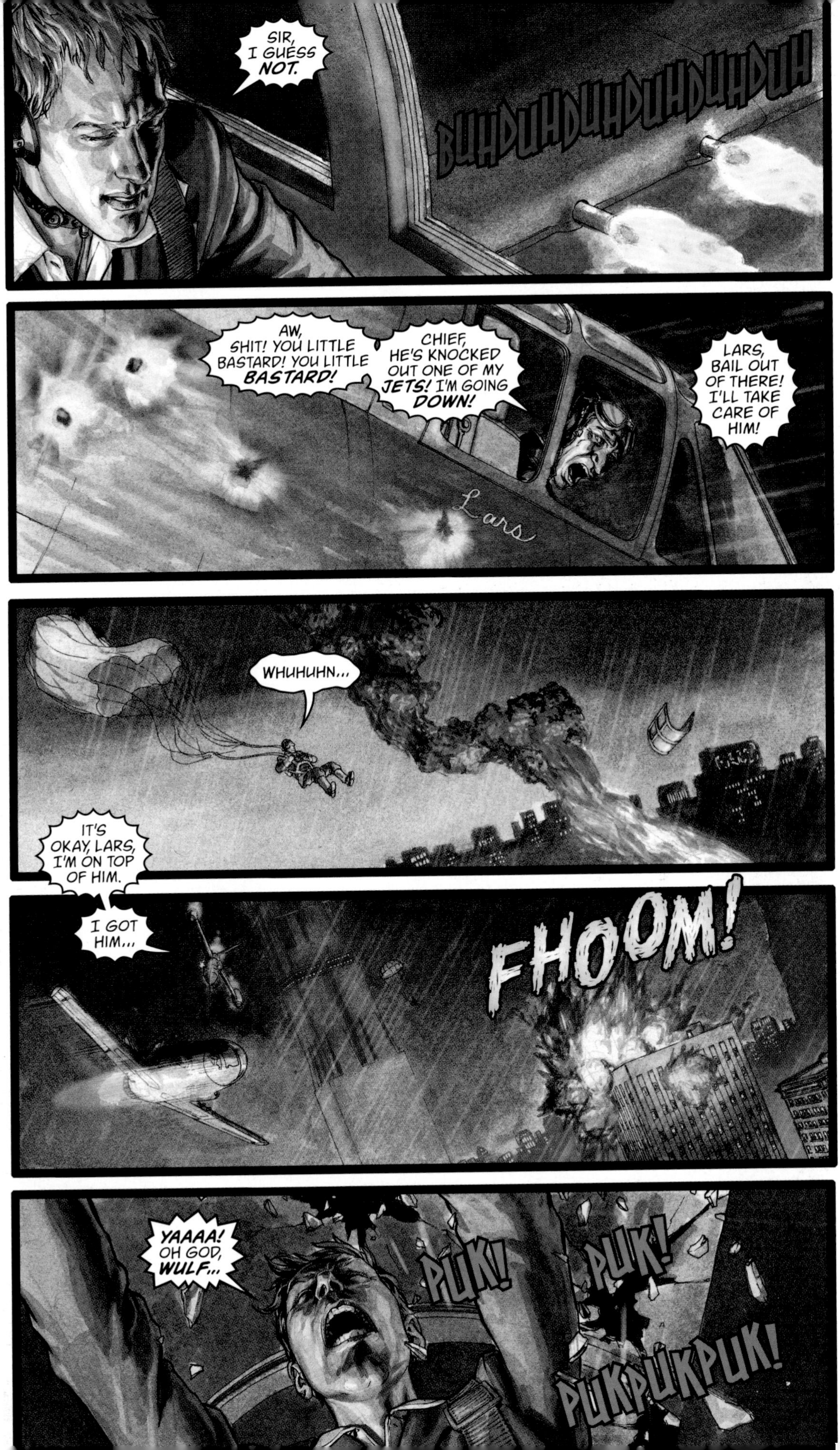
SIR, I GUESS NOT.
BUHDUHDUHDUHDUHDUH
AW, SHIT! YOU LITTLE BASTARD! YOU LITTLE BASTARD!
CHIEF, HE'S KNOCKED OUT ONE OF MY JETS! I'M GOING DOWN!
LARS, BAIL OUT OF THERE! I'LL TAKE CARE OF HIM!
Lars
WHUHUHN...
IT'S OKAY, LARS, I'M ON TOP OF HIM.
I GOT HIM...
FHOOM!
YAAAA! OH GOD, WULF...
PUK!
PUK!
PUKPUKPUK!

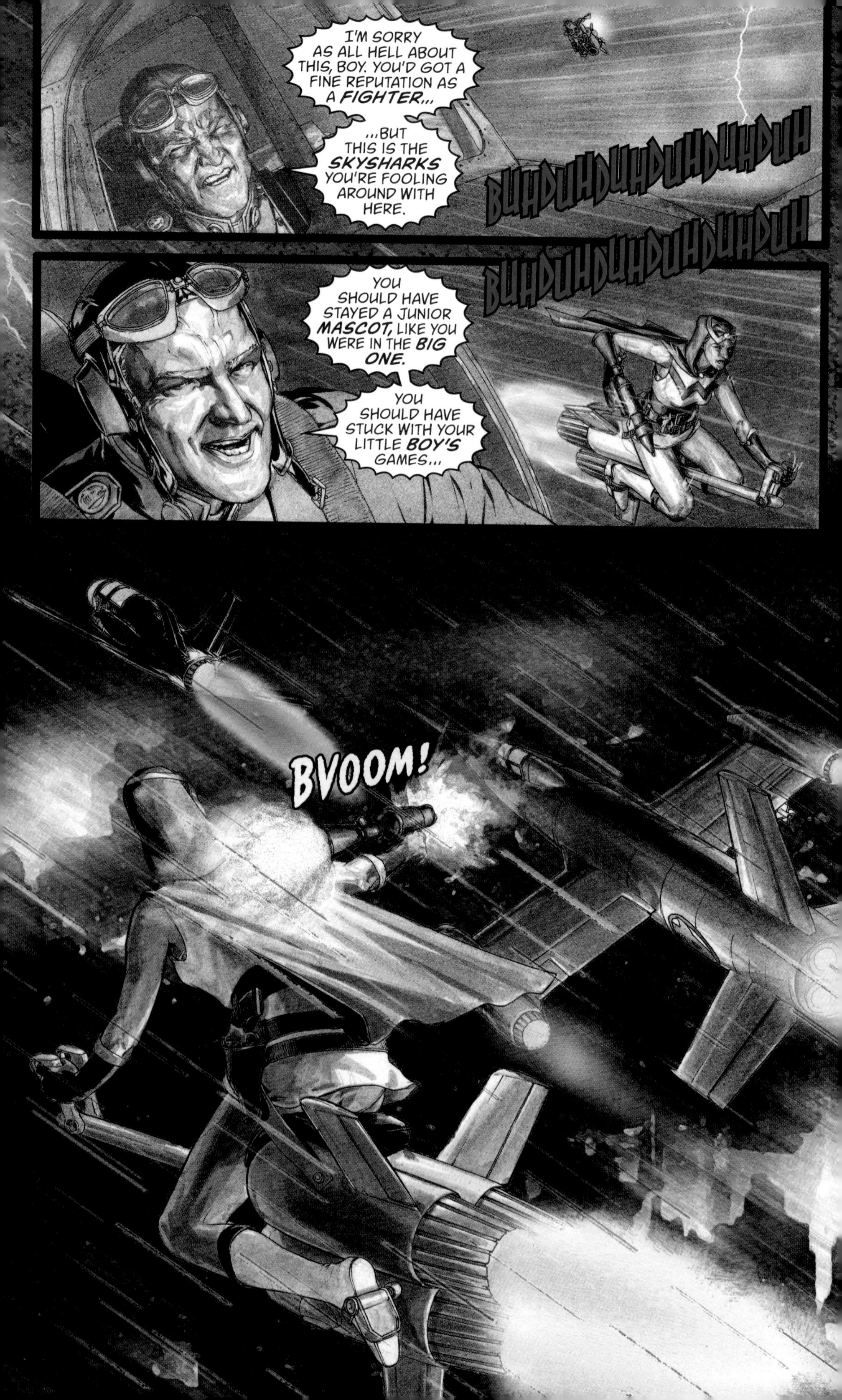
I'M SORRY AS ALL HELL ABOUT THIS, BOY. YOU'D GOT A FINE REPUTATION AS A FIGHTER...
...BUT THIS IS THE SKYSHARKS YOU'RE FOOLING AROUND WITH HERE.
BUHDUHDUHDUHDUHDUH
BUHDUHDUHDUHDUHDUH
YOU SHOULD HAVE STAYED A JUNIOR MASCOT, LIKE YOU WERE IN THE BIG ONE.
YOU SHOULD HAVE STUCK WITH YOUR LITTLE BOY'S GAMES...
BVOOM!

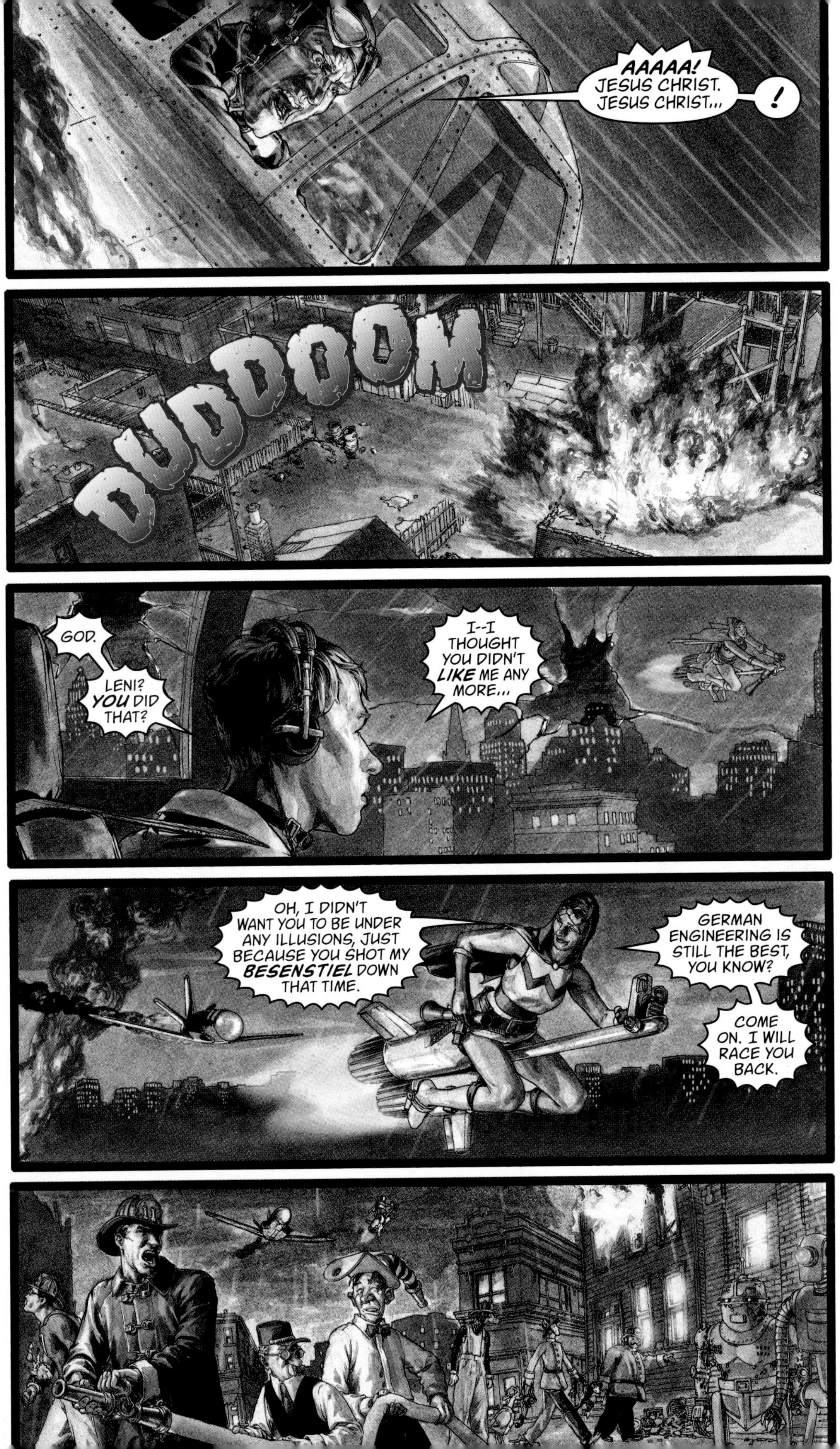

AAAAA! JESUS CHRIST. JESUS CHRIST...
!
DUDDOOM
GOD.
LENI? YOU DID THAT?
I--I THOUGHT YOU DIDN'T LIKE ME ANY MORE...
OH, I DIDN'T WANT YOU TO BE UNDER ANY ILLUSIONS, JUST BECAUSE YOU SHOT MY BESENSTIEL DOWN THAT TIME.
GERMAN ENGINEERING IS STILL THE BEST, YOU KNOW?
COME ON. I WILL RACE YOU BACK.

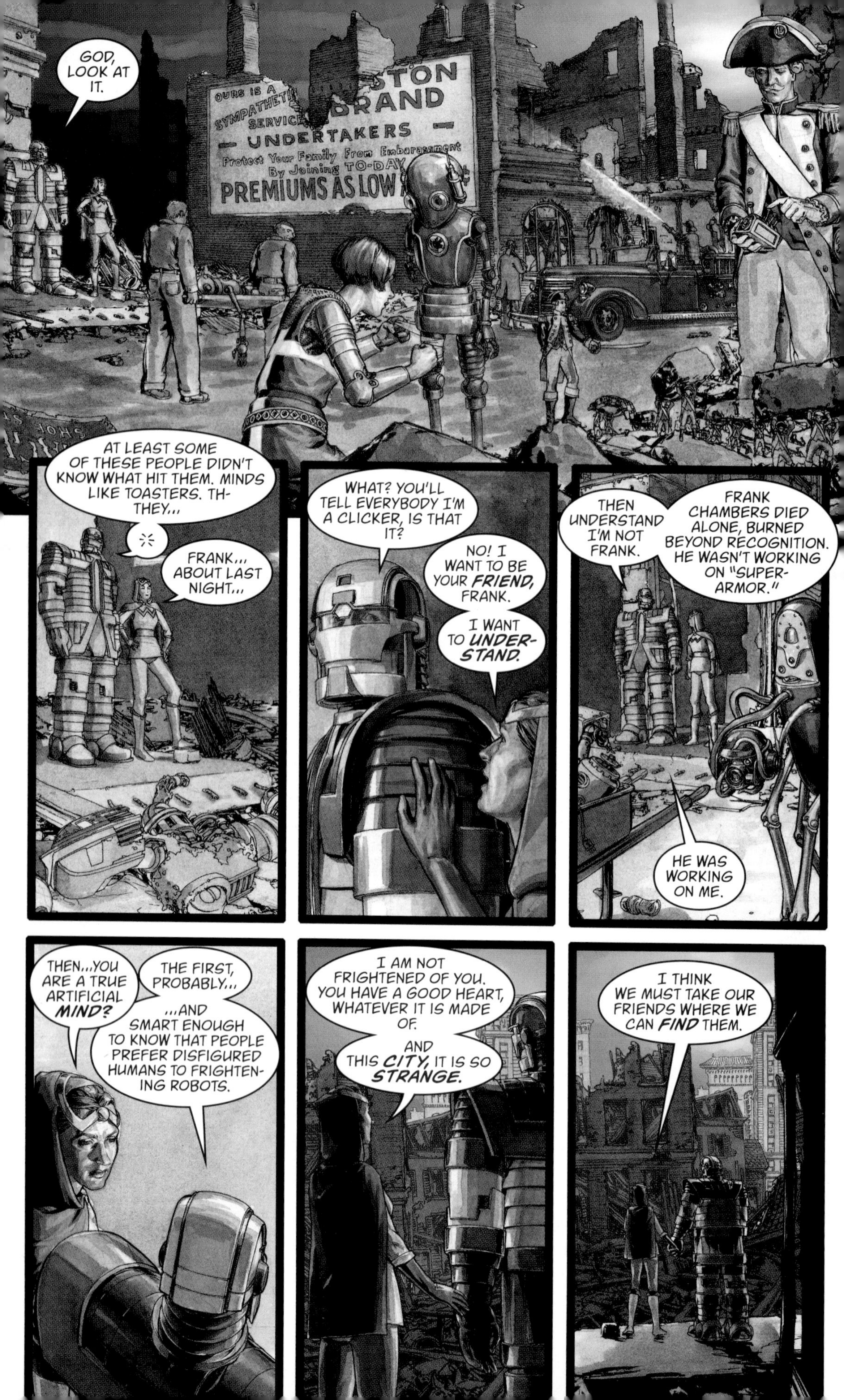
GOD, LOOK AT IT.
OURS IS A SYMPATHETIC SERVICE
BRAND
— UNDERTAKERS —
Protect Your Family From Embarassment By Joining TO-DAY
PREMIUMS AS LOW
AT LEAST SOME OF THESE PEOPLE DIDN'T KNOW WHAT HIT THEM. MINDS LIKE TOASTERS. TH-THEY...
FRANK... ABOUT LAST NIGHT...
WHAT? YOU'LL TELL EVERYBODY I'M A CLICKER, IS THAT IT?
NO! I WANT TO BE YOUR FRIEND, FRANK.
I WANT TO UNDERSTAND.
THEN UNDERSTAND I'M NOT FRANK.
FRANK CHAMBERS DIED ALONE, BURNED BEYOND RECOGNITION. HE WASN'T WORKING ON "SUPER-ARMOR."
HE WAS WORKING ON ME.
THEN...YOU ARE A TRUE ARTIFICIAL MIND?
THE FIRST, PROBABLY...
...AND SMART ENOUGH TO KNOW THAT PEOPLE PREFER DISFIGURED HUMANS TO FRIGHTENING ROBOTS.
I AM NOT FRIGHTENED OF YOU. YOU HAVE A GOOD HEART, WHATEVER IT IS MADE OF.
AND THIS CITY, IT IS SO STRANGE.
I THINK WE MUST TAKE OUR FRIENDS WHERE WE CAN FIND THEM.

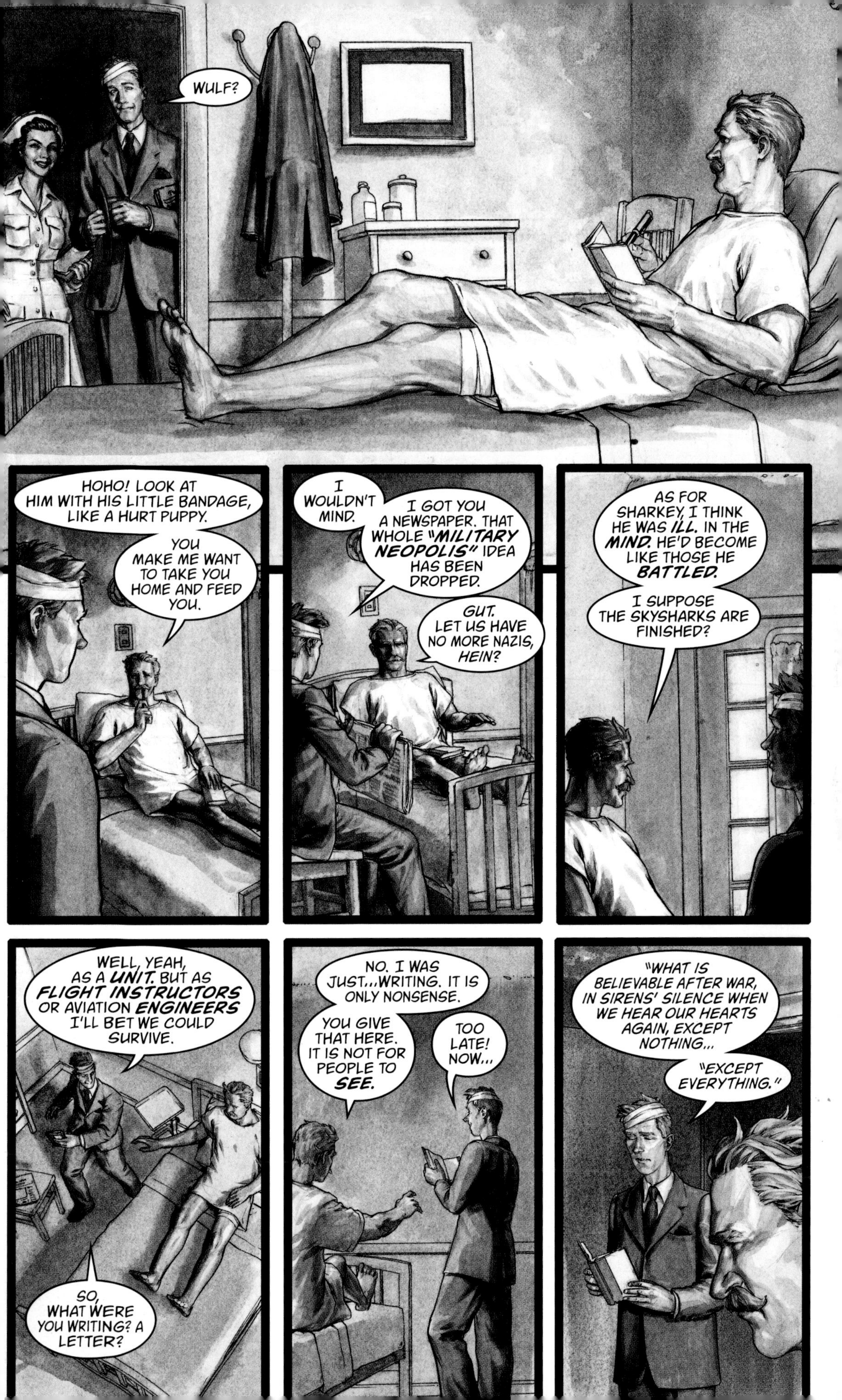
WULF?
HOHO! LOOK AT HIM WITH HIS LITTLE BANDAGE, LIKE A HURT PUPPY.
YOU MAKE ME WANT TO TAKE YOU HOME AND FEED YOU.
I WOULDN'T MIND.
I GOT YOU A NEWSPAPER. THAT WHOLE "MILITARY NEOPOLIS" IDEA HAS BEEN DROPPED.
GUT. LET US HAVE NO MORE NAZIS, HEIN?
AS FOR SHARKEY, I THINK HE WAS ILL. IN THE MIND. HE'D BECOME LIKE THOSE HE BATTLED.
I SUPPOSE THE SKYSHARKS ARE FINISHED?
WELL, YEAH, AS A UNIT. BUT AS FLIGHT INSTRUCTORS OR AVIATION ENGINEERS I'LL BET WE COULD SURVIVE.
SO, WHAT WERE YOU WRITING? A LETTER?
NO. I WAS JUST...WRITING. IT IS ONLY NONSENSE.
YOU GIVE THAT HERE. IT IS NOT FOR PEOPLE TO SEE.
TOO LATE! NOW...
"WHAT IS BELIEVABLE AFTER WAR, IN SIRENS' SILENCE WHEN WE HEAR OUR HEARTS AGAIN, EXCEPT NOTHING...
"EXCEPT EVERYTHING."

CONTRIBUTORS

ALAN MOORE is perhaps the most acclaimed writer in the graphic story medium, having garnered many awards for works such as WATCHMEN, V FOR VENDETTA, FROM HELL, MIRACLEMAN, SWAMP THING and SUPREME. He is currently masterminding the America's Best Comics line, with writing credits that include PROMETHEA, TOM STRONG, TOP 10, THE LEAGUE OF EXTRAORDINARY GENTLEMEN and TOMORROW STORIES. Alan is also overseeing and plotting the upcoming series ALBION, written by Leah Moore and John Reppion. He lives in central England.

GENE HA is the Eisner Award-winning artist and co-creator of TOP 10 and THE FORTY-NINERS. Recently he has also drawn GLOBAL FREQUENCY and covers for Wizard Magazine and Marvel Comics. Gene feels very odd talking about himself in the third person. He draws at a small table in Oak Park, Illinois, and rants about comics and politics at www.geneha.com. His patient and lovely wife Lisa and their two beagle-bassets take care of Gene as he gets older and crankier.

ART LYON, colorist of THE FORTY-NINERS, has been in and out of the comic book industry for twenty years as a penciler, inker, colorist, retailer, and all-around sequential guy. He recently returned to comics as a colorist with GLOBAL FREQUENCY #12, and a pin-up in the ASTRO CITY GUIDEBOOK. Ellen Starr Lyon, a talented painter in her own right, has been his assistant on GLOBAL FREQUENCY and THE FORTY-NINERS, handling the lion's share of the ink washes. They married in 1999, live in Bloomington, Indiana, and have two delightful children, Finnian and Odessa.

TODD KLEIN has lettered and designed nearly all of the ABC line of comics and collected editions. He began lettering comics in 1977 and has won numerous Eisner, Harvey and CBG Fan awards for his work. Todd lives in rural southern New Jersey with his wife Ellen and a small menagerie of animals.

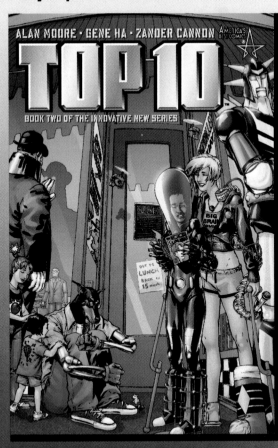

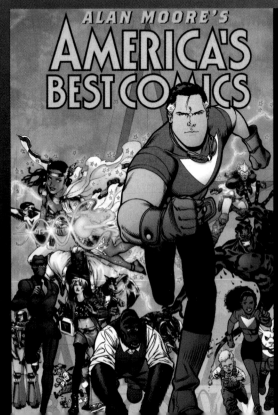

Look for these and other fine ABC Editions at a comics retailer or bookstore near you.

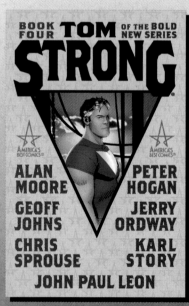

TOM STRONG
BOOKS 1 to 4
Moore/Sprouse/Gordon/
Story/Various

PROMETHEA
BOOKS 1 to 4
Moore/Williams III/Gray
Cox/Villarrubia

THE LEAGUE OF
EXTRAORDINARY GENTLEMEN
VOLUMES 1 & 2
Moore/O'Neill

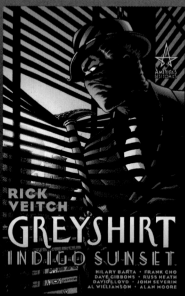

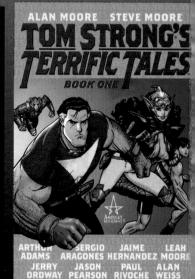

TOMORROW STORIES
BOOKS 1 & 2
Moore/Various

GREYSHIRT:
INDIGO SUNSET
Veitch/Various

TOM STRONG'S TERRIFIC
TALES BOOKS 1 & 2
Moore/Moore/Various

To find more books and comics from America's Best Comics, call 1-888-COMIC BOOK for the comics retailer nearest to you